THE DELL
WAR SERIES

The Dell War Series takes you onto the battle-field, into the jungles, and beneath the oceans with unforgettable stories that offer a new look at the terrors and triumphs of America's war experience. Many of these books are eyewitness accounts of the duty-bound fighting forces. From the intrepid foot soldiers, sailors, pilots, and commanders to the elite warriors of the Special Forces, here are stories of those who fight because their lives depend on it.

PRAISE FROM ACROSS THE
POLITICAL SPECTRUM
FOR HARRY G. SUMMERS, JR.'S
ASTONISHING MILITARY CLASSIC

ON STRATEGY: A CRITICAL ANALYSIS OF THE VIETNAM WAR

"Just about the best thing I have read on Vietnam."

—Drew Middleton, *The New York Times*

"A penetrating analysis of our strategy during the Vietnam war—no one concerned with the future of American foreign policy can afford to ignore it."

—*The New Republic*

"Extends well beyond the battlefield to Congress, the political leadership, and the people."

—*Foreign Affairs*

"I have read *On Strategy* with great interest and much profit."

—Dean Rusk, Secretary of State under
Lyndon Johnson

"The most important analytical military literature since Alfred Thayer Mahan wrote his great treatise on sea powers almost a century ago."

—General Andrew P. O'Meara, former commander in
chief, U.S. Army, Europe

Also by Harry G. Summers, Jr.

ON STRATEGY: A CRITICAL ANALYSIS OF THE
VIETNAM WAR

A CRITICAL
ANALYSIS
OF
THE GULF WAR

Harry G. Summers, Jr.

A DELL BOOK

Published by
Dell Publishing
a division of
Bantam Doubleday Dell Publishing Group, Inc.
666 Fifth Avenue
New York, New York 10103

ISBN: 0-440-21194-8

Printed in the United States of America

Published simultaneously in Canada

February 1992

10 9 8 7 6 5 4 3 2 1

OPM

Contents

Part III
THE REMARKABLE WAR

Acknowledgments

Ten years ago, in his foreword to the first *On Strategy,* General Jack N. Merritt, then commandant of the U.S. Army War College, noted that it was "important for the reader to understand what this book is and what it is not. It is not, nor was it intended to be, a history of the Vietnam war. It is not a detailed account of day-to-day tactical operations. . . . What was intended was a narrow focus on the war in the area of major concern to the Army War College—'the application of military science to the national defense.' Using Clausewitzian theory and the classic principles of war, the book attempts to place the Vietnam war in domestic context as well as in the context of war itself."

A decade later, General Merritt's words apply as well to *On Strategy II,* a direct descendant of that earlier work. Again I must acknowledge my enormous debt to General Merritt and to then Army chief of staff General Edward C. "Shy" Meyer and to the many others who made that earlier work possible, for without *On Strategy* there could have been no *On Strategy II.*

Ironically, my initial involvement with the Persian Gulf war came not through the military but through the media. NBC News Pentagon correspondent Fred Francis championed me from the very first as a strategic military analyst, and his good offices led to some 125 TV appearances during the war, primarily on NBC and CNN, but also on ABC, CBS, Fox, C-Span, and Canada's CBC-Newsworld, and to scores of radio interviews across the United States and abroad.

Serving as NBC News military analyst for their *America at War* special reports during Operation Desert Storm, I was able to gain a unique insight into the war. For that, much thanks to NBC senior vice president Timothy J. Russert; to Nancy Nathan, Washington producer of the *Today* show; to NBC Washington Bureau's Betty Nevins, Marcie Rickun, and Colleen Halpin, and to Kristin Moore and Alison Rosenberg in New York. Special thanks also to Tom Brokaw and Jane Pauley of NBC News, and to the *Today* show's Bryant Gumbel, Deborah Norville, Faith Daniels, and Katie Curic.

In the first three months of Desert Shield, thanks to CNN Pentagon correspondent Wolf Blitzer, Washington Bureau chief Bill Headline, and CNN vice president Gail Evans in Atlanta, I served as the military analyst for CNN's *Crisis in the Gulf* reports. My appreciation to them, to Pat Reap and Jill Neff, and to news anchors Bernard Shaw, John Holliman, Reid Collins, and David French.

Thanks also to the producers and production staffs of CNN's several talk shows and their hosts, including Marlene Fernandez's *Telemundo;* *Crossfire*'s Pat Buchanan and Michael Kinsley; *Larry King Live*'s Larry King; and Bob Franken of *Newsmaker Sunday*.

In addition to my weekly syndicated newspaper column, Shelby Coffee, the editor-in-chief of the *Los Angeles Times,* asked me to be their "Drew Middleton"—for many years the distinguished military correspondent for *The New York Times*—and to write a series of analyses of the strategic issues of the war.

Special gratitude to Shelby Coffee for that great honor, as well as to my editor, Tony Day, and the staff of the newspaper's War Desk for their help in that endeavor. Also most helpful, as usual, were the *Los Angeles Times* Syndicate's managing editor, Steve Christiansen, and copy editors Connie Cloos and Tim Lange.

Another great honor was Congressman Les Aspin's invitation to testify before his House Armed Services Committee on the situation in the Gulf, and Senator Herbert Kohl's invitation to testify before his Governmental Affairs Committee on media coverage of the Gulf war. Much thanks to them and to their staffers for that special opportunity.

When I wrote my critical analysis of the Vietnam war it was six years after the war's end, and there were over six thousand books already in print from which to glean my data. This work was completed some six months after the end of the Gulf war, and only a handful of books were available. As is evident from my footnotes, most of the material came from news accounts and from official government documents.

From Julie Damgard of White House Media Relations came copies of presidential speeches and announcements. Colonel F. William Smullen III, the special assistant to the chairman of the Joint Chiefs of Staff, provided copies of documents on reserve mobilization and on the chairman's views on future military force structures, and provided sound advice and commentary from an old friend as well.

Major Doug Hart of the office of the assistant secretary of defense for public affairs provided data on the reserve components. Lieutenant Colonel John Olsen of the U.S. Central Command provided copies of General H. Norman Schwarzkopf's postvictory briefings, reproduced as an appendix to this work, as well as information on military-media relations. And Major Jim Bates of the Military Airlift Command provided data on airlift and deployment of the Civil Reserve Air Fleet.

Colonel Bill Mulvey (who later deployed to the Gulf) and Colonel Dave Kiernan and others in Army public affairs were most helpful in providing or locating data on the war, as were the public affairs officers of the Navy, Air Force, and Marine Corps.

A particular debt of gratitude to the readers of the first drafts of this work, including Colonel Donald E. Lunday, the deputy commandant of the Army War College; Colonel Ralph L. Allen, the chairman of the Army War College's Department of Military Strategy, Planning, and Operations; and Lieutenant Colonel Larry F. Icenogel, the War College's public affairs officer who served on temporary duty in the Gulf.

Major thanks also to Dr. David MacIsaac of the Air University for his advice and for the documents he provided on Air Force doctrine. And special thanks to Major Mark

Clodfelter of the Air University for his critical commentary on the chapter on aerospace doctrine.

Thanks likewise to Dr. Mackubin Owens (colonel, USMCR) of the Naval War College for reviewing my chapter on naval doctrine and for providing a forum for discussion of my chapters on doctrine before a Naval War College symposium. Also appreciation to Mr. Frank Uhlig, editor of the *Naval War College Review,* for the documents he provided on the evolution of naval doctrine.

Many others directly or indirectly helped with this work, including Brigadier General Tim Grogan of the Army's Training and Doctrine Command, for his explanation of the evolution of joint doctrine; Navy captain Danny McGinn and the other members of the Naval War College's Strategic Studies Group for their discussion of strategic futures; and Air Force chief of staff General Merrill A. McPeak for his discussions of stealth technologies and the future of the Air Force.

A final word of thanks to my editor, E. J. McCarthy of Dell Publishing, who not only provided the original inspiration for this book but who also provided kind words and encouragement along the way; and to my wife, Eloise, and our two sons, Major Harry G. Summers III and Major David Cosgrove Summers, U.S. Army. And special thanks to our daughter-in-law, Chief Warrant Officer Kathy L. Summers, who gave the war a personal dimension as she raced across Kuwait and into Iraq with the lead brigade of the U.S. VII Corps' 3d Armored Division.

In expressing my thanks to those who provided comments and advice, I must add that the conclusions and such errors as the books may contain are solely my responsibility.

H.G.S.
Bowie, Maryland
February 1, 1992

HOW THE
WAR WAS WON

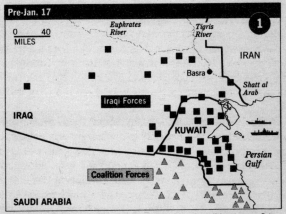

Before the air war began, Iraqi forces outnumbered coalition troops 3 to 2. U.S. and coalition forces were concentrated and aligned opposite the enemy in Kuwait, reinforcing Iraq's belief that an attack would come over the Saudi-Kuwaiti frontier. An active naval presence in the gulf presented the threat of an amphibious landing.

With Iraq's ability to perform air reconnaissance wiped out by the air war, coalition forces shifted to the west unobserved, gaining the vital element of surprise. Logistics bases were created by moving thousands upon thousands of tons of supplies. U.S. Special Forces (★) were dropped behind enemy lines to provide friendly reconnaissance.

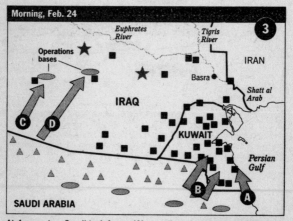

At 4 a.m., two Saudi task forces (**A**) moved up the coast, penetrating Iraqi defenses. The 1st and 2nd Marine divisions (**B**) punched through the border near where Iraq expected an assault to begin. The biggest surprise took place to the west: French forces and one brigade from the U.S. 82nd Airborne Division (**C**) drove toward As Salman air field. Hours later, the 101st Airborne Division (**D**) moved north to establish a forward fuel and ammunition base.

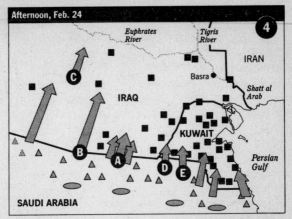

Afternoon, Feb. 24

Later that day the surprise invasion in the west continued as the U.S. VII Corps (**A**), which included the 1st British Armored Division, mounted a massive assault into Iraq. The 24th Mechanized Infantry Division (**B**) also broke over the western border, and the 101st Airborne (**C**) continued pressing north to the Tigris-Euphrates Valley. That afternoon an Egyptian-led Arab force (**D**) and a second Saudi force (**E**) broke across the Kuwaiti border farther to the east.

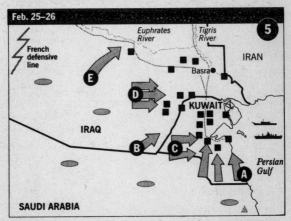

Feb. 25–26

Saudi troops (**A**) continued driving up the Kuwaiti coast. Off the coast, U.S. Special Forces pursued mine-clearing operations, keeping alive the threat of an amphibious landing. British forces (**B**) drove east, as did additional Arab forces (**C**) and the VII Corps (**D**). The 24th Division (**E**) thrust to the Euphrates River and blocked east-west roads, cutting off Iraqi forces. French troops set up a defensive line in the west.

Introduction

Forging Victory
from Defeat

America was regarded as a paper tiger. . . . It was beaten like a wet rat in Vietnam and because of this we tended to underestimate it. But the Gulf war has changed all that.

An Asian diplomat in Beijing, as reported by
Michael Breen, "North Korea in 'Gulf 'shock.' "
The Washington Times (March 12, 1991), p. A1.

If you would understand America's victory in the Persian Gulf war you must first understand America's defeat in Vietnam. Combat experience in the jungles of Vietnam was the common thread that bound all the senior U.S. commanders in the Persian Gulf war, from the chairman of the Joint Chiefs of Staff, General Colin Powell, to General H. Norman Schwarzkopf, the U.S. commander in the field, to the senior Army, Navy, Air Force, and Marine Corps generals to their colonels commanding the regiments and brigades.

But as will be seen, the lessons they drew from the jungles of Vietnam were light-years away from the perceptions held not only by the Asian diplomat

1

quoted above but also by many people around the world, including some Americans. Seen as a loser that had been defeated by a ragtag peasant army in Vietnam, plagued by a series of mishaps at Desert One in Iran and at the Marine barracks in Beirut, their successes in Grenada and Panama overshadowed by reports of things gone wrong, they were ridiculed in the media as "the gang that couldn't shoot straight."

No wonder that those who knew the military only from what they had read in the newspapers or seen on television had such a low opinion of America's fighting forces. Even at the beginning of the Persian Gulf crisis there were all kinds of stories about how the high-tech equipment wouldn't work in the desert, how the military had prepared for the wrong war at the wrong place, and how in any case the peacetime "all-volunteer" military would fall apart at the first sound of the guns.

Future conspiracy theorists will have a field day, for from a distance it surely will look like an enormous media disinformation campaign orchestrated by the U.S. government designed to lull Saddam Hussein into a false sense of complacency. And that would not have been hard to do, for by several accounts he had already gained his impressions of American impotence from discussions with bragging North Vietnamese "guest workers" sent abroad to earn hard currency for their bankrupt socialist regime.

Although they would later complain about being used by the government, the media's own nattering-nabobs-of-negativism style of reporting, which tends to hype bad news and ignore the good, was the unintended culprit. It is a news style that Americans understand and almost unconsciously discount, but it can be totally misinterpreted overseas. In any event, it gave the United States an enormous psychological warfare advantage in the Persian Gulf war, an advantage all the more sweet for being fortuitous.

As events were to dramatize, the notion that America was a paper tiger, fierce in appearance but toothless in reality, was (to use H. L. Mencken's words) "neat, plausible . . . and wrong." The reason it was wrong is what this book is all about.

Like its predecessor, *On Strategy: A Critical Analysis of the Vietnam War,* this work is not intended as a history of the Persian Gulf war. It is not a day-to-day account of tactical operations or a recounting of strategic and operational events. It is rather a *critical analysis* of the war—critical not in the first sense of that word, "tending to find fault," but in its second— "characterized by careful analysis and judgment."

Using Clausewitzian theory and the classic principles of war, *On Strategy II* examines how the victory in the Persian Gulf was forged from the defeat in Vietnam. Among other things, it deflates some of the mythology surrounding the Vietnam war, examines the postwar renaissance in the military that passed almost unnoticed in the larger community, and looks at the doctrinal changes that radically transformed the American way of war by propelling it not so much into the future as by returning it to its conventional-war past.

The intent, as with the earlier work, is to provide a deeper appreciation of strategy and the art of war so that Americans can "know the instrument they mean to use" to provide for their security and protection in what continues to be a most dangerous and uncertain world.

THE REMARKABLE TRINITY

As a total phenomenon its dominant tendencies always make war a remarkable trinity. . . .

The first of these three aspects mainly concerns the people; the second the commander and his army; the third the government. The passions that are to be kindled in war must already be inherent in the people; the scope which the play of courage and talent will enjoy in the realm of probability and chance depends on the particular character of the commander and the army; but the political aims are the business of government alone.

These three tendencies are like three different codes of law, deep-rooted in their subject and yet variable in their relationship to one another. A theory that ignores any one of them or seeks to fix an arbitrary relationship between them would conflict with reality to such an extent that for this reason alone it would be totally useless.

Carl von Clausewitz, *On War*,
Book I, chap. 1, p. 89

1

The Vietnam Syndrome and the American People

> It's a proud day for Americans and by God, we've licked the Vietnam syndrome once and for all.
>
> President George W. Bush, March 1, 1991[1]

The Vietnam Syndrome

President Bush called it a "Vietnam syndrome." Over a decade earlier President Jimmy Carter had called it a national malaise. By whatever name, it was a widespread perception that in the aftermath of the Vietnam war America had somehow lost its nerve. That perception has far-reaching consequences, for while American military *power* remained formidable after Vietnam, its military *authority* declined precipitously.

Simply stated, military power, based on physical factors that can be counted and computerized, is the aggregate of the size of a nation's armed forces; the strength of its weaponry, arms, and equipment; and the sufficiency of its sustaining logistical base. Military authority, on the other hand, is based on the more intangible perceptions by other nations that such power will be used, if need be, in pursuit of national interests. While unquantifiable, it is nonetheless real.

In its heyday, the British Empire fostered the perception that if you harmed a British citizen anywhere in the world, sooner or later—maybe not today, maybe not tomorrow, or maybe not even next week or next month, but *inevitably*—something bad was going to happen to you. And the British were not alone.

When the advancing Japanese Imperial Army swept·into Hankow, China, in 1938, noted John Paton Davies, Jr., then an American diplomat with the U.S. consulate general there, they overran the entire city except for the French concession, which was guarded by a corporal's guard of French businessmen and Tonkinese colonial mercenaries. But it was not the military power of that motley force that kept the Japanese at bay. It was military authority. "The French," Davies pointed out, "still had in 1938 the advantage of a martial reputation, the best army in Europe, and therefore the world."[2]

The United States enjoyed just such military authority after its overwhelming victories in World War II. As Ambassador Bui Diem, the Republic of Vietnam's former envoy to the United States, remarked, South Vietnamese "faith in the U.S. was total simply because . . . they thought that the powerful and disinterested U.S. could not be wrong, and all the more so because the U.S. had never lost a war in its history."[3]

National Will

But after the Vietnam war all that changed. Although U.S. military power remained potent, American military authority practically disappeared. "While mindful of superior American muscle," an Asian diplomat said in the aftermath of the Gulf war, his country "had until now figured that the United States would lack the will to fight."[4]

It was a bad rap. As discussed at length in an earlier work,[5] it was not right to blame the loss of the Vietnam war on a failure of American will. Having deliberately never been built, it could hardly be said that the national will collapsed.

At the very beginning of the war then president Lyndon B. Johnson had made a conscious decision not to mobilize the American people—to invoke the national will—for the Vietnam war for fear it would jeopardize his "Great Society" social programs. As he told his biographer:

> History provided too many cases where the sound of the bugle put an immediate end to the hopes and dreams of the best reformers: The Spanish American War drowned the populist spirit; World War I ended Woodrow Wilson's New Freedom; World War II brought the New Deal to a close. Once the [Vietnam] war began, then all those conservatives in the Congress would use it as a weapon against the Great Society. . . .[6]

Johnson's decision to attempt to fight the Vietnam war without arousing the passions of the American people was reinforced by the theories of the academic limited-war theorists. As Harvard University's Stephen Peter Rosen found, one of the most influential of these theorists, political scientist Robert Osgood, "concluded that even though the American people will be hostile, because of their traditions and ideology, to the kind of strategy he proposes, that strategy must still be adopted."[7]

Factoring the American people out of the strategic

equation was one of the most consequential and far-reaching mistakes of the Vietnam war. As former secretary of state Dean Rusk commented, "Since we wanted to limit the war, we deliberately refrained from creating a war psychology in the United States. We did not try to stir up the anger of the American people over Vietnam, and we did not have military troops parading through our cities or put on big war bond drives. Neither did we send movie actors across the country, whipping up enthusiasm for the war. . . . We tried to wage this war as 'calmly' as possible, treating it as a 'police action' rather than as a full-scale war."[8]

"We tried to do in cold blood perhaps what can only be done in hot blood, when sacrifices of this order are involved," Rusk said. "At least that's a problem that people have to think of if any such thing, God forbid, should happen again."[9]

And think about it they did. "Vietnam was a reaffirmation of the peculiar relationship between the American Army and the American people," observed General Fred C. Weyand, the last U.S. commander in Vietnam and 1974–76 Army chief of staff. "The American Army really is a people's Army in the sense that it belongs to the American people who take a jealous and proprietary interest in its involvement. . . . In the final analysis, the American Army is not so much an arm of the Executive Branch as it is an arm of the American people."[10]

Reinvolving the American people in the strategic equation became a matter of some concern within the military, especially after President Richard Nixon suspended the draft in January 1973 and opted for an "all-volunteer" military. As will be discussed in greater detail in subsequent chapters, General Creighton W. Abrams, Weyand's predecessor as Army chief of staff, set out in 1974 to create an active duty-reserve component "total Army" where the "citizen soldiers" of the Army National Guard and Army Reserves served as a bridge between the active Army and the American people.[11] This decision would have a profound effect on the conduct of the Persian Gulf war.

Another decision that would have a profound effect on that war was the adoption of Princeton University Press's new 1976 translation of Carl von Clausewitz's classic *On War* as the foundation for military strategy, doctrine, and theory. Particularly apt was Clausewitz's emphasis on the "remarkable trinity" of the people, the government, and the army as the essential basis for military operations. He could have been talking about Vietnam when he warned that "A theory that ignores any of them . . . would conflict with reality to such an extent that for this reason alone it would be totally useless."[12]

Public Support

Putting the lie to Osgood and the other limited-war theorists who preached that war was the business of government alone, Clausewitz stressed that "the only source of war is politics—the intercourse of governments and peoples."[13] In November 1984, that Clausewitzian tenet was reintroduced into U.S. politico-military doctrine by Secretary of Defense Caspar W. Weinberger himself. Speaking before the National Press Club on "the uses of military power," Weinberger emphasized the criticality of public support. Among his six preconditions for the commitment of U.S. forces to combat was his conviction that "before the U.S. commits combat forces abroad, there must be some reasonable assurance we will have the support of the American people and their elected representatives in the Congress."[14]

The Vietnam era "we experts know best what's good for you" fallacy did not die without a fight.

Speaking for the coterie of self-appointed academic and media elitists who saw military policy as their private preserve, *The New York Times* columnist William Safire sarcastically commented that "Secretary Weinberger's stunning doctrine suggests that we take a poll before we pull a trigger. No more unpopular wars—if the public won't hold a big parade to send us off, we're not going."[15]

But it was Safire who was off-target. In denouncing what he called Weinberger's "doctrine of only the fun wars" he was in fact denouncing the Constitution itself. Having just gone through a divisive eight-year war to win American independence, the framers of the Constitution—twenty-three of whom were veterans of that conflict—knew how difficult it was to maintain public support in wartime. As historian Dave R. Palmer pointed out in his history of Revolutionary War strategy, the biggest threat facing British troops in Philadelphia was not the Continental Army but the venereal disease rate.[16]

To ensure public support and to enshrine the moral principle that those whose tax monies paid "to provide for the common defense" and whose sons' (and now daughters') lives would be emperiled on the battlefield, the Constitution would make the military an instrument of the American people themselves. As Alexander Hamilton explained:

The whole power of raising armies [is to be] lodged in the *Legislature*, not in the *Executive*; This Legislature [is] to be a popular body, consisting of the representatives of the people, periodically elected. . . .

The power of the President would be inferior to that of the Monarch. . . . That of the British King extends to the *Declaring* of war and to the *Raising and Regulating* of fleets and armies; All which by the Constitution . . . would appertain to the Legislature.[17]

These precepts were incorporated in Article I, Section 8 of the Constitution: "The Congress shall have power: . . . To declare war. . . . To raise and support armies. . . . To provide and maintain a navy. To make rules for the government and regulation of the land and naval forces. To provide for calling forth . . . organizing, arming, and disciplining the militia. . . ."

And if these moral considerations are not sufficient to provide the necessity of public support, the practical considerations are even more compelling. As Article 1, Section 9 of the Constitution makes clear, "No money shall be drawn from the Treasury but in consequence of appropriations made by law. . . ." As will be examined in more depth in the following chapter, by controlling appropriations, Congress—and hence the American people—have absolute control not only over the military's ability to wage war but over their very existence as well.

Thus, Safire and his ilk notwithstanding, Secretary Weinberger was absolutely right. Public support is an essential precondition for the conduct of military operations. And in making that point clear, Weinberger set the stage for the successful prosecution of the Persian Gulf war.

Antimilitarism

One of the reasons public support and the national will had been factored out of the strategic equation during the Vietnam war was that it was almost impossible to quantify. As Clausewitz had noted a century and a half earlier, "To assess these things in all their ramifications and diversity is plainly a colossal task . . . to master all this complex mass by sheer methodical examination is obviously impossible, [Napoleon] Bonaparte was quite right when he said that [Isaac] Newton himself would quail before the algebraic problems it could pose.''[18]

American national will is particulary difficult to predict. As Kaiser Wilhelm, Adolf Hitler, Hideki Tojo, Kim Il Sung, Muammar al-Qaddafi, Manuel Noriega, and Saddam Hussein found to their sorrow, it is easy to reach the erroneous conclusion that Americans lack the will to fight. One American character trait that can be especially misleading is antimilitarism.

''Americans have a long and proud tradition of irreverence toward and distrust of their military,'' General Fred Weyand observed in the aftermath of the Vietnam war. American antimilitarism springs from a variety of causes—historical, cultural, and social. It has been a constant since the beginning of the republic. ''There's no use agonizing over it,'' General Weyand said. ''If we cannot be loved, we can be trusted and respected.''[19] Even he would have been surprised by the degree to which this came true during the Persian Gulf war.

But during the Vietnam war this basic antimilitarism was aggravated by several factors. One was the decision to grant draft deferments to students. ''This policy,'' observed General William C. Westmoreland, America's commander in Vietnam from 1964 to 1968, ''contributed to antiwar militance on college campuses in that young men feeling twinges of conscience because they sat out the war while others fought could appease their conscience if they convinced themselves the war was immoral.''[20]

Antiwar activism was not peculiar to the Vietnam war. Every American war had sparked protests of one kind or another. ''Militarism [is] an evil from which it has been our glory to be free,'' said the American

Anti-Imperialist League in 1899 during the Spanish-American War. "[While] we deplore the sacrifices of our soldiers and sailors, whose bravery deserves admiration even in an unjust war, [we believe] the United States cannot act on the ancient heresy that might makes right."[21]

But in the Vietnam war antiwar activists directed their venom against the military itself. It was a tactic that would cost them much public support. As the University of Rochester's professor John Mueller found, contrary to the folklore that has grown up around it, "the Vietnam protest movement, at least through 1968, actually was somewhat counterproductive in its efforts to influence public opinion—that is, the war might have been somewhat more unpopular had the protest not existed. . . .

"[T]he Vietnam protest movement generated negative feelings among the American public to an all but unprecedented degree. In a poll conducted by the University of Michigan in 1968, the public was asked to place various groups and personalities on a 100-point scale. Fully one-third of the respondents gave Vietnam War protesters a zero, the lowest possible rating. . . . Opposition to the war came to be associated with violent disruption, stink bombs, desecration of the flag, profanity and contempt for American values."[22]

In the aftermath of the war, *mea culpas* from former draft dodgers were commonplace, such as James Fallows's "What Did You Do in the Class War, Daddy?,"[23] which fatuously predicted a class war between those who fought the war and those "elites" who evaded it. Fallows and his fellow antiwar activists misjudged their own importance. Within a decade the war protesters had fallen from their high moral plateau to the depths of derision. Addressing a student group at the State University of New York at Stony Brook in the mid-1980s, a former antiwar activist said that the reason he opposed the war was to bring our boys home safely. A student then contemptuously asked, "When you spit at them, and called them baby-killers, and threw rocks at them, was that just your way of saying 'Glad to see you'?"[24]

This about-face in American attitudes was revealed in an unlikely source, Garry Trudeau's April 21, 1991, *Doonesbury* cartoon. At an outdoor reception "Congresswoman Davenport" is being served by a college student bartender. Both agree that they had supported the Persian Gulf war. But when she asks, "Do you think you should have fought in it?," he replies "Uh . . . No, not really. I mean, it was a just war and all. . . . But I'm not so sure the country's best and brightest should be on the front lines."

"And yet, there they were" was her caustic reply.

Not understanding the volatility of American public opinion, Saddam Hussein missed this shift in attitudes and may well have believed that the antiwar movement would stay America's hand as he believed it had done in Vietnam. And for a moment it looked like he might be right. Within two weeks of Iraq's invasion of Kuwait, protests broke out across America. But they soon fizzled out. Ridiculed by the media as the work of the professional protester class, their demonstrations drew relatively few supporters outside of their own fevered ranks and were generally ignored. Their influence on U.S. policy was nil.

Instead American public opinion overwhelmingly supported the president and his Persian Gulf policies. One reason was that with the end of the draft in 1973, all of the military forces committed to the war, active and reserve, were volunteers. Not themselves immediately liable for military service, college students had no particular incentive to protest.

And when some antiwar groups attempted to exploit the handful of "conscientious objectors" who refused to serve in the Gulf, this, too, backfired. Most Americans had little sympathy for those who only discovered the horrors of military service after they got orders to go overseas. If they were so opposed to war, most asked, why had they enlisted in the first place?

Yet another reason, noted Peter Braestrup, whose classic *Big Story* (New Haven, Conn.: Yale University Press, 1983) analyzed media coverage of the Vietnam war, was that "during Vietnam the left adopted [North Vietnamese leader] Ho Chi Minh as a good guy. In contrast, during the Persian Gulf crisis no one has adopted [Iraqi president] Saddam Hussein as the good guy."[25]

Building a National Consensus

But a more important reason was that, after several false starts, President Bush, wittingly or unwittingly, had followed Caspar Weinberger's advice and set out to garner public and congressional support for his Persian Gulf policies. That had never been done during the Vietnam war.

As former assistant secretary of defense for public affairs Phil G. Goulding admitted, "In my four-year tour [1965–69] there was not once a significant organized effort by the Executive Branch of the federal government to put across its side of a major policy issue or a major controversy to the American people. Not once was there a 'public affairs program' . . . worthy of the name."[26]

That was yet another key failing. "Since war is . . . controlled by its political object," Clausewitz emphasized, "the value of this object must determine the sacrifices to be made for it in *magnitude* and also in *duration*."[27]

By its nature the media can be counted on to show the cost of war, and the antiwar movement, not surprisingly, will do everything in its power to magnify those costs. But "costs" only have meaning in relationship to value, and it is the responsibility of the government to set national objectives and in so doing establish the value of military operations.

In World War II the political objective was survival of the nation, and we paid over a million casualties in its pursuit. In Vietnam, as will be discussed later in more detail, the objective was never clear. Because the value was never fixed, the costs soon became exorbitant.

At first President Bush seemed to be falling into the same trap. "By refusing to go on television to address the American people, George Bush is leaving the same vacuum Lyndon Johnson did during and after [the 1968] Tet [offensive]," warned Peter Braestrup in November 1990. "Like Johnson, more and more Bush is turning the stage over to the anti-war people."[28]

But that same month President Bush went on the offensive. At every opportunity he explained America's political objectives in the Persian Gulf. Writing in the November 26, 1990, *Newsweek,* he reiterated them once again:

> Our goals have not changed since I first outlined them to the American people last August. First, the immediate and unconditional withdrawal of all Iraqi forces from Kuwait. Second, the restoration of Kuwait's legitimate government. Third, security and stability for the Gulf— an important national interest of the United States since the time of Harry Truman. And fourth, the protection of American citizens abroad.[29]

It was a masterful campaign. As General Abrams had predicted, Bush's decision to mobilize and deploy units of the Army and Air National Guard and the Army, Air Force, Navy, Marine Corps, and Coast Guard reserves involved communities across the nation in the war effort and built a bridge between the military and the American people.

Coalition-building among the Arab nations and among U.S. allies around the world also garnered public support, as did the administration's decision to seek formal approval at the United Nations for U.S. actions. And although President Bush did not ask Congress for a formal declaration of war, on January 7, 1991, he did finally ask Congress to authorize the use of "all necessary means" to drive Iraq out of Kuwait. After an intensive debate, a war resolution was forthcoming on January 12, 1991, five days before the outbreak of the war.

This time we had done it right. The American people were back in the strategic equation. According to an ABC poll on January 18, 1991, the day after the air war began, 83 percent of Americans supported the war, while 71 percent disapproved of domestic protesters. At war's end a *Washington Post*-ABC poll gave President Bush an unprecedented 90 percent approval rating.[30] No wonder he could proclaim, "By God, we've licked the Vietnam syndrome once and for all."

NOTES

1. President George W. Bush, quoted in Ann Devroy and Guy Gugliotta, "Bush to 'Move Fast' on Mideast Peace," *The Washington Post* (March 2, 1991), p. A13.

2. John Paton Davies, Jr., *Dragon by the Tail* (New York: W. W. Norton & Company, 1972), p. 200.

3. Bui Diem, "Reflections of a Vietnamese on the Vietnam War," discussion paper, Fourteenth Military History Symposium, U.S. Air Force Academy (October 17–19, 1990), p. 4.

4. Quoted in Michael Breen, "North Korea in Gulf 'shock,' " *The Washington Times* (March 12, 1991), p. A1.

5. Harry G. Summers, Jr., *On Strategy: A Critical Analysis of the Vietnam War* (New York, Dell Publishing, 1984), pp. 33–34. (Hereafter cited as *On Strategy*.)

6. Lyndon B. Johnson, quoted in Doris Kearns, *Lyndon Johnson and the American Dream* (New York: Harper & Row, 1976), p. 252.

7. Stephen Peter Rosen, "Vietnam and the American Theory of Limited War," *International Security* (Fall 1982), p. 85.

8. Dean Rusk, *As I Saw It* (New York: W. W. Norton & Company, 1990), pp. 499–500.

9. Dean Rusk, quoted in Michael Charlton and Anthony Moncrief, *Many Reasons Why: The American Involvement in Vietnam* (New York: Hill & Wang, 1978), p. 115.

10. Fred C. Weyand, "Vietnam Myths and American Military Realities," *CDRS CALL* (September–October 1976), quoted in *On Strategy,* p. 33.

11. Harry G. Summers, Jr., *On Strategy: The Vietnam War in Context* (Washington, D.C.: U.S. Government Printing Office, 1981), pp. 111–13. This government version of *On Strategy* differs from the commercial version only in its subtitle and its epilogue, which is more oriented toward a military audience.

12. Carl von Clausewitz, *On War,* ed. and trans. (Princeton, N.J.: Princeton University Press, 1976), p. 89. (Hereafter cited as *On War*.)

13. Ibid., p. 605.

14. Caspar W. Weinberger, "The Uses of Military Power," News Release 609–84 (Washington, D.C.: Office of the Assistant Secretary of Defense for Public Affairs, November 28, 1984), p. 6.

15. William Safire, "Only the 'Fun' Wars," *The New York Times* (December 3, 1984), p. A23.

16. Dave R. Palmer, *The Way of the Fox: American Strategy in the War for America 1775–1783* (Westport, Conn.: Greenwood Press, 1975), pp. 81–148.

17. Alexander Hamilton, "The Federalist No. 24 (December 19, 1787)" and "The Federalist No. 69 (March 14,

1788)," *The Federalist,* ed. by James E. Cooke. (Middletown, Conn.: Wesleyan University Press, 1961), pp. 153, 465.

18. *On War,* p. 586.

19. Fred C. Weyand, "Serving the People: The Need for Military Power," *Military Review* (December 1976), p. 8.

20. William C. Westmoreland, *A Soldier Reports* (Garden City, N.Y.: Doubleday & Company, 1976), p. 297.

21. "Platform of the American Anti-Imperialist League," October 18, 1899, in Henry Steele Commager, ed., *Documents in American History,* vol. 2 (New York: Appleton-Century-Crofts, 1963), pp. 11–12.

22. John Mueller, "Reflections on the Vietnam Antiwar Movement and on the Curious Calm at the War's End," *Vietnam As History,* ed. Peter Braestrup. (Washington, D.C.: University Press of America, 1984), pp. 151–52.

23. James Fallows, "What Did You Do in the Class War, Daddy?," *Washington Monthly* (October 1975), pp. 5–19.

24. Author's notes.

25. Peter Braestrup, quoted in Don Kowet, "Are the Media Inventing a New Anti-War Movement?," *The Washington Times* (November 23, 1990), p. E1.

26. Phil G. Goulding, *Confirm or Deny: Informing the People on National Security* (New York: Harper & Row, 1970), pp. 81–82.

27. *On War,* p. 92.

28. Braestrup quoted in Kowetz, p. E6.

29. George Bush, "Why We Are in the Gulf," *Newsweek* (November 26, 1991), p. 29.

30. Joseph P. Englehart, ed., *Desert Shield and Desert Storm: A Chronology and Troop List* (Carlisle Barracks, Pa.: Strategic Studies Institute, U.S. Army War College, 1991), pp. 31, 71.

2

The Vietnam Syndrome and the Government

> Our firm view is that the president has no legal authority, none whatsoever, to commit American troops to war in the Persian Gulf or anywhere else without congressional authorization.
>
> Senator George J. Mitchell (D., Me.)[1]

War and the Constitution

The conviction that war is a shared responsibility of the people, the government, and the military is as old as the nation itself. On September 17, 1787, some forty-five years before Carl von Clausewitz's people-government-army "remarkable trinity" theory[2] was promulgated, the Constitution of the United States incorporated that concept into law.

Emerging from the bitter eight-year war for American independence, the framers of that Constitution sought to ensure that the United States would not enter into war lightly. War powers were deliberately split between the Executive and the Legislative branches. The president was made commander in chief of the armed forces, while the power to raise armies and to declare war was reserved to the Congress.

As James Wilson of Pennsylvania, one of the Constitution's primary drafters, explained, "This system will not hurry us into war; it is calculated to guard against it. It will not be in the power of a single man or a single body of men, to involve us in such distress."[3]

Declaration of War

For most of our history, that principle was well understood. In his war message on June 1, 1812, President James Madison deferred the decision to go to war on to the Congress. "Whether the United States shall continue passive . . . or, opposing force to force in defense of their national rights . . . is a solemn question which the Constitution wisely confides to the legislative department of the Government," he said.[4]

And even though he claimed that "Mexico has . . . invaded our territory and shed American blood on the American soil," in his war message to the Senate and House of Representatives on May 11, 1846, President James K. Polk did not fall back on his powers as commander in chief of the armed forces under Article II of the Constitution to repel the invasion. Instead he invoked "the prompt action of Congress to recognize the existence of the war, and to place at the disposal of the Executive the means of prosecuting the war with vigor. . . ."[5]

Likewise, President William McKinley did not act unilaterally, even after the U.S. battleship *Maine* had been blow up in Havana Harbor on February 15, 1898, sending the nation into a paroxysm of jingoistic war fever. Rather, after asking the Congress on April 11, 1898, for authority "to use the military and naval forces of the United States as may be necessary," he allowed that "The issue is now with the Congress. It is a solemn responsibility. I have exhausted every effort to relieve the intolerable condition of affairs which is at our doors. Prepared to execute every obligation imposed upon me by the Constitution and the law, I await your action."[6]

And when President Woodrow Wilson addressed a joint session of Congress on April 2, 1917, to "advise that the Congress declare the recent course of the Imperial German Government to be in fact nothing less than war against the government and people of the United States," he began by stating, "I have called the Congress into extraordinary session because there are serious, very serious, choices of policy to be made, and made immediately, which it was neither right nor constitutionally permissible that I should assume the responsibility of making."[7]

Finally even after the Japanese had launched a devastating sneak attack on U.S. naval and military forces in the Hawaiian Islands, Guam, and the Philippines, President Franklin D. Roosevelt still thought it necessary to appear before Congress on December 8, 1941, and "ask that the Congress declare that since the unprovoked and dastardly attack by Japan on Sunday, December seventh, a state of war has existed between the United States and the Japanese Empire."[8]

Significantly, public antiwar sentiment was then so high in America that Roosevelt did not at the same time ask for a declaration of war against Germany. On December 11, 1941, that problem was solved when Adolf Hitler declared war against the United States. That same day Roosevelt asked Congress to affirm that "a state of war exists between the Government of

Germany and the government and the people of the United States.''[9]

Korea: A Terrible Precedent

After such formal declarations of war, it would seem that the precedent for shared war powers between the Executive and Legislative branches had been well established. Ironically, it was to become unglued during the Korean war, not so much by design as by accident. President Harry S Truman had no intention of usurping the Constitution when on June 27, 1950, he responded to a call from the UN Security Council for all members of the United Nations to assist South Korea in repelling the North Korean cross-border invasion that had begun two days earlier.

That very day, without seeking congressional approval, he "ordered United States air and sea forces to give the Korean Government troops cover and support." Three days later he would authorize use of ground troops as well.

"The attack upon Korea makes it plain beyond all doubt," he said, "that Communism has passed beyond the use of subversion to conquer independent nations and will now use armed invasion and war." Accordingly he "ordered the Seventh Fleet to prevent any attack on Formosa [Taiwan]," directed that "United States Forces in the Philippines be strengthened," and in a move that would ultimately have fatal consequences, "similarly directed acceleration in the furnishing of military assistance to the forces of France and the Associated States of Indo-China and the dispatch of a military mission to provide close working relations with those forces."[10]

Truman's failure to seek a congressional declaration of war (which he could have had for the asking) before committing American armed forces to sustained combat would set far-reaching precedents, but at the time it went virtually unchallenged. The Congress's "endorsement of President Truman's firm response to the North Korean invasion reflected the general tone of public opinion," noted the late Republican senator Jacob Javits of New York. "[T]here was little disposition to invoke the Constitution against a President who had already gained a considerable reputation as a man of the people. HST simply didn't have the look of a 'usurper' about him."[11]

And the military also took little notice. During the "Great Debate" on the Korean war (the 1951 Joint Senate Armed Services and Foreign Affairs Committees hearings), General of the Army Douglas A. MacArthur, who had just been relieved as commander in chief of the Far East Command and as commander in chief of the UN Command, was asked whether the United States should have declared war against North Korea or China.

"The actions of the United Nations might well be regarded as [the] declaration of war," MacArthur replied. When pressed, he said that he "had never given special consideration to the *technical question* of whether a declaration of war should be made or not."[12] The confusion was evident in the comments of General of the Army Omar N. Bradley, the chairman of the Joint Chiefs of Staff. "Someone might question whether technically or not [the Korean War] was a war because normally Congress declares war and I don't believe Congress has declared a war," he said. "The question of when to declare war in this case, how to do it, and how you explain it to the people, the exact nature of it I don't know."[13]

But to its credit, the Congress did recognize the danger involved. One of the principal concerns of the congressional joint committee was that the Korean war not set a political-military precedent for future wars. "The United States should never again become involved in a war without the consent of the Congress," read its final report.[14]

Vietnam: The Error Compounded

Ironically, President Lyndon B. Johnson, who as a senator had been a member of that committee, wrote in his autobiography, "I believed that President Truman's one mistake in courageously going to the defense of South Korea in 1950 had been his failure to ask Congress for an expression of its backing. He could have had it easily, and it would have strengthened his hand. I made up my mind not to repeat that error."[15]

But that's exactly what he did. Instead of fully involving the Congress in his decision to go to war in Vietnam after U.S. destroyers were attacked by North Vietnamese motor torpedo boats in the Gulf of Tonkin in August 1964, President Johnson asked instead for a congressional resolution empowering him to "take all necessary measures to repel an armed attack against the forces of the United States and to prevent further aggression." This Southeast Asia Resolution (better known as the "Gulf of Tonkin Resolution") passed the Senate by a vote of 88–2 and the House by a unanimous voice vote of 426–0.[16]

Not only was it not a declaration of war, but also some in the Congress saw it as precisely the opposite. "In voting unlimited presidential power most members of Congress thought they were providing for retaliation for an attack on our forces," said Senator Javits, "and *preventing* a large-scale war in Asia."[17]

The error was compounded several months later, when in March 1965 President Johnson ordered American ground forces into the war. Instead of going back to the Congress, Johnson deliberately played down the action, and "efforts were made to make this change as imperceptible as possible to the American people."[18] The irony, as one of his severest critics later acknowledged, was that "Johnson could certainly have obtained congressional authorization beyond the Tonkin Gulf resolution for a limited war in Vietnam in 1965. He might even, had he wished (but no one wished), have obtained a declaration of war."[19]

But not all the blame lay with the Executive Branch. "Whatever President Johnson's position," acknowledged Senator Javits, "Congress had the obligation to make an institutional judgement as to the wisdom and the propriety of giving such a large grant of its own power to the Chief Executive. . . . The power of decision . . . had not been stolen. It had been surrendered."[20]

And many in the Congress preferred it that way. They had the luxury of being all things to all people. Even the most vociferous Congressional opponents of the war consistently voted the funds for the war's continuation as long as American forces were involved, while at the same time undercutting public support for the war by railing against it at every opportunity.

"I do think that we should have gone to the Congress each year for a vote up or down on the Tonkin Gulf Resolution," said Dean Rusk, President Johnson's secretary of state. "[But] it was the Congressional leadership who strongly urged President Johnson not to do that. . . . Nevertheless, in retrospect I think we should have held the feet of Congress to the fire and required them to make up their minds."[21]

General William C. Westmoreland, America's military commander in Vietnam from 1964 to 1968, agreed. "When dissent [against the war] developed in 1966 and 1967, [President Johnson] would have been well advised to have gone back to the Congress for reaffirmation of the commitment to South Vietnam, a vote either of confidence or rejection. . . . [He] should have forced the Congress to face its constitutional responsibility for waging war."[22]

But instead Johnson repudiated Congress's role completely. "We stated then, and we repeat now," he said in an August 18, 1967, news conference, "we did not think the [Gulf of Tonkin] resolution was necessary to do what we did and what we're doing."[23] Earlier, in March 1966, the State Department's legal adviser told the Senate Committee on Foreign Relations that "There can be no question . . . of the president's authority to commit U.S. Forces to the defense of South Vietnam. The grant of authority to the President in article II of the Constitution extends to the actions of the United States currently undertaken in Vietnam."[24] When he took office in 1969, President Richard M. Nixon also fell back on his authority as commander in chief as the legal basis for the prosecution of the Vietnam war.[25]

A year later, the Gulf of Tonkin Resolution was terminated. "The Executive Branch has already . . . disavowed a reliance on the Gulf of Tonkin resolution as authority or support for its conduct of the war in Indochina," noted the Senate Committee on Foreign Relations in its May 1, 1970, report. "The committee [also] does not regard the Tonkin resolution as a valid legal authorization for the war in Indochina. This being the case, repeal of the resolution will not create but simply confirm and clarify the existence of a legal vacuum."[26]

And repeal did not resolve the fundamental issue, either: "the proper locus within our constitutional system of the authority to commit our country to war." As the Senate Committee on Foreign Relations report noted, "It is the Executive's view . . . that the President, in his capacity as Commander-in-Chief, is properly empowered to commit the Armed Forces to hostilities in foreign countries. It is the committee's view—*conviction* may be the better word—that the authority to initiate war, as distinguished from acting to repel a sudden attack, is vested by the Constitution in the Congress and in the Congress alone."[27]

The Congress could have forced the issue at any time of its choosing, either by impeachment of the president for exceeding his constitutional warmaking powers or by refusing to appropriate the funds necessary for the prosecution of the war. But those actions would have come at a considerable political cost, and the Congress supinely chose to do neither.

Congress's Codified Vietnam Syndrome

Instead, on November 7, 1973, seven months after all U.S. forces were withdrawn from Vietnam in accordance with the so-called Paris Peace Accords, the Congress, over President Nixon's veto, passed the War Powers Resolution. Its purpose, stated its preamble, was "to fulfill the intent of the framers of the Constitution of the United States and insure that the collective judgement of both the Congress and the President will apply to the introduction of United States Armed Forces into hostilities, or into situations where imminent involvement in hostilities is clearly indicated by the circumstances, and to the continued use of such forces in hostilities or in such situations."[28]

The resolution required the president to consult with the Congress before military forces were committed. Military action could continue for sixty days, and for another thirty days thereafter if the president certifies in writing that the safety of the force so required. Unless Congress specifically authorized it by a declaration of war, resolution, or legislation, the involvement cannot be continued beyond the ninety days.

In truth the War Powers Resolution should have been named the "Congressional Vietnam Syndrome Resolution," for it was a pitiful restatement of its lack of backbone during that conflict. As the University of Virginia's Robert F. Turner put it, "It was, in essence, an act of political subterfuge which allowed members of Congress to pretend to their constituents that 'they' were not responsible for the horrors of Vietnam."[29]

A Congress that lacked the will to use its considerable powers to force the president to abide by the Constitution during the Vietnam war could hardly be expected to have the strength of character to force future presidents to abide by a mere resolution that in effect watered down rather than strengthened Congress's constitutional warmaking authority.

Seeing it for what it was, every president since its enactment has ignored the War Powers Resolution with impunity. Declaring the resolution unconstitutional, they all refused to be limited by its provisions. That was true when President Gerald Ford committed American forces to the evacuation of Saigon and to the rescue of the *Mayaguez* in the spring of 1975. And it was true in April 1980, when President Jimmy Carter put American troops in harm's way at Desert One in Iran. And President Ronald Reagan flagrantly flouted the War Powers Resolution when he sent U. S. Marines into Beirut in 1983, when he sent troops into Grenada that same year, and when he bombed Libya in April 1986.

Ironically, as was discussed earlier, one of the strongest voices for congressional participation in military action came from Reagan administration defense secretary Caspar W. Weinberger. In his November 28, 1984, National Press Club speech calling for public support as a precondition for commitment of U.S. forces to combat, he called for congressional support as well. "Before the U.S. commits combat forces abroad," he said, "there must be some reasonable assurance we will have the support of the American people and their elected representatives in the Congress. . . . We cannot fight a battle with the Congress at home while asking our troops to win a war overseas."[30]

But there did not seem to be any "battle with the Congress" involved. Weinberger's words notwithstanding, the War Powers Resolution was once again contemptuously flouted on December 20, 1989, when, while Congress was in recess, President George Bush launched Operation Just Cause, the U.S. invasion of Panama to depose Panamanian strongman Manuel Antonio Noriega.

In each incidence the Congress did nothing to enforce its own writ. It did not vote to impeach the president for failing to uphold the War Powers Resolution, which was, in fact, the law of the land, enacted on November 7, 1973, as Public Law 93-148. It did not force a confrontation with the Executive Branch, which would have required the U.S. Supreme Court to decide the issue once and for all. And it did not use its power of the purse to restrain presidential warmaking powers. In the face of this congressional pusillanimity, the Executive Branch, it seemed, had successfully arrogated war powers to itself alone.

The Vietnam war and its aftermath had not been the Legislative Branch's finest hour. "A Congress that lets the president call the shots on war and peace," wrote Stanford University professor John Hart Ely on the eve of the Persian Gulf war, "and devotes itself instead to the construction of private political bomb shelters, is not what the framers of the Constitution had in mind in vesting the war power in the legislative process."[31]

The Persian Gulf Crisis

That was the sad state of affairs when the Persian Gulf crisis erupted on August 2, 1990. Although the president did issue Executive Order 12722 that day declaring a national emergency "to address the threat to the national security and foreign policy of the United States posed by the invasion of Kuwait by Iraq," he did not invoke the War Powers Resolution, nor did he ask Congress for a declaration of war.

Like Presidents Johnson and Nixon before him in the Vietnam war, President Bush fell back on his authority as commander in chief under Section II of the Constitution. Once again the same tired arguments were dredged up to support that position. Making war is the president's business, ran one argument, and Congress would be exceeding its constitutional mandate if it chose to interfere. It would be "micromanaging" the war.

But oversight of military operations is certainly within congressional purview, the first such incidence being its investigation of the disaster suffered by Major General Arthur St. Clair in his clash with Indian leader Little Turtle on the banks of the Wabash River on November 4, 1791.[32] "It is about as clear as anything can be in constitutional interpretation," noted *The New Republic*'s Michael Kinsley, "that the Framers did not intend to give the president carte blanche. . . .

"That fact prompts the second counterargument:" writes Kinsley, "forget the Framers. In real life, over two centuries, the president has taken on the war power. A favorite statistic is that the United States has sent forces abroad some 200 times, while there have been only five declarations of war."[33]

But while perhaps statistically correct, that argument is specious as well. First invoked by President Thomas Jefferson in 1801, when, without seeking prior

congressional approval, he dispatched the newly
formed U.S. Navy to put down the Barbary pirates,
the authority of the president in his role as commander
in chief under Article II of the Constitution to dispatch
troops to repel invasion or otherwise counter immediate threats to American security is well established.[34]

But until the Korean war, in every major military
conflict in which the United States has been involved—the War of 1812, the war with Mexico, the
Spanish-American war, World War I, and World War
II—the president has deferred to the Congress and
asked for a declaration of war. As Professors Francis
D. Wormuth and Edwin B. Firmage noted in their pre-
Gulf war analysis of congressional war powers, "No
contemporaneous congressional interpretation attrib-
utes a power of initiating war to the President. The
early Presidents, and indeed everyone in the country
until the year 1950, denied that the President possessed such a power."

Debunking the notion "that in the course of our
history the President has very frequently exercised the
power to make war without congressional authorization—and that he has done so on one or two hundred
occasions," they find that allegation "entirely unsup-
ported by fact." Even if the claim was true, they point
out, quoting U.S. Supreme Court justice Felix Frank-
furter, "Illegality cannot attain legitimacy through
practice."

Most of the "wars" were naval landings for the
protection of citizens (specifically authorized by the
Congress) where no collision of hostile forces or no
bloodshed ensued or "trivial actions undertaken by a
naval officer in a distant port on personal responsibility." Except for the Korean and Vietnam wars, most
of the others were enforcement of the laws against
piracy, reprisals against aborigines, various Caribbean
interventions, and the like.

They concluded, "It can only be audacity or desperation that leads the champions of . . . presidential usurpations to state that 'history had legitimized the practice of presidential warmaking.' "³⁵ But throughout the Persian Gulf crisis the "two-hundred-war" canard was repeated time and again at the highest levels of the government.

While President Bush vowed that a Gulf war "would not be another Vietnam," Congress at first seemed to be following the same feckless course they had followed in that conflict, nattering on about the president's actions but, in what Robert Turner called a "spirit of legislative timidity," refusing to assert their own warmaking powers. That inaction continued throughout the 1990 congressional election campaign, where the Gulf crisis was virtually ignored.

The Constitution Rediscovered

But all that changed on November 8, 1990, when President Bush, with the intent of developing an adequate offensive military option against Iraq, ordered another 150,000 American troops, including the VII Corps, with its two armored divisions and armored cavalry regiment to the Gulf to augment the 230,000 already there. As Senator Sam Nunn (D., Ga.), the chairman of the Senate Armed Services Committee, said in a television interview on CBS, the president's new troop levels meant that Gulf policy had undergone a "fundamental change."³⁶

And so, at long last, had the attitude of the Congress. On November 21, 1990, forty-five members of the Congress (later increased to fifty-four members) filed suit in federal court to bar President Bush from taking offensive action in the Persian Gulf without obtaining a declaration of war "or other explicit authority from the Congress." Led by Representative

Ronald V. Dellums (D., Ca.), the group, significantly, cited Article I, Section 8 of the Constitution as the basis for their action. They did not cite the 1973 War Powers Resolution, Dellums said, because it was "a meaningless piece of legislation."[37]

Their petition was rejected by U.S. District Court judge Harold Greene on December 13, 1990, in part because it was unclear that war was imminent. But as a *Washington Post* editorial noted, his decision broke new ground. "Judge Greene specifically found that courts do have the power to determine what is war and what is not; that hostilities involving hundreds of thousands of American troops in the Gulf would, in fact, be war; and that in such a situation Congress would have the right to vote on a declaration of war, and a court *could* enjoin the president from acting without such a declaration."[38]

Meanwhile, Senator Nunn, also no friend of the War Powers Resolution, began hearings before his Senate Armed Services Committee on November 27, 1990. From the lead witness, former defense secretary James Schlesinger through two former chairmen of the Joint Chiefs of Staff, Air Force general David C. Jones and Navy admiral William J. Crowe, Jr., the consensus was that economic sanctions ought to be given more time to work.[39]

But it was Secretary of Defense Dick Cheney's testimony on December 3, 1990, the last day of the hearings, that touched off a fire storm. Asked by Senator Edward Kennedy (D., Mass.) whether he agreed that the president must obtain the approval of Congress in advance before launching an attack on Iraq, Cheney replied, "I do not believe the President requires any additional authorization from the Congress before committing U.S. forces to achieve our objectives in the Gulf."[40]

The next day the House Democratic Caucus, on a

vote of 177–37, adopted a nonbinding policy statement declaring that President Bush should not initiate any offensive military action in the Persian Gulf without the formal approval of Congress unless American lives were in danger.[41] It appeared that the bipartisan coalition in support of President Bush's policy in the Persian Gulf was in imminent danger of collapse.

Meanwhile, on December 4, 1990, while the House Democratic Caucus was still meeting, Representative Les Aspin (D., Wis.), chairman of the House Armed Services Committee, opened hearings on the Gulf crisis. "Action that isn't backed by consensus will mean disaster," he said. "Whatever we do, the country, the Congress and the President must do it standing on common ground." The committee then set out "to look at the three broad policy options open to us to resolve the crisis. Sanctions, war and diplomacy."[42] After calling some thirty-four witnesses, the author included, the committee adjourned on December 20, 1990.

While Senator Nunn had concluded that more time should be given for sanctions to work, Representative Aspin came to a quite different conclusion. "On a vote to authorize the President to use force to liberate Kuwait," he wrote in his January 8, 1991, white paper on the hearings, "the right vote is 'yes.' "[43]

But would the Congress be given an opportunity to vote? That was the question when the 102nd Congress convened on January 3, 1991. As *The New York Times* editorialized, "Will Congress debate and vote on President Bush's war policy in the Persian Gulf? Will Mr. Bush ask it to? . . . Until now, the Congress has shirked its constitutional duty to debate a declaration of war. . . . That's unconscionable. While hundreds of thousands of young Americans gird for battle in the deserts of Arabia, their elected representatives can't summon up the courage to confront their responsibilities at home.''

The editorial concluded, ''A deferred debate on a declaration of war invites divisiveness at the worst possible time—after Mr. Bush takes the country to war.''[44] Adding to the pressure, a *USA TODAY* poll conducted on December 29–30, 1990, found that seven of ten Americans ''say [President Bush] should get congressional approval before ordering any major military action against Iraq.''[45]

In an unusual move, the Congress canceled its normal January recess and remained in session. ''These are not normal times,'' said Senator Tom Harkins (D., Ia.); ''American men and women may be dying in combat,'' and Congress should debate whether to go to war before it starts rather than after. Representative David R. Obey (D., Ws.) said he thought it was an ''impeachable offense'' to order offensive military operations without a declaration of war.[46] Notably, it was the constitutionally mandated declaration of war, not the War Powers Resolution, that was the focus of attention.

Speaker Thomas S. Foley (D., Wash.) announced on January 7, 1991, that the House would begin debate on January 10 on a resolution authorizing President Bush to use force to oust Iraq from Kuwait. Senate majority leader George J. Mitchell (D., Me.) said the Senate would probably also begin debate on a resolution. After distainfully dismissing congressional participation for months, the White House suddenly sat up and took notice.

''Bush began calling Senate and House Republicans that night to obtain a head count,'' reports Bob Woodward in his chronicle of the crisis. ''He personally typed out the draft of a letter he could send to the Congress requesting that both houses endorse the 'all necessary means' language of the United Nations resolution [i.e., U.N. Resolution 678 of November 29, 1990, which authorized member states to use all necessary means to uphold previous U.N. Security Council resolutions unless Iraq withdraws from Kuwait by January 15, 1991]."

On January 8, 1991, President Bush presided over a meeting in the White House Cabinet Room to discuss whether the letter should be dispatched. Deputy Attorney General William P. Barr was asked his opinion. "War is in the gray area," he said. "The war power is a shared power with Congress; the Constitution intends it to be shared. . . . As with any shared power, our hand is strongest when the executive branch and Congress agree. . . . The situation most closely resembling the current crisis was the Korean War," he concluded, "when Truman acted without Congress under a United Nations resolution somewhat similar to the current one."

But Bush wisely refused to repeat that terrible mistake that had poisoned the warmaking process for over a generation. "The lawyers reworked the letter, and within the hour it was on its way to the Hill."[47]

After three days of debate, on January 12, 1991, the Congress voted President Bush authority to go to war against Iraq. The "Authorization for Use of Military Force Against Iraq Resolution" passed the Senate 52–47 and the House 250–183.[48]

Although a "resolution" rather than a declaration of war, it was a far cry from the Tonkin Gulf "Resolution" of the Vietnam war. This time the Congress knew precisely what it was doing: giving the president authority "to use United States armed forces pursuant to United Nations Security Council 678." And five days later, on January 17, 1991, that's exactly what Bush did.

Although many in the Congress who had voted against the authorization for the use of force had wanted more time for sanctions to work, when the war began they closed ranks with the president. "The Congress commends and supports the efforts and leadership of the President as Commander-in-Chief in the Persian Gulf hostilities," read Senate Concurrent Resolution 2, enacted by the Senate on a 96–6 vote, and on January 18, 1991, by the House of Representatives by a 399–6, and "unequivocally supports the men and women of our armed forces who are carrying out their missions with professional excellence, dedicated patriotism and exemplary bravery."[49] Congress's Vietnam syndrome had finally been put to rest.

NOTES

1. George J. Mitchell, quoted in Ruth Marcus, "Congress and the President Clash Over Who Decides on Going to War," *The Washington Post* (December 14, 1990), p. 46.

2. Carl von Clausewitz, *On War,* trans. and ed. Michael Howard and Peter Paret. (Princeton, N.J.: Princeton University Press, 1976), pp. 13–32.

3. Marcus, "Congress and the President," p. 46. See also Jacob K. Javits, *Who Makes War: The President versus Congress* (New York: William Morrow & Company, 1973), pp. 12–15.

4. "Madison's War Message," in *Documents of American History,* vol. I, ed. Henry Steele Commager (New York: Appleton-Century-Crofts, 1963), pp. 207–9. (Hereafter cited as *Commager.*)

5. "Polk's Message on War With Mexico," *Commager,* vol. I, pp. 310–11.

6. "McKinley's War Message," *Commager,* vol. II, pp. 1–4.

7. "Wilson's Speech for Declaration of War Against Germany," *Commager,* vol. II, pp. 128–32.

8. "President Roosevelt's Message Asking for War Against Japan," *Commager,* vol. II, 451–52.

9. "Declaration of War on Germany," *Commager*, vol. II, pp. 452–53.

10. "Truman's Statement on the Korean War," *Commager*, vol. II, pp. 560–61.

11. Javits, *Who Makes War*, p. 250.

12. 82nd Cong., 1st sess., U.S. Senate, Hearings Before the Committee on Armed Services and the Committee on Foreign Relations, *Military Situation in the Far East*, Part I (Washington, D.C.: U.S. Government Printing Office, 1951), pp. 227–28, 305–6 (emphasis added).

13. *Ibid.*, Part II, pp. 794–95, 852, 1065–66.

14. *Ibid.*, Part V, pp. 3600, 3605.

15. Lyndon B. Johnson, *The Vantage Point: Perspectives of the Presidency 1963–1969* (New York: Popular Library, 1971), p. 115.

16. Ibid., pp. 116–19.

17. Javits, *Who Makes War*, pp. 260–61 (emphasis added).

18. Herbert Y. Schandler, *The Unmaking of a President: President Lyndon Johnson and Vietnam* (Princeton, N.J.: Princeton University Press, 1977), pp. 20–22.

19. Arthur M. Schlesinger, Jr., *The Imperial Presidency* (Boston, Mass.: Houghton Mifflin Company, 1971), p. 181.

20. Javits, *Who Makes War*, pp. 260–61.

21. Dean Rusk, letter to the author (August 4, 1981). See also Dean Rusk, *As I Saw It* (New York: W. W. Norton & Company, 1990), pp. 501–2.

22. William C. Westmoreland, *A Soldier Reports* (Garden City, N.Y.: Doubleday & Company, 1976), p. 412.

23. 91st Cong., 2nd sess., Committee on Foreign Relations, U.S. Senate, *Termination of Middle East and South Asia Resolutions*, Report to Accompany Senate Concurrent Resolution 64, May 15, 1970 (Washington, D.C.: U.S. Government Printing Office, 1970), p. 7.

24. Ibid.

25. Ibid.

26. Ibid, p. 3.

27. Ibid.

28. 94th Cong., 2nd sess., Committee on International Relations, U.S. House of Representatives, *The War Powers*

Resolution (Washington, D.C. U.S. Government Printing Office, 1975), p. 1.

29. Robert F. Turner, "War Powers and the Gulf Crisis," *Freedom at Issue* (November–December 1990), pp. 6–10.

30. Caspar W. Weinberger, "The Uses of Military Power," New Release 609–84 (Washington, D.C.: Office of the Assistant Secretary of Defense for Public Affairs, November 28, 1984), pp. 1, 6.

31. John Hart Ely, quoted in "Constitution's Conflicting Clauses Underscored by Iraq Crisis," *Congressional Quarterly* (January 5, 1991), pp. 33–36.

32. James T. Currie, "The First Congressional Investigation: St. Clair's Military Disaster of 1791," *Parameters: US Army War College Quarterly,* vol. XX, no. 4 (December 1990), pp. 95–102.

33. Michael Kinsley, "The War Powers War," *The New Republic* (December 31, 1990), p. 4.

34. Javits, *Who Makes War,* pp. 36–52.

35. Francis D. Wormuth and Edwin B. Firmage, *To Chain the Dog of War: The War Power of Congress in History and Law,* (2nd ed.) (Urbana, Ill.: University of Illinois Press, 1989), pp. 135–51.

36. "Gulf Policy: Complex Signals," *The Economist* (November 17, 1990), p. 29.

37. Martin Tolchin, "45 in House Sue to Bar Bush from Acting Without Congress, *The New York Times* (November 21, 1990), p. 11.

38. "Judges and War Powers," *The Washington Post* (December 17, 1990), p. 20. See also Tracy Thompson, "Two Federal Judges Reject Challenges to Bush's Actions," *The Washington Post* (December 14, 1990), p. 45.

39. 101st Cong., 2nd sess., Hearings Before the Committee on Armed Services, U.S. Senate, *Crisis in the Persian Gulf Region: U.S. Policy Options and Implications* (Washington, D.C.: U.S. Government Printing Office, 1990), pp. 113–257.

40. Ibid. See pp. 701–3 for an exchange between Kennedy and Cheney on war powers.

41. Susan F. Rasky, "House Democrats Caution Bush on War," *The New York Times* (December 5, 1990), p. 20.

42. 101st Cong., 2nd sess., Hearings Before the Committee on Armed Services, U.S. House of Representatives, *Crisis in the Persian Gulf: Sanctions, Diplomacy and War* (Washington, D.C.: U.S. Government Printing Office, 1991), p. 1.

43. Ibid., p. 917.

44. "Where Is Congress on the Gulf?" *The New York Times* (January 3, 1991), p. 20.

45. Sharon Shaw Johnson, "Public Wants Congress to OK Actions," *USA Today* (January 3, 1991), p. 1.

46. Helen Dewar and Tom Kenworthy, "Canceling Recess, Lawmakers Prepare to Debate War Powers," *The Washington Post* (January 4, 1991), p. 19.

47. Bob Woodward, *The Commanders* (New York: Simon & Schuster, 1991), pp. 356–58.

48. Adam Clymer, "Congress Acts to Authorize War in Gulf; Margins are 5 Votes in Senate, 67 in House," *The New York Times* (January 14, 1991), p. 1.

49. "Supporting U.S. Presence in the Persian Gulf," *Congressional Record,* vol. 137, no. 13 (January 18, 1991), pp. H566–H596. Helen Dewar and Tom Kenworthy, "Senate Commends Bush, Backs Troops," *The Washington Post* (January 18, 1991), p. A29.

3

The Vietnam Syndrome and the Military

> The group of leaders who are in the key positions, we were all about the same rank during the Vietnam days, majors and lieutenant colonels, and I think all of us were shaped by that, all of us were shaped by the low point in the military in the early '70s. All of us then determined we were going to rebuild an Army and we did.
>
> General Carl E. Vuono,
> chief of staff, U.S. Army,
> (October 1, 1990)[1]

Tactical Victory, Strategic Defeat

As General Vuono's remarks testify, the mood of the post-Vietnam officer corps was not a defeatist "Vietnam syndrome," but instead a determination to rebuild the military on a firm foundation of solid military values.

Paradoxical as it may seem, those then junior officers who actually fought the war at the platoon, company, and battalion levels had no hangdog attitude about the war, mainly because they knew they weren't the ones who lost it. The United States as a nation may have lost the Vietnam war when its ally the

Republic of Vietnam was overrun by the multidivision North Vietnamese Army (NVA) crossborder blitzkrieg in the spring of 1975. But the armed forces of the United States were not defeated for the simple reason that they weren't there to be defeated. They had departed the battlefield two years earlier, in accordance with the terms of the 1973 Paris Peace Accords.

Although some, like the Asian diplomat quoted earlier, believe that the U.S. military was "beaten like a wet rat in Vietnam," the North Vietnamese themselves knew better. "You know you never beat us on the battlefield," I said to my North Vietnamese Army Four-Party Joint Military Team counterpart in Hanoi a week before the fall of Saigon. He pondered the remark a moment, then said, "That may be so. But it is also irrelevant."[2]

His reply was a short lesson in military strategy, a lesson at least twenty-one centuries old. In January 202 B.C., at the end of an eight-year struggle for power following the death of China's first emperor, General Hsiang Yu, who had won most of the battles, committed suicide. "Heaven has forsaken me," he said. "I have never made a military error."[3] It was a lesson the United States especially should have known full well. It our own eight-year struggle for independence, the British redcoats and their Hessian and Tory allies also won most of the battles. But in the end it was General George Washington and his Continental Army who emerged victorious.

How could one win all the battles and lose the war? The answer involves an understanding that wars are fought on three synergetic levels: the engagement or tactical level, which involves actual fighting; the theater of war or operational level, which involves a series of such engagements to achieve set objectives; and the strategic level, which involves use of national power to achieve the objectives of national policy.

The tactical and operational levels are primarily the province of the military and involve defeat of the enemy's armed forces on the battlefield. But at the strategic level the military is only one of the several actors involved. "Strategy," states the official Joint Chiefs of Staff (JCS) definition, involves "the art and science of developing and using political, economic, psychological and military forces . . . in order to increase the probabilities and favorable consequences of victory and to lessen the chances of defeat."[4]

On the wall of the Army General Staff's War Plans Directorate in the Pentagon used to hang a poster of a World War II infantryman with rifle and fixed bayonet advancing against the enemy. "At the end of the most grandiose plans and strategies," read its caption, "is a soldier walking point." The message to those staff officers formulating plans and strategies was that their directives had to be capable of execution by soldiers on the ground; otherwise they were meaningless scraps of paper.

But Vietnam proved that the reverse was also true. No matter how well the soldiers performed on the battlefield—and most American men and women in Vietnam performed well indeed—it was all meaningless if the plans and strategies were flawed.

The sad tragedy of Vietnam was that at the tactical and operational levels our soldiers, sailors, airmen, marines, and coast guardsmen did everything we asked of them and more. They won every major battle, beginning with the battle of the Ia Drang Valley in November 1965, when the newly arrived U.S. 1st Cavalry Division (Airmobile) defeated an NVA attempt to cut South Vietnam in two by attacking from its sanctuaries in Laos eastward to the South China Sea.[5]

And at Hue and Khe Sanh and a hundred battles in between, the Marine Corps fought bravely and well.

The same was true in the air and at sea. The U.S. Air Force and their Navy and Marine compatriots won total air superiority over Indochina, including the skies over North Vietnam; and the U.S. Navy and Coast Guard not only reigned supreme on the high seas, but also, with their riverine "brown-water navy" units, controlled much of South Vietnam's inland waterways as well.

As the University of California at Berkeley's Douglas Pike, one of the world's leading experts on the North Vietnamese military, noted, "the historic fact to emerge [from the Vietnam war] was that the U.S. Army during its entire stay, from 1965 to 1973, did not lose a single important battle. It was a record unparalleled in the history of modern warfare."[6]

Critics, most persuasively the Army's Andrew F. Krepinevich, Jr.,[7] have argued that the military ignored its own counterinsurgency doctrine in the prosecution of the war. But that argument is moot. Perhaps in spite of itself, the United States and its allies won the counterinsurgency war against the Viet Cong guerrillas. It was the conventional war against the NVA regulars that was ultimately lost by our South Vietnamese ally.

As former CIA director William S. Colby observed:

[When the North Vietnamese Army entered Saigon on April 30, 1975] an NBC television crew caught one of the more significant pictures of the event. It filmed a huge North Vietnamese tank with its obscenely monstrous cannon as it broke open the main gate of the Presidential Palace. The people's war was over, not by the work of a barefoot guerrilla but by the most conventional of military forces. . . .

The ultimate irony was that the people's war launched in 1959 had been defeated, but the soldiers' war, which the

United States had insisted on fighting during the 1960s with massive military forces, was finally won by the enemy.[8]

The war was lost not at the tactical or operational level but at the strategic level. And it was lost because we failed to address the most fundamental strategic question of all. "The first, the supreme, the most far-reaching act of judgement that the statesman and commander have to make is to establish . . . the kind of war on which they are embarking," warned Carl von Clausewitz, "neither mistaking it for, nor trying to turn it into, something that is alien to its nature. This is the first of all strategic questions, and the most comprehensive."[9]

As will be discussed in more detail in Part II, "The Remarkable Renaissance," the U.S. government was so mesmerized by its new and trendy counterinsurgency strategies that it failed to see the duality of the war, which involved both internal and external adversaries. As a result, it pursued policies and strategies that almost guaranteed ultimate defeat.

The Civilian Strategists

One self-defeating notion, discussed in an earlier chapter, was that the American people could be factored out of the strategic equation. Another was the absurd idea that the armed forces' primary purpose was not for fighting a war but instead for use as a kind of signaling device.

"What had happened to American military strategy?" asked Harvard's Stephen Peter Rosen in his landmark 1982 article on the Vietnam war. "Its absense became painfully obvious in 1968, but it was missing from 1964 on. The answer, in part, is that we had adopted a limited war signalling strategy."[10] Led by such academic limited-war theorists as Robert Osgood and Thomas Schelling, who shared "the happy belief that the study of limited war in no way depended on any actual knowledge about war," the focus was not on war but on diplomacy and bargaining.

According to Osgood, "military problems are no proper part of a theory of limited war . . . because limited war is an essentially diplomatic instrument, a tool for bargaining with the enemy." According to these theories, "Military forces are not for fighting but for signalling."[11]

This was more than mere academic prattle. "[T]he greater the costs and risks of a military measure," Rosen found, "the greater the tendency for the men at the higher levels of government to talk and act as if they were guided by the academic theory of limited war. . . . This approach to the problem seemed to minimize risk and offer victory without combat. This [was] true for the civilians but, to a surprising extent, also true of military men, particularly Maxwell Taylor."[12]

Rosen quotes General William C. Westmoreland on a particularly idiotic application of this mind-set. "In 1965, we observed the construction of the first surface-to-air missile [SAM] sites in North Vietnam, and the military sought permission to attack them before they were completed to save American casualties. [Assistant Secretary of Defense for International Affairs John] McNaughton ridiculed the idea.

" 'You don't think the North Vietnamese are going to use them!' he scoffed to [Seventh Air Force commander] General [Joseph H.] Moore. 'Putting them in is just a political ploy by the Russians to appease Hanoi.' It was all a matter of signals, said the clever civilian theorist in Washington. We won't bomb the SAM sites, which signals the North Vietnamese not to use them."[13] But our enemies were not playing Washington's silly games. A month later the United States lost its first aircraft to a SAM.

Graduated Response

But that was not the worst of it. McNaughton (a former Harvard Law School professor) was also the architect of the disastrous "slow squeeze" strategy of graduated response. As then colonel Dave Palmer (who would later rise to lieutenant general and become superintendent of the U.S. Military Academy) pointed out in his 1978 analysis of the war, "Civilian planners wanted to start out softly and gradually increase the pressure by precise increments which could be unmistakingly recognized in Hanoi. Ho Chi Minh would see the tightening pattern, the theory went, and would sensibly stop the war against South Vietnam. . . .

"Assistant Secretary of Defense John McNaughton dubbed the strategy 'slow squeeze.' . . . The Joint Chiefs of Staff . . . argued that if force was to be used at all it should be applied hard and fast to obtain maximum impact with minimum loss. To start lightly and escalate slowly, they held, would be like pulling a tooth bit by bit. . . .

"President Johnson overrode the objections of his . . . military advisors. Indeed it is not at all clear whether Secretary [of Defense Robert S.] McNamara ever even bothered to convey their arguments to him. Ambassador [Maxwell D.] Taylor, still addressed as 'General,' had given his blessings to their theory, approval of which apparently cancelled the objections of the Joint Chiefs of Staff. Thus was born the strategy of 'graduated response.' "[14]

Stab-in-the-Back Syndrome

What this combination of battlefield success and strategic failure could have produced was something far more serious than a "Vietnam syndrome." It could have produced a "stab-in-the-back syndrome" within the ranks of the Army in particular that could have threatened the very foundations of the Republic.

That's what happened in Germany after World War I, when the Weimar Republic was undermined by the notion among German war veterans, including Adolf Hitler, that civilians in Berlin had betrayed the soldiers at the front. And, except for the intervention of General Charles de Gaulle that aborted the planned coup, that's what would have also happened in France in 1959 after the loss of Algeria.

But that never happened here. One reason, as the Congress acknowledged at the time of his retirement, was the superb leadership of General Fred C. Weyand, America's last commander in Vietnam and Army chief of staff at the time of Saigon's fall.[15]

Another was the fact that most military officers tended to blame not the American government but instead the military's senior leadership for what went wrong in Vietnam.[16] General William C. Westmoreland, the senior U.S. commander in Vietnam from 1964 to 1968, took most of the heat. In what may have been his greatest contribution to his country, he drained off the animosity of the officer corps and thus helped defuse a "stab-in-the-back syndrome."

It was terribly unfair, for Westmoreland, the war's tactical commander, had had little to say at the Washington strategic level, where the most serious errors were made. Who really deserved the blame, said General Bruce Palmer, Jr., in one of the most hard-hitting critiques of the war, were the Joint Chiefs of Staff, by law the principal military advisers to the president.

A Lapse in Moral Courage

First they allowed the civilian "strategists" such as McNaughton and other McNamara amateurs to run roughshod over the military professionals and dictate the strategies for the conduct of the war. One could not imagine General of the Army George C. Marshall, Army chief of staff during World War II, or his Navy counterpart, Fleet Admiral Ernest J. King, permitting some Harvard dilettante to usurp their prerogatives. They would have resigned in protest rather than countenance such an affront to their authority.

But, made of lesser stuff, the Vietnam-era senior military leadership supinely acquiesced. It was the culmination of a trend that had begun after World War II. In his study of the Korean war, historian T. R. Fehrenbach was talking about Congress, but his words apply to the Vietnam-era defense bureaucrats as well.

"The generals could have told them to go to hell and made it stick. A few heads would have rolled, a few stars would have been lost. But without acquiescence [they] could no more emasculate the Army than [they] could alter the nature of the State Department. [They] could have . . . weakened it even more than [they] did—but [they] could not have changed its nature."[17]

But the generals did not tell the interlopers to go to hell. Instead they allowed themselves to be politicized and their integrity compromised.

A prime example of such politicization was General Maxwell D. Taylor, personal military adviser to both Presidents John F. Kennedy and Lyndon B. Johnson and chairman of the Joint Chiefs of Staff (CJCS) during the critical October 1962–July 1964 period when fundamental decisions on Vietnam were being made.

"Having just served in the White House as a close personal advisor to the president, [General Taylor] had become in effect the number one military advisor to the Kennedy administration," observed General Bruce Palmer. "Thus when Kennedy brought him out of retirement to be chairman, Taylor possessed far more clout than the average CJCS. At the same time, having been closely associated with the inner political-military thinking of the administration, Taylor's objectivity and independence of mind had to be somewhat compromised."[18]

Proof came in October 1963, when Lieutenant Colonel John Paul Vann, an early critic of American policy in Vietnam who "probably knew Vietnam better than any other American of his day," was scheduled to brief the JCS. The meeting "was cancelled at the last minute by direction of General Taylor." As Palmer goes on to say, "It is almost impossible to resist the conclusion that Taylor and McNamara were playing U.S. presidential politics—the 1964 elections were only a year away."[19]

The climate had been set. "Not once during the war did the JCS advise the commander-in-chief or the secretary of defense that the strategy being pursued most probably would fail and that the United States would be unable to achieve its objectives. The only explanation of this failure is that the chiefs are imbued with the 'can do' spirit and could not bring themselves to make such a negative statement or to appear disloyal."[20]

It's not as if they did not know better. Almost ten years after his retirement from active duty, a colleague asked General Harold K. Johnson, who had served as Army chief of staff—and thus a member of the JCS—

from July 1964 to July 1968, "If you had your life to live over again, what would you do differently?"

With some emotion, General Johnson replied: "I remember the day I was ready to go over to the Oval Office and give my four stars to the president and tell him, 'You have refused to tell the country they cannot fight a war without mobilization; you have required me to send men into battle with little hope of their ultimate victory; and you have forced us in the military to violate almost every one of the principles of war in Vietnam. Therefore I resign and will hold a press conference after I walk out your door.' "

With a look of anguish, General Johnson concluded: "I made the typical mistake of believing I could do more for my country and for the Army if I stayed in than if I got out. I am now going to my grave with that lapse in moral courage."[21]

Resetting the Moral Compass

Such behavior on the part of the senior leadership evoked a sense of disgust and revulsion among the military's then junior officers, officers such as Lieutenant Colonels Colin Powell and Norman Schwarzkopf, who more than two decades later would be the senior officers who led American forces to victory in the Persian Gulf. Ironically, within the Army it was the much-maligned General William C. Westmoreland who took the first steps to reset the moral compass. On April 18, 1970, while the war in Vietnam was still raging, General Westmoreland, then Army chief of staff, directed the Army War College to conduct an immediate analysis of the moral and professional climate in the Army.[22]

The results were a shocker. There was a sense of moral outrage among both company- and field-grade officers (i.e., lieutenants through colonels) that their seniors had sold out to careerism and venal self-interest. "Duty, honor, country" had become mere words, not a code to live by. "The younger officers appear to have higher ideals than the senior officers," reported one of the professionalism study's field seminars; they "were more idealistic about the Army's standards."[23]

Those who recall General Schwarzkopf's angry reaction against "body count" during the Persian Gulf war will find echoes over twenty years earlier. "One of the most violent reactions we got," noted another of the professionalism study's field seminars, "was from the body count, particularly from the young combat arms officers recently back from Vietnam. . . . In fact, they expressed concern that the President of the United States was making decisions on totally invalid information."[24]

That emphasis on integrity and moral courage would be one of the hallmarks of the post-Vietnam military. As will be examined in more depth in Part II, it was part of a "back to basics" reaction to the Vietnam war that permeated not only the Army but the Navy, Air Force, and Marine Corps as well. General Bernard W. Rogers, then Army chief of staff, could have been speaking for all the armed services in his February 1, 1977, letter to Army general officers worldwide:

> Our ability to share in the effort of protecting and defending our Nation's vital interests depends in large measure on public perceptions of the integrity of our Officer Corps. If the American people cannot trust our word, if they cannot rely on our conduct, we can hardly expect them to trust us with the lives of their sons and daughters.

It seems to be that we have tended toward a toleration of those officers who would violate our ethical and professional standards. If we are to have the confidence of the public—and an Officer Corps worthy of the name—we must recapture our sense of indignation. We must treat those persons who disgrace our good name with the disapproval they deserve. . . .

The standards are all there—in the oath of office, in the officer's commission, in the tradition of our Officer Corps, and in the code of an honorable man: *"I will not lie, cheat nor steal, nor tolerate one who does."*. . .

You are, by the very fact of your commission, the conscience of the Army. I expect you—and every officer in the United States Army—to act like it. Ensure that those officers subordinate to you understand what is expected of them.[25]

"In war," Napoleon Bonaparte observed, "the moral is to the material as three to one."[26] In Vietnam the failure was not in material. Supposedly when President Richard Nixon took office in January 1969 a Pentagon computer was fed all the data on the United States and North Vietnam—size of population, gross national product, steel production, numbers of ships, tanks, aircraft, and the rest. It was then asked, "When will we win?" The answer was instantaneous: "You won in 1964!"

By any statistical measure, the United States could not lose in Vietnam. But as Napoleon said, there is more to war than what can be counted. In Vietnam the failure was moral, not material. In rediscovering its moral compass the American military came to grips with its bitter experience in the Vietnam war.

It was to make a critical difference in the Persian Gulf. "Playing against type," wrote *The Washington Post*'s Jim Hoagland on the eve of the war, "America's

generals are refusing to fight the last war again. . . .
The Persian Gulf crisis represents the professional
military's revenge for Vietnam. . . ."[27] As will be seen
in Part III, "The Remarkable War," it would be sweet
revenge indeed.

NOTES

1. Carl E. Vuono, *U.S. News & World Report* (October
1, 1990), p. 30.

2. Author's notes. The Four-Party Joint Military Team
(FPJMT) was set up by the Paris Peace Accords to deal with
the POW/MIA issue. With members from the United States,
the South Vietnamese, the North Vietnamese and the Viet
Cong, it required liaison trips between Saigon and Hanoi on
a regular basis.

3. Pan Ku, *Han Shu* in Homer H. Dubs, trans., *History
of the Former Han Dynasty,* 3 vols. (Baltimore: Waverly
Press, 1938–55), pp. 1B–2A.

4. "Dictionary of Military and Associated Terms," *JCS
Pub. 1* (Washington, D.C.: Joint Chiefs of Staff, July 1,
1987), p. 350.

5. Harry G. Summers, Jr., "The Bitter Triumph of Ia
Drang," *American Heritage* (February 1984), pp. 50–58.

6. Douglas Pike, *PAVN: People's Army of Vietnam* (Novato, Calif.: Presidio Press, 1986), p. 227.

7. Andrew F. Krepinevich, Jr., *The Army and Vietnam*
(Baltimore: The Johns Hopkins University Press, 1986).

8. William Colby with James McCargar, *Lost Victories:
A Firsthand Account of America's Sixteen-Year Involvement
in Vietnam* (New York: Contemporary Books, 1989), pp.
365–66.

9. Carl von Clausewitz, *On War,* trans. and ed. Michael
Howard and Peter Paret (Princeton, N.J.: Princeton University Press, 1976), pp. 88–89.

10. Stephen Peter Rosen, "Vietnam and the American
Theory of Limited War," *International Security* (Fall 1982),
repr. *Military Strategy: Theory and Application,* ed. Arthur

F. Lyke, Jr. (Carlisle Barracks, Pa.: U.S. Army War College, 1984), pp. 12–28.

11. Ibid., pp. 12–23.

12. Ibid.

13. Ibid., pp. 12–26. See also Jack Broughton, *Going Downtown: The War Against Hanoi and Washington* (New York: Orion Books, 1988), pp. 173–74.

14. Dave Richard Palmer, *Summons of the Trumpet: U.S.-Vietnam in Perspective* (Novato, Calif.: Presidio Press, 1978), pp. 75–76. See also Rosen, pp. 12-25–12-26.

15. Fred C. Weyand, "Troops to Equal Any," *Vietnam* (Summer 1988), p. 25.

16. Ward Just, *Military Men* (New York: Alfred A. Knopf, 1970), p. 186.

17. T. R. Fehrenbach, *This Kind of War: A Study in Unpreparedness* (New York: The Macmillan Company, 1963), p. 431.

18. Bruce Palmer, Jr., *The Twenty-Five-Year War: America's Military Role in Vietnam* (Lexington, Ky.: The University Press of Kentucky, 1984), p. 20. See also Douglas Kinnard. *The Certain Trumpet: Maxwell Taylor and the American Experience in Vietnam* (New York: Brassey's, 1991).

19. Ibid., pp. 22–23. See also Neil Sheehan, *A Bright Shining Lie: John Paul Vann and America in Vietnam* (New York: Random House, 1988), pp. 337–42.

20. Ibid., pp. 45–46.

21. Letter to the author, Brigadier General Albion W. Knight, USA (Ret.), August 4, 1984. See also Harry G. Summers, Jr., "A Survivor of Bataan in World War II and Unsan in Korea, Harold K. Johnson's Undoing Was the War in Vietnam," *Vietnam* (December 1990), p. 56. See also Mark Perry, *Four Stars* (Boston: Houghton Mifflin Company, 1989), pp. 163–66.

22. William C. Westmoreland, letter, chief of staff, U.S. Army, "Analysis of Moral and Professional Climate in the Army" (April 18, 1970).

23. *Study on Military Professionalism* (Carlisle Barracks, Pa.: U.S. Army War College, June 30, 1970), p. B-1-8.

24. Ibid., p. B-1-10.

25. Bernard W. Rogers, letter, the chief of staff, U.S. Army (February 2, 1977).

26. Napoleon I, quoted in *Dictionary of Military and Naval Quotations,* ed. Colonel Robert Debs Heinl, Jr., USMC (Ret.). (Annapolis, Md.: U.S. Naval Institute, 1966), p. 196.

27. Jim Hoagland, "Congress, Bush and the Generals," *The Washington Post* (November 22, 1990), p. 31.

THE REMARKABLE RENAISSANCE

It should be clear, and well worth mature reflection on the part of our officers, that . . . an absence of doctrine is a serious danger to any military force. . . . Universal understanding and acceptance of common doctrine is necessary before concerted action by a large force engaged in hostilities is possible; it is an essential element of command, and an essential prelude to great success in war.

Lieutenant Commander, Dudley W. Knox, USN,
"The Role of Doctrine in Naval Warfare"
U.S. Naval Institute Proceedings,
vol. 41, no. 2 (March–April 1915) p. 340

4

Back to Basics

The way of the superior man is like that of the
archer. When he misses the center of the target
he turns and seeks the cause of his failure in
himself.

Confucius (c. 551–479 B.C.), *Analects*[1]

Strategic Fundamentals

Instead of developing a "Vietnam syndrome" or a
"stab-in-the-back syndrome" after the Vietnam war,
the military, appropriately enough, took a Confucian
approach to its Southeast Asian travail. Although it
had not been defeated on the battlefield, it had not hit
"the center of the target," either.

The very purpose of the military is to assist in
achieving the foreign policy objectives of the United
States, and after the enemy's 1968 Tet offensive it
became apparent that the foreign policy objective of
guaranteeing a free and independent South Vietnam

had been written off. It was abandoned, not because of enemy action but because American public and political support for the war had collapsed. With Richard Nixon's assumption of the presidency in 1969, the focus changed from winning the war to getting out as gracefully as possible.

In that same year, six years before the end of the war, two American combat divisions—the Army's 9th Infantry Division and the 3rd Marine Division—left Vietnam. In ensuing years the drawdowns continued apace. By August 1972, almost three years before the end of the war, the last American ground combat unit—the 3rd Battalion, 21st Infantry—had been withdrawn from Vietnam.

During that prolonged withdrawal period the military turned "to seek the cause of its failure in itself." Particular attention was paid to several unique features of the war. As discussed earlier, one was that it was the first war in which the American people—and, in the final stages, the U.S. Congress—had been deliberately excluded from the strategic equation.

It was the first time that nuclear science and social science, not military science, dictated battlefield doctrines and where basic strategies were formulated by civilian amateurs rather than military professionals. And it was also the first major war in U.S. history where the military's reserve components—the Army and Air National Guard and the Army, Navy, Air Force, Marine Corps, and Coast Guard reserves—did not play a major role on the battlefield.

Doctrinal Confusion

Since 1945, military war-fighting doctrines and strategies had been dominated by the phantasmagoric notions of civilian nuclear strategists, who claimed that in the atomic age all past military theories and philosophies; all past military doctrines; and, most importantly, all past military battlefield experiences were totally irrelevant. Only these nuclear theorists, not the generals and admirals, knew what was needed for future wars.

Writing in 1915, on the eve of America's involvement in the First World War, Navy lieutenant commander (later commodore) Dudley W. Knox warned that "to reach the ultimate goal of war efficiency . . . we must build from the foundation upwards and not from the roof downwards."[2] But that's exactly what happened. Nuclear "strategy" was forced on the military from "the roof downwards" by the Eisenhower administration, primarily for budgetary, not strategic reasons. While the conventional (i.e., nonnuclear) elements of all the armed forces were seriously affected, the Army in particular was hard hit.

As military historian Russell F. Weigley noted, "A national military policy and strategy relying upon massive nuclear retaliation for nearly all the uses of force left the Army uncertain of its place in the policy and strategy, uncertain that civilians recognized a need even for the Army's existence and uncertain therefore of the service's whole future."[3]

The result was a near-paralysis in military thinking for almost a generation. Adding to this paralysis was another set of phantasmagoric notions, this time from social scientists rather than nuclear scientists. As Harvard's J. Bower Bell explained:

> Even before Vietnam . . . guerrilla revolution had become a fashionable challenge to be met by elegant and complex ways but ways which needed the talents, the scope, the capacities and the experience of various available careerists. . . .

For the American intellectual theoreticans of order, the nature of the appropriate response—intricate and highly calculated reforms to transform Vietnamese society—fit the prejudices and aspirations of the moment . . . the guerrilla could be met by using the advanced tools of social science for the benefit of man.[4]

Nothing if not fashionable, the Kennedy administration jumped on the "new kind of war." General Maxwell Taylor was brought in from retirement as the president's special military representative and assigned the duties of monitoring counterinsurgency efforts.[5] Except for Taylor, now thoroughly politicized, the professional military were cut out of the action, for "counterinsurgency strategy," like "nuclear strategy" before it, required no knowledge of warfare itself.

Forced into retirement because he disagreed with the Eisenhower administration's nuclear war dogma, Taylor ironically played a leading role in foisting off counterinsurgency dogma on the military. When Army chief of staff General George H. Decker, a World War II combat infantryman, "stoutly stood up to [President John F. Kennedy] with the assurance that 'any good soldier can handle guerrillas,' " he was eased from office and replaced by General Earle G. Wheeler, a Taylor protégé.

President Kennedy "dropped a broad hint that future promotions of high-ranking officers would depend upon their demonstration of experience in the counter-guerrilla or sublimited field."[6]

Ironically, it was General Decker, not Kennedy, who ultimately was proved to be correct. The Viet Cong were destroyed, not by the fanciful nation-building doctrines of the social scientists, but by the riflemen of the Army and Marine Corps, backed by the supporting arms of their own services and by Navy and Air Force firepower. By the end of 1968 the Viet Cong had ceased to exist as an effective fighting force.

For the next seven years the war was primarily a North Vietnamese Army affair. And they weren't following a social-science script, either. "Like us, Hanoi failed to win the 'hearts and minds' of the South Vietnamese peasantry," noted Stuart A. Herrington in his account of the war in the countryside. "Unlike us, Hanoi's leaders were able to compensate for this failure by playing their trump card—they overwhelmed South Vietnam with a twenty-two-division force."[7]

And the assumptions of the nuclear strategists proved equally bankrupt. In the closing days of the war my North Vietnamese Army counterpart crowed, "This just goes to prove you can't stamp out a revolutionary idea with force."

"That's nonsense and you know it," I replied. "In the thirteenth century Genghis Khan did a pretty good job of stamping out a revolutionary idea with force when the Moslems in central Asia declared a jihad against him. He killed some seventeen million people and turned the area into a howling desert for the next seven hundred years.

"And you'd be hard pressed to find anyone in southern France today able to recite the Albigensian Code. When that heresy was put down in A.D. 1250, the military commander asked the bishop, 'How do you tell the heretics from the true believers?' The terrible answer was, 'Kill them all! God will know his own.'

"You know, with our nuclear weapons, we had the capability many times over to wipe North Vietnam from the face of the map."

"We knew that," he said. "We also knew you'd never do it."[8]

When it came to anything less than nuclear war

itself, our vaunted nuclear deterrent force had one critical flaw: It did not deter.

Failure to Mobilize

Another major failing was in the area of military manpower. Unlike all previous wars, there had been no major mobilization of America's reserve components—the Army and Air National Guard and the Army, Navy, Air Force, Marine Corps, and Coast Guard reserves. Instead, reliance had been placed on conscription (i.e., the draft) to raise the necessary manpower. But on March 27, 1969, President Nixon appointed a commission headed by former secretary of defense Thomas S. Gates to study the prospects of ending the military draft and relying on an all-volunteer force for America's defenses.

As then Harvard professor Eliot A. Cohen noted, it was a commission dominated by economists, not strategists. "The dominance of economists in defense policy was not an isolated phenomenon; it was part of a much larger development, the rise of systems analysis, a mode of strategic thought derived from economics that was at its height during the tenure of Robert S. McNamara as secretary of defense during the 1960s."

Using a McNamarian framework for their analysis, the "commissioners started from the premise that 'conscription is a form of taxation, the power to conscript is the power to tax.' . . . Manpower became a commodity, an input into the machinery of national defense, in the same way that weapons or installations were."[9]

Not only was the military repulsed by such a cynical prostitution of the ideal, expressed in the preamble to the Constitution, that the responsibility of providing for the common defense was the responsibility of every American citizen, they also were concerned that the end of the draft would further weaken the bridge between the American public and their military, a bridge already on the verge of collapse because of the Vietnam war.

The government's response was to put a gag order on the military, forbidding any criticism of the end of the draft, which was formally suspended by President Nixon in January 1973. America's defenses would henceforth rest on an "all-volunteer force." That decision was one of the factors that led to a "total force" concept, which involved reliance on the reserve components to a degree not true since the Korean war.

Citizen Soldiers

The argument of whether to rely on a standing military or the "citizen soldiers" of the reserve components for our national defenses is older than the Republic itself. Debated in the *Federalist Papers* that preceded the Constitution, the argument was incorporated into that document by Article I, Section 8, which gives the Congress power "to provide for calling forth the militia [and] to provide for organizing, arming, and disciplining the militia." Further, the Second Amendment specifically provides that "A well-regulated militia, being necessary to the security of a free State, the right of the people to keep and bear arms, shall not be infringed."

To implement these provisions, the Militia Act of 1792 (which remained in effect until 1903) required every able-bodied male citizen between eighteen and forty-five years of age to be "enrolled in the militia [and] be constantly provided with a good musket or fire-lock [and] a sufficient bayonet and belt."[10]

Although unworkable in its original form, by the turn of the century a "new National Guard" had evolved, which divided the militia into two classes, "one of which is the active or organized forces and the other is the mass of able-bodied citizens liable for military service." The job of the regular army was to "serve as a training school for officers, and to provide a nucleus for the large armies necessary in time of war." America's first line of defense would be the new National Guard, whose duty was to "act at decisive points on the outbreak of hostilities."[11]

During the Spanish-American war the Regular Army totaled some 58,688 while the National Guard provided 8,207 officers and 162,747 enlisted men. Although prior to World War I the Regular Army was named by Congress as America's first line of defense, during that war the National Guard and the newly organized Army Reserve provided 208,000 men to the Regular Army's 127,588 at the war's beginning. Forty percent of the forty-three U.S. divisions in the AEF (American Expeditionary Force) were National Guard personnel.

In World War II the first American division to deploy overseas was the National Guard's 34th Infantry Division, which deployed to Northern Ireland in January–March 1942, and the first American division to see offensive action was the National Guard's 32nd Infantry Division, in New Guinea in September 1942. During that war the National Guard brought 300,034 men into active service and the Army Reserve an additional 77,000.

The Korean war would have been lost without the reserve components. More than 50 percent of the 7th Marine Regiment, which stormed ashore at Inchon in September 1950, were reservists, having been called to active duty only a month before. The Army Reserve contributed 244,300 officers and men, most as fillers for active units, and beginning in August 1950, a total of 1,457 Army National Guard units, including eight combat divisions, were mobilized, comprising some 138,600 officers and men.

Two of these divisions, California's 40th Infantry Division and Oklahoma's 45th Infantry Division, fought on the front lines in Korea. Another two, Pennsylvania's 28th Infantry Division and New England's 43rd Infantry Division (with units from Maine, Vermont, Connecticut, and Rhode Island) were sent to Europe to bolster NATO's defenses.[12]

But in the Vietnam war no such large-scale mobilization took place. Although there was a limited mobilization in January 1968, primarily of Air National Guard units and Air and Navy reservists, and another in April 1968, when seventy-six Army National Guard and Army Reserve units were called up, by and large the National Guard and Reserves played little part in the war.

Total Force

It was not because they did not want to. And it was not because the Pentagon didn't want them. The reason was purely political. As historian Herbert Y. Schandler found, "When [President Lyndon B. Johnson] began to search for the elusive point at which the costs of Vietnam would become unacceptable to the American people, he always settled on [reserve] mobilization."[13] Defense analyst Lewis Sorley put it even more directly:

Lyndon Johnson astonished the defense establishment by his refusal to call up the reserves . . . perhaps the most fateful decision of the entire conflict. Johnson's refusal was apparently motivated in part by reluctance to spread the effects of the war throughout the population—certainly many more families and virtually every town and city would be affected by a call-up of any proportions, with a much different class cross-section and much greater political impact than draft calls affecting only those who could not engineer a deferment. . . .

[T]he President's failure to call the reserves had an effect of lasting significance. In Jim Webb's powerful novel of the war, *Fields of Fire*, a young Marine crouched in a foxhole somewhere in Vietnam experiences a sudden flash of insight. He turns to his buddy and says of the war, "It isn't *touching* anybody." And that was exactly so. Except for those who were actually out there fighting it, Lyndon Johnson's policy of trying to fight the war on the cheap, on the sly almost, and without involving the larger community, meant that the general population had no stake in it, and hence no motivation to ensure that the sacrifices of those who did serve were in some way validated by the eventual outcome. Perhaps that was the most fateful result of all.[14]

General Creighton W. Abrams, Jr., who as COMUSMACV (Commander, U.S. Military Assistance Command Vietnam) presided over the U.S. drawdown in Vietnam and who served as Army Chief of staff from 1972 until his death in office in 1974, saw clearly the critical role played by the reserves. Although in most American wars their reinforcing capabilities had been critical, more important was their function as a bridge between the wartime military and the American public. Thus the reserves were the ideal instrument to revitalize the "remarkable trinity" by stiffening the congressional backbone and ensuring Congress's active support for wartime operations.

In March 1974 Abrams directed that instead of a cut from thirteen to ten divisions, the Army would go from thirteen to sixteen divisions. This would be done by "rounding out" active Army divisions with combat brigades from the National Guard and by closely affiliating the Army National Guard and Army Reserve with active Army units in what he called the "Total Army."

As Sorley explains, "Abrams built into the 16-division structure a reliance on reserves such that the force could not function without them, and hence could not be deployed without calling them up. . . . There can be little doubt that the steps taken were meant deliberately to ensure that the reserves would be available in any future conflict of significant dimensions.

" 'They're not taking us to war again without calling up the reserves,' [General John Vessey] heard Abrams say on many occasions. Vessey [who later served as Chairman of the Joint Chiefs of Staff] was asked whether part of the thinking in integrating the reserves so deeply into the active force structure was that it would make it very difficult, if not impossible, for the President to deploy any significant force without calling up the reserves. 'That's it, with malice aforethought,' said Vessey, 'the whole exercise.' "[15]

Sixteen years later, on the eve of the Persian Gulf war, reserve components made up 58 percent of Army total strength, 31 percent of the Air Force, 29 percent of the Navy and Marines, and 32 percent of the Coast Guard.

More to the point, 86 percent of the Army's heavy-equipment maintenance units, most of its water resupply units, 74 percent of POL (petroleum, oil, and lubricant) companies, 69 percent of hospital units, 64 percent of military police units, 62 percent of ammunition companies, and 58 percent of truck companies were in the reserve components.

Fifty-nine percent of the Air Force's theater airlift aircraft, 22 percent of refueling tanker aircraft, 93 percent of aeromedical evacuation aircrews, 71 percent of aerial port units, and 59 percent of combat logistics support units were also in the reserves. So were 93 percent of the Navy's cargo handling units, 85 percent of Military Sealift Command personnel, 65 percent of the SEABEE mobile construction battalions, and 53 percent of fleet hospitals.[16]

In November 1990, commenting on the critical differences between the Vietnam war and the looming war in the Persian Gulf, *The Washington Post*'s Jim Hoagland noted that the Bush administration "look[s] honest and open by comparison to the effort by Johnson's White House 'to go to war without arousing the public ire.'

"Bush has little choice to arouse the public. . . . The generals saw to that in 1973, when the draft was ended. The new 'total force' Army that Gen. Creighton Abrams designed works only if reserve units are called up to round out active-duty forces in a massive deployment abroad.

"Johnson had refused to call up the reserves because of the political alarm bells it would have set off in congressional districts. Abrams and his successors made sure future presidents would not have that option. The generals have already curbed the president's powers, quietly and indirectly, but more efficiently than have all the congressional critics of Executive War."[17]

Back to the Beginning

While to some degree that may have been the effect of his actions, General Abrams did not set out to curb presidential power. He set out to reinvigorate the "remarkable trinity" of the people, the government, and the military that had been the basis of American warmaking policy for most of this nation's existence. The reason for this attempt was simple. As Abrams's

successor as Army chief of staff, General Fred C.
Weyand, explained:

> Vietnam was a reaffirmation of the peculiar relationship
> between the American Army and the American people.
> The American Army really is a people's Army in the
> sense that it belongs to the American people who take a
> jealous and proprietary interest in its involvement. When
> the Army is committed the American people are com-
> mitted; when the American people lose their commit-
> ment it is futile to try to keep the Army committed. In
> the final analysis, the American Army is not so much an
> arm of the Executive Branch as it is an arm of the
> American people. The Army, therefore, cannot be com-
> mitted lightly. It can only be committed when there is a
> consensus among the American people that vital inter-
> ests of such critical importance are involved that the
> commitment of the Army is warranted.[18]

What were those vital interests? That was one of
the questions posed to the "Astarita Group," an in-
house think tank formed by General Abrams in 1973
to examine the post-Vietnam strategic environment.
Named after its director, Colonel Edward Astarita,
who had been instrumental in devising the glide path
for the Vietnam troop withdraw, the group found that
despite Vietnam, the United States was in a position
of relative advantage. It was allied with the world's
two major power centers—Western Europe and Japan—and its two then adversaries, China and the
Soviet Union, were also adversaries with each other.

The challenge for the Army and the other services,
the group concluded in its 1974 report, was to assist in
maintaining that position of advantage.[19] Instead of the
delusions of nuclear and counterinsurgency "strategy," the focus was on commonsense conventional-
war strategies. Instead of the jungles of Southeast

Asia, the focus was on air and sea control and the plains of Central Europe. In March 1981, General John W. Vessey, Jr., later to become chairman of the Joint Chiefs of Staff, commented that "[T]he Astarita Report . . . marked a turning point in the post-Vietnam Army."[20]

Responding to critics who claimed that the report merely revalidated the obvious, General Weyand replied with a line from T. S. Eliot: "At the end of all our exploring/Will be to arrive where we started/And know the place for the first time."[21] The comment was particularly apt, for as a result of its post-Vietnam self-analysis, the Army (and, as we will see, the other services as well) had indeed arrived back at the beginning. That was particularly true when it came to war-fighting doctrine.

NOTES

1. Confucius, in Arthur Waley, trans., *The Analects of Confucius* (London: George Allen & Unwin, 1939). p. 59

2. Dudley W. Knox, "The Role of Doctrine in Naval Warfare," *U.S. Naval Institute Proceedings,* vol. 41, no. 2 (March–April 1915). p. 352.

3. Russell F. Weigley, *The American Way of War: A History of United States Military Strategy and Policy* (New York: Macmillan Publishing Company, 1973), p. 418.

4. J. Bower Bell, *The Myth of the Guerrilla: Revolutionary Theory and Malpractice* (New York: Alfred A. Knopf, 1971), pp. 257–58.

5. Douglas A. Blaufarb, *The Counterinsurgency Era: U.S. Doctrine and Performance 1950 to the Present* (New York: The Free Press, 1977), p. 52.

6. Lloyd Norman and John B. Spore, "Big Push in Guerrilla War," *Army* (March 1962), pp. 33–34.

7. Stuart A. Herrington, *Silence Was a Weapon: The Vietnam War in the Villages* (Novato, Calif.: Presidio Press, 1982), p. 203.

8. Author's notes.

9. Eliot A. Cohen, *Citizens & Soldiers: The Dilemmas of Military Service* (Ithaca, N.Y.: Cornell University Press, 1985), p. 167.

10. Francis V. Greene, "The New National Guard," *The Century Magazine* (vol. XLIII, no. 4 (February 1892), p. 484.

11. Ibid., pp. 491, 496.

12. John D. Stucky and Joseph H. Pistorius, *Mobilization of the Army National Guard and Army Reserve: Historical Perspective and the Vietnam War* (Carlisle Barracks, Pa.: U.S. Army War College, 1984), pp. 7–15.

13. Herbert Y. Schandler, *The Unmaking of a President: Lyndon Johnson and Vietnam* (Princeton, N.J.: Princeton University Press, 1977), p. 56.

14. Lewis Sorley, "Creighton Abrams and Active-Reserve Integration in Wartime," *Parameters: U.S. Army War College Quarterly,* vol. XXI, no. 2 (Summer 1991), pp. 37–39.

15. Ibid., p. 45. See also Harry G. Summers, Jr., "The Army after Vietnam," in Kenneth J. Hagen and William R. Roberts, eds., *Against All Enemies* (Westport, Conn.: Greenwood Press, 1986), p. 363.

16. *Defense 90 Almanac* (Washington, D.C.: U. S. Government Printing Office, 1990), pp. 15–18.

17. Jim Hoagland, "Congress, Bush and the Generals," *The Washington Post* (November 22, 1990), p. 31.

18. Fred C. Weyand and Harry G. Summers, Jr., "Vietnam Myths and American Realities," *CDRS CALL* (Washington, D.C.: Department of the Army Pamphlet 360–828 (July–August 1976), p. 7.

19. Harry G. Summers, Jr., *The Astarita Report: A Military Strategy for the Multipolar World* (Carlisle Barracks, Pa.: Strategic Studies Institute, U.S. Army War College, 1981), pp. 40–45.

20. Ibid., p. v.

21. Fred C. Weyand and Harry G. Summers, Jr., "Serving the People: The Need for Military Power," *Military Review,* vol. LVI, no. 12 (December 1976), p. 10.

5

Maritime Strategy and Amphibious Warfare

To get [Naval War College students just returned from Vietnam] in a room and try to dispassionately talk about whether we should or should not have been in Vietnam and what were the strategic implications of a sea power going into a prolonged engagement overseas would have been impossible. Yet they talked about Vietnam when they talked about the Peloponnesian War and they understood.

Vice Admiral Stansfield Turner
president, U.S. Naval War College (1972–74)[1]

Back to Basics

"This year's shift of emphasis toward a deeper study of strategy," said the newly appointed President of the U.S. Naval War College, Vice Admiral Stansfield Turner, on August 24, 1972, "represents[s] a return to our great traditions—to the strategic and historical contribution of men like Mahan; to the tactical and operational studies of men like William Sims, Raymond Spruance, Kelly Turner who were the experts in naval warfare of their day."

But it was the final part of his address that was the real shocker—"the announcement that the first meeting to discuss Thucydides' *The Peloponnesian War* would take place that day immediately after lunch. For many students, that was an unknown book about an apparently irrelevant war by an author with an unpronounceable name. Yet to Turner it was the essence of his approach, 'the best example of how you could use historical case studies to teach contemporary or strategic problems.' "[2]

The "Turner Revolution" was at hand, a renaissance in military thinking that would sweep the armed forces and revitalize the long-suppressed study of conventional war. The curriculum at the Naval War College was completely revamped, and among the changes was a return to the roots of naval warfare.

Once again the texts of the great naval strategists held sway, including the writings of Alfred Thayer Mahan. Author of some 20 books and 137 articles, Mahan's most influential works were his 1890 *The Influence of Sea Power upon History, 1660–1783* and his 1892 *The Influence of Sea Power upon the French Revolution and Empire, 1793–1812*. Both books had originated as lectures delivered by Captain Mahan at the Naval War College.

"There may be another Alfred Thayer Mahan in this year's class or the next," Admiral Turner said. "We cannot afford to miss him."[3] As Philip A. Crowl, Ernest J. King Professor of Maritime History Emeritus at the Naval War College noted, the most important aspect of a return to Mahan was not his answers, many long since overtaken by events, but his questions—questions that went to the heart of naval warfare:

> He constantly asked his listeners and readers to give serious thought to such matters as the meaning of the concept of national interest; the moral dimensions of military force; the responsibilities as well as the opportunities of world power; the nature of American depen-

dence on sea-lines of communications; the composition of fleets; the logistical requirements of warfare; and, most importantly, the uses of navies as instruments of national power.[4]

And there was another critical aspect as well: Mahan's conviction that *"it must be a fundamental principle to assure defense by means of offense."* As British naval writer Anthony Preston emphasized, Mahan grasped that a major problem of sea power "is the indivisibility of the sea, which means there cannot be partial control of it; it has no frontiers to be defended and no natural features to strengthen the defense . . . command of the sea can only be guaranteed by destroying or neutralizing hostile forces in that sea. Once that command of the sea is established the weaker side is totally excluded from it, and although sporadic raids can be mounted against the superior power they can never be more than pinpricks."[5]

Another important text was Sir Julian S. Corbett's 1911 work *Some Principles of Naval Strategy.* In his advocacy of sea power Mahan has been accused of being too parochial and of seeing naval strategies as an end in themselves. But Corbett, Britain's greatest maritime strategist, saw matters in a broader context. In an earlier work he noted, "We speak glibly of 'sea power' and forget that its true value lies in its influence on the operations of armies."[6]

His words were echoed in the Naval War College's classic *Sound Military Decisions,* first published in 1936 and reprinted in September 1942, at the beginning of World War II. "The final outcome" of war, it emphasized, "is dependent on ability to *isolate, occupy or otherwise control the territory of the enemy.* The sea, though it supplements the resources of land areas, is destitute of many essential requirements of man, and affords no basis, alone, for the secure development of human activities. *Land is the natural habitat of man.*"[7]

Clausewitz Rediscovered

Corbett not only refined the works of Mahan, he also served as a link to another important theorist and philosopher of war. "[I]nspired by reading Clausewitz's *On War,* [Corbett] applied a general, philosophical approach to the specific issues of naval conflict," wrote naval historians John B. Hattendorf and Wayne P. Hughes, Jr., in the preface to the U.S. Naval Institute's reprint of Corbett's seminal work. "Corbett wrote . . . the first successful attempt at a comprehensive synthesis of [naval conflict], linking it both to a general theory of warfare and to the specific problems of sea power, strategy and naval battle."[8]

By a stroke of amazing good fortune, just at the time this renaissance in military thought was underway at the Naval War College, Princeton University Press was in the process of publishing a new version of Clausewitz's work. Rejecting the bowdlerizations of earlier versions, Oxford University's Michael Howard and Stanford's Peter Paret returned to the original 1832 texts unearthed by the keeper of the Clausewitzian flame, Muenster University professor Werner Hahlweg, and published in his 1952 edition of *Vom Kriege.*

Howard and Paret's masterful 1976 translation—including the introductory essays by Paret, Howard, and the University of California at Los Angeles's professor Bernard Brodie, as well as the commentary and reader's guide by Brodie—was to become the Rosetta stone for the post-Vietnam military.[9]

Appropriately, given the joint (i.e., Army, Navy, Air Force, Marine Corps) nature of post-Vietnam military theory and doctrine, the *éminence grise* behind the inclusion of the new translation of *On War* into the

War College curricula—the Naval War College in 1976, the Air War College in 1978, and the Army War College in 1981—was an Air Force exchange officer on the faculty at Newport, Lieutenant Colonel David MacIsaac (of whom more later). Working with a distinguished military historian, Professor Philip A. Crowl, chairman of the Naval War College's Department of Strategy, MacIsaac was instrumental in integrating Clausewitzian philosophy into the college's course of study.

A Doctrine of War

With the philosophical basis for a "general theory of warfare" established, attention then shifted to "the specific problems of sea power, strategy and naval battle." Here another seminal work came into play, Lieutenant Commander (later Commodore) Dudley W. Knox's pre-World War I classic, "The Role of Doctrine in Naval Warfare." Knox could have been writing about the post-Vietnam War Navy sixty years later when he emphasized, "[I]t is important to determine whether our strategic and tactical operations shall be offensive or defensive in character. . . . The determination of such matters as these produces a 'conception' of war which furnishes a point of origin, without which we are as uncertain of our bearings as a vessel in a fog."[10]

Following Knox's prescription, in the late 1970s and early 1980s the Naval War College produced "Sea Plan 2000," an offensive strategic concept that established the Navy's post-Vietnam point of origin and that would become the basis for the later Maritime Strategy. "Working with the fleet commanders-in-chief and testing the development and employment concept through repeated wargaming at the Naval War College," noted F. J. West, Jr., who played a major role in the study, "two successive [chiefs of naval operations]—Admirals Thomas Hayward and James D. Watkins—steadily developed an overall concept for the wartime employment of naval forces [and] a conceptual strategy for maritime forces."[11]

Assisting in this effort was the Strategic Studies Group (SSG), founded at the Naval War College in 1981. As former secretary of the navy John Lehman, Jr., described it, "This elite group of midgrade officers, navy and marine, is selected from the fleet to spend a year working on strategy. Each year a new SSG is formed, and changing perspectives help to keep the strategy from solidifying into dogma."[12]

Then there was the remarkable reemergence of strategic thinking among senior naval officers at the highest levels. As Navy captain Linton F. Brooks found, "only three articles by flag officers [i.e., admirals and generals] on *any* aspect of strategy appeared in a typical five-year period in the 1960s. Of 719 articles in *Proceedings* [the professional journal of the Navy and Marine Corps] during 1964–1968, only two were directly concerned with overall naval strategy." By contrast, in an eight-month period in 1985–86, articles by the chief of naval operations, the commander in chief (CINC) of the Atlantic Fleet, the CINC of the Pacific Fleet, and the commander of Strike Force Atlantic appeared in *Proceedings* and *Naval War College Review*.[13]

The Maritime Strategy

"Both ashore and afloat," wrote Commander Knox in 1915, "we . . . imperatively need first of all a *conception of war*. Once this is created we will be able to proceed, with our eyes open and our course well marked, toward a coherent comprehensive scheme of naval life. Doctrine, methods and rules may be made to flow consistently and logically therefrom. Strategy, tactics, logistics, gunnery, ship design . . . every ramification of the profession—may be developed with confidence and wisdom. . . .''[14]

The Maritime Strategy provided just such a conception. And from that conception flowed not only naval doctrines and tactics but the composition and organization of the fleet as well. Ballyhooed as the "600-ship Navy" by Secretary of the Navy John F. Lehman, Jr., to sell it to the Congress, the strategy envisioned fifteen carrier battle groups, four battleship surface action groups, one hundred attack submarines, an adequate number of ballistic missile submarines, and lift for the assault echelons of a Marine amphibious force and a Marine amphibious brigade. "When escort, mine warfare, auxiliary, and replenishment units are considered," Lehman said, "about 600 ships emerge from this accounting. . . .''[15]

Publicly announced in January 1986 as a supplement to the *Proceedings* of the U.S. Naval Institute in a joint statement by the secretary of the Navy, the chief of naval operations, and the commandant of the Marine Corps, the Maritime Strategy set the course for the naval forces that would fight the Persian Gulf war.

Technically, it was not a "strategy" per se. Rather it was "the maritime component of the National Military Strategy." As then chief of naval operations Admiral James D. Watkins explained, "The Maritime Strategy is firmly set in the context of national strategy, emphasizing coalition warfare and the criticality of allies, and demanding cooperation with our sister services."[16]

One thing the Maritime Strategy did for sure: It got the naval service out of its Vietnam war doldrums and reoriented it toward offensive operations. I once asked then Navy secretary John F. Lehman, Jr., if he was serious about conducting naval operations against the Soviets in the Norwegian fjords (one of the strategy's more controversial aspects) or whether that was simply a way of building an offensive "carry the fight to the enemy" mind-set throughout the fleet. He allowed that creating a warrior spirit was the most critical part, but that forward operations were still an important element of the strategy.[17]

The Maritime Strategy's primary focus was on a protracted conventional (i.e., nonnuclear) war with the Soviet Union. Instead of defensive "Maginot Line" measures such as closing the "GIUK gap" (i.e., the sea passages between Greenland, Iceland, and the United Kingdom) to deny Soviet submarines access to the high seas, the Navy would instead take the offensive, carrying the war to the Soviets and bottling them up in their home ports. With control of the seas thus assured, the SLOCs (sea lines of communication) would be secured, paving the way for creation of a sea bridge to Europe so that the mobilization capabilities of the United States could be brought to bear on the critical NATO Central Front.

Meanwhile, with its carrier battle groups and surface action groups, the Navy would add a new dimension to the war through horizontal escalation—applying pressure on the flanks through force projection in the Pacific and Indian oceans, the Persian Gulf, and the Mediterranean and Norwegian seas.

Although the goal of 600 ships was never reached, on the eve of the Persian Gulf war the Navy did have some 534 warships, including 34 strategic nuclear submarines armed with SLBMs (nuclear-tipped submarine-launched ballistic missiles) and 91 tactical submarines. Principal surface combatants included 14 aircraft carriers (and 13 attack carrier air wings), 4 battleships, 43 cruisers, 59 destroyers, and 100 frigates. In addition, there were 30 patrol and coastal

combatants, 29 mine warfare ships, 65 amphibious
warfare ships, and 63 underway support, maintenance,
and logistics ships. Another 67 ships of the Military
Sealift Command Fleet Auxiliary Force, and 11 civil-
ian-operated survey and research ships were also part
of the force.[18]

Admiral Watkins called the Maritime Strategy a
"dynamic concept," and that's exactly what it proved
to be. Although initially designed for a major protracted conventional war with the Soviet Union, it also
provided for war on the flanks as well.

Thanks to almost twenty years of internal reflection and reform, when the crisis erupted in the Middle
East in August 1990, the Navy was ready. The Maritime Strategy had provided it with the offensive spirit,
warfighting doctrine, and warships necessary for successful naval operations in the Persian Gulf.

The Marine Corps

"Marines are naval forces. The Marine Corps and the
Navy form the naval service of the United States,"
emphasized then Lieutenant General Carl E. Mundy,
Jr. (now commandant of the Marine Corps) at the
Center for Naval Analyses' 1986 Seapower Symposium. "Although this relationship is established in law
and practiced daily around the globe, few people outside naval circles understand it well, and it sometimes
eludes a few within naval circles. . . . The laws of the
United States direct the Marine Corps to provide 'fleet
marine forces of combined arms, together with supporting air components, for service with the fleet . . .
in prosecution of a naval campaign' or for 'such additional duties as the president may direct.' "[19]

Thus as part of the naval service the Marine Corps
was intimately involved in the post-Vietnam renaissance at the Naval War College. Marines were students

there, members of the faculty, and part of its Strategic Analysis and Wargaming groups.

Like the Navy, the Marine Corps returned to fundamentals. "We are pulling our heads out of the jungle and getting back into the amphibious business," said General Robert E. Cushman, the commandant of the Marine Corps, in April 1972. "We are redirecting our attention seaward and reemphasizing our partnership with the Navy and our shared concern in the maritime aspects of our national strategy."[20]

But for a while in the post-Vietnam era it appeared that the Marine Corps' primary reason for being—amphibious, forcible entry operations—had been written off as "outmoded or suicidal in the modern age." Critics maintained that "the Marine Corps didn't need to be tied to the Navy and that there was plenty for the Corps to contribute in the battles for Central Europe without being shackled to an amphibious mission . . . initiatives . . . would have 'heavied-up' the Marine Corps to create a mechanized clone of existing Army divisions."[21]

Amphibious Forces

To do so "would likely have emasculated the Corps' naval and utilitarian character," General Mundy pointed out at the 1986 symposium. "[T]he Marine Corps is a global force. Historically it has maintained a readiness to be 'first to fight' in 'every clime and place.' To do so, the Corps has resisted regional specialization and scenario-dependent reorganization of our basic structure."[22]

The Marine Corps had unlikely saviors: Iran's Ayatollah Ruhollah Khomeini and the Soviet Union's Leonid I. Brezhnev. The 1979 Iranian Islamic fundamentalist revolution and the Soviet intervention in Afghanistan that same year shifted the focus of American strategic interests toward a more global perspective. In January 1980 President Jimmy Carter proclaimed the "Carter Doctrine," which declared the oil supplies of the Persian Gulf to be a vital American interest. And on February 4, 1980, the Rapid Deployment Joint Task Force (the forerunner of the U.S. Central Command) was formed at MacDill Air Force Base near Tampa, Florida; the unit was under the initial command of Marine General P. X. Kelley, who would later serve as commandant of the Marine Corps.

"While trying to form a Rapid Deployment Force to implement the Carter Doctrine, our government leaders soon found that carrier battle groups and amphibious forces were the only military assets capable of establishing an American presence in the Arabian area," General Kelley later noted. "The equipment for a Marine amphibious brigade (MAB) was quickly put aboard a set of near-term prepositioning ships and rushed to Diego Garcia."[23]

A movement that would have profound long-term consequences, it led to the creation of the Maritime Prepositioning Ships (MPS) program. Initially known as the Near-Term Prepositioning Ships (NTPS) program, "by the summer of 1980 six ships loaded with a MAB's equipment and fifteen days' supplies were steaming toward the Indian Ocean. The NTPS grew to a total of eighteen ships by 1982, and they supported not only a MAB, now with thirty days of supply, but also carried war material for Army and Air Force units as well."

As the MPS program developed, three squadrons, each with four or five commercial roll-on/roll-off (RO/RO) ships with a MAB's worth of equipment and thirty days' supply, were deployed. "The first squadron deployed to the eastern Atlantic in July 1984. The second squadron replaced the Marine Corps portion of the NTPS in Diego Garcia in December 1985. The last squadron to be put into service sailed into Guam and Tinian in October 1986.''[24] All would see service in the Persian Gulf war.

Meanwhile, the organization for the Marine airground task forces (MAGTF) was also being refined:

Each MAGTF consists of a headquarters element, a ground combat element, an aviation combat element and a combat service support element. The smallest element is a Marine Expeditionary Unit (MEU), which is designed around an infantry battalion and a composite helicopter squadron. [Next] is a Marine expeditionary brigade (MEB), which has an infantry regiment as its ground combat element and an aircraft group as its aviation combat element. The largest MAGTF is a Marine expeditionary force (MEF), consisting notionally of a division, wing and FSSG [force service support group.][25]

As in the Vietnam war, a Marine expeditionary force (then called a Marine amphibious force [MAF]) can control more than one division and thus be equivalent to an Army corps headquarters. This was the case with the III MAF, which at one time in 1968 commanded the 1st and 3d Marine divisions, the 1st Marine Aircraft Wing, two Marine regimental landing teams, and the Army's Americal Division, 1st Cavalry Division (Airmobile), 101st Airborne Division, and a brigade from the 5th Infantry Division (Mechanized).[26]

The Marine Corps' organization for combat was complete. In the Persian Gulf, ''the I Marine Expeditionary Force would be structured very much like the III Marine Amphibious Force in Vietnam: two divisions, a very large [air] wing, and a substantial service support command.'' In addition, the Army's 1st Brigade, 2nd Armored Division—the ''Tiger Brigade''—with its some forty-two hundred soldiers and more than a hundred M1A1 Abrams—tanks would also be under the I MEF's operational command. Afloat with the U.S. Seventh Fleet would be "two Marine Expeditionary Brigades and a special-operations-capable Marine Expeditionary Unit . . . offering a very powerful landing force for any contemplated amphibious operation."[27]

Amphibious Warfare Strategy

When it came to strategic doctrine, the Marine Corps played a major role in formulating the Maritime Strategy discussed above. As then Marine commandant General P. X. Kelley wrote in January 1986, "the development of strategic concepts for the employment of naval forces is an ongoing effort by the Navy and Marine Corps. . . . In June 1985, the Chief of Naval Operations and the Commandant of the Marine Corps approved the publication of the Amphibious Warfare Strategy . . . as a subset of the Maritime Strategy."[28]

The Amphibious Warfare Strategy had several components. One was the Marine Corps' role in low-intensity conflict, a mission with which the Marine Corps was intimately familiar. "From the end of the nineteenth century until 1934 the U.S. Marine Corps engaged primarily in the conduct of small wars," noted Professor Ronald Schaffer in a 1972 article. "In the three decades beginning in 1893, Marines landed in the Philippines, Cuba, Puerto Rico, Honduras, Mexico, Guam, Samoa, China, Nicaragua, and the Dominican Republic." As a result of those experiences the Marine Corps published its first *Small Wars Manual* in 1935 and a final version in 1940.[29] Part of the "back to basics" movement that pervaded all of the services in the wake of Vietnam, this classic was reprinted by the Marine Corps in 1987.[30]

Also part of the "back to basics" movement was a

reemphasis on warfighting. "No matter how . . . sound the strategy may be," General Kelley said in 1986, "the lack of a ready, well-equipped, and professional amphibious force will make all else irrelevant." To keep that from happening, "Marines are working on the refinement of tactics that will increase the effectiveness of the MAGTF ashore. Our schools have become hotbeds for the development of new initiatives, and the volume and quality of the tactical debate in our military journals indicate that the scope, depth and enthusiasm of this effort runs deeply through the Corps."[31]

A major portion of that tactical debate had to do with maneuver warfare—"a warfighting philosophy that seeks to shatter the enemy's cohesion through a series of rapid, violent, and unexpected actions which create a turbulent and rapidly deteriorating situation with which he cannot cope." Centered at the Marine Corps' Command and Staff School and Amphibious Warfare School at Quantico, Virginia, this debate led to the publication of Marine Corps FMFM 1, *Warfighting,* in March 1989 and its companion volume, FMFM 1-1, *Campaigning,* in January 1990.

The Vietnam loop had been closed. As then Marine commandant General A. M. Gray emphasized in the foreword to *Campaigning,*

> *Tactical success in combat is not enough, because tactical success of itself does not guarantee victory in war.* What matters ultimately in war is success at the level of strategy, the level directly concerned with attaining the ends of policy. That these two levels are connected and that there is an art to the way tactical results are used to advance the strategic purposes are beyond doubt. With this thought as its point of departure, *this book discusses this intermediate operational level which links strategy and tactics, describing the military campaign as the*

primary tool of operational warfare [and] establishes the authoritative doctrinal basis for military campaigning in the Marine Corps, particularly as it pertains to a Marine Air-Ground Task Force (MAGTF).[32]

"We believe that there is ample evidence to suggest that we have entered a renaissance period in the evolution of amphibious operations," General Kelley concluded in his January 1986 elaboration on the Amphibious Warfare Strategy.[33] Events would prove his assessment to be absolutely correct.

NOTES

1. Stansfield Turner in John B. Hattendorf, B. Mitchell Simpson III, and John R. Wadleigh, *Sailors and Scholars: The Centennial History of the U.S. Naval War College* (Newport, R.I.: Naval War College Press, 1984), p. 285.

2. Hattendorf et al., *Sailors and Scholars,* pp. 284–85.

3. Stansfield Turner, "Challenge!," *Naval War College Review* (September–October 1972), p. 2, quoted in Philip A. Crowl, "Alfred Thayer Mahan: The Naval Historian," *Makers of Modern Strategy from Machiavelli to the Nuclear Age,* ed. Peter Paret (Princeton, N.J.: Princeton University Press, 1986), p. 477.

4. Crowl, *Makers of Modern Strategy,* p. 477.

5. Anthony Preston, "Introduction," Alfred Thayer Mahan, *The Influence of Sea Power upon History, 1660–1783* (Novato, Calif.: Presidio Press, 1987), p. 9. Emphasis added.

6. Julian S. Corbett, *The Successors of Drake,* quoted in Robert Debs Heinl, Jr., *Dictionary of Military and Naval Quotations* (Annapolis, Md.: U.S. Naval Institute, 1966), p. 289.

7. *Sound Military Decisions* (Newport, R.I.: U.S. Naval War College, 1942), p. 46. Emphasis in original.

8. John B. Hattendorf and Wayne P. Hughes, Jr., *Classics of Sea Power: Julian S. Corbett, Some Principles of Maritime Strategy* (Annapolis, Md.: Naval Institute Press, 1988), preface.

9. Carl von Clausewitz, *On War,* ed. and trans. Michael Howard and Peter Paret, with introductory essays by Peter Paret, Michael Howard, and Bernard Brodie, with a commentary by Bernard Brodie (Princeton, N.J.: Princeton University Press, 1976).

10. Dudley W. Knox, "The Role of Doctrine in Naval Warfare," *U.S. Naval Institute Proceedings,* vol. 41, no. 2 (March–April 1915), repr. *The Art of War Colloquium* (Carlisle Barracks, U.S. Army War College, November 1983), pp. 68–69.

11. F. J. West, Jr., "Maritime Strategy and NATO Deterrence," *Naval War College Review* (September/October 1985), p. 5.

12. John F. Lehman, Jr., *Command of the Seas: Building the 600-Ship Navy* (New York: Charles Scribner's Sons, 1989), p. 129. The SSG continues apace. On April 18, 1991, the author was briefed by Captain Denny McGinn, USN, and other members of the SSG "Gold Team" on their concept of the future strategic environment and its implications for the nation and the Navy.

13. Linton F. Brooks, "Naval Power and National Security: The Case for the Maritime Strategy," *International Security,* vol. 11, no. 2 (Fall 1986), p. 58.

14. Knox, "The Role of Doctrine in Naval Warfare," p. 70.

15. John F. Lehman, Jr., "The 600-Ship Navy," *The Maritime Strategy,* supplement to *U.S. Naval Institute Proceedings* (January 1986), pp. 35–36.

16. James D. Watkins, "The Maritime Strategy," in *The Maritime Strategy,* p. 4.

17. Author's notes.

18. *The Military Balance: 1990–91* (London: International Institute for Strategic Studies, 1990), pp. 19–20.

19. Carl E. Mundy, Jr., "Amphibious Warfare," in *The U.S. Marine Corps: The View from the Late 1980s,* ed. James L. George and Christopher Jehn (Alexandria, Va.: Center for Naval Analyses, 1988), pp. 9–10.

20. General Robert E. Cushman, quoted in Edwin H. Simmons, *The United States Marines: 1775–1975* (New York: The Viking Press, 1976), p. 299. General Cushman

commanded the III Marine Expeditionary Force in Vietnam from 1967 to 1969.

21. P. X. Kelley, "The Amphibious Warfare Strategy," *The Maritime Strategy,* p. 20. For example, see Martin Binkin and Jeffrey Record, *Where Does the Marine Corps Go from Here?* (Washington, D.C.: The Brookings Institution, 1976).

22. Mundy, "Amphibious Warfare," p. 10.

23. Kelley, "The Amphibious Warfare Strategy," pp. 23–24.

24. George Akst, "Deployment Concepts," in *The U.S. Marine Corps: The View from the Late 1980s,* pp. 23–24.

25. In 1988, Marine commandant General A. M. Gray reinstated the traditional title of "Expeditionary" forces, replacing the "Amphibious" forces euphemism used during the Vietnam war. MAFs, MABs, and MAUs became MEFs, MEBs, and MEUs. See Edwin H. Simmons, "Getting Marines to the Gulf," *U.S. Naval Institute Proceedings,* vol. 117, no. 5 (May 1991), p. 53.

26. Harry G. Summers, Jr., *The Vietnam War Almanac* (New York: Facts on File, 1985), p. 339.

27. Simmons, "Getting Marines to the Gulf," pp. 60, 63.

28. Kelley, "The Amphibious Warfare Strategy," pp. 24–25.

29. Ronald Schaffer, "The 1940 Small Wars Manual and the 'Lessons of History,' " *Military Affairs* (April 1972), p. 46.

30. *Small Wars Manual* (reprint of 1940 ed.) (Washington, D.C.: U.S. Marine Corps, 1987).

31. Kelley, "The Amphibious Warfare Strategy," pp. 27–28.

32. A. M. Gray, *FMFM 1-1, Campaigning* (Washington, D.C.: U.S. Marine Corps, 1990), foreword. Emphasis in original.

33. Kelley, "The Amphibious Warfare Strategy," p. 29.

6

Aerospace Doctrine

Airpower is the only answer available to our
country in this circumstance. . . . [To attempt to
beat Iraq on the ground risks] destroying Kuwait
in order to save it. [By using air power against
targets in Iraq] you would attempt to convince
his population that [Saddam Hussein] and his
regime cannot protect them. If there is a nation
that cannot defend its people against these in-
truding foreigners—protect their lines of communication, their means of production, their
cities—that brings a great burden for their
leaders. . . . Airpower in peace and war brings a
special kind of psychological impact. . . .

General Michael J. Dugan,
chief of staff, U.S. Air Force[1]

Doctrinal Schizophrenia

On September 17, 1990, on the eve of the Persian Gulf
war, Air Force chief of staff General Michael J. Dugan
was relieved from office for these and other such
comments to John M. Broder of the *Los Angeles
Times,* and simultaneously to Rick Atkinson of *The
Washington Post,* concerning U.S. strategy for the
forthcoming military campaign. "Ground forces may
be needed to reoccupy Kuwait," Dugan was para-
phrased as saying in *The Washington Post*'s account
of the interview, "but only after air power has so

shattered enemy resistance that soldiers can 'walk in and not have to fight' a pitched battle."[2]

"There are some things we never discuss." said Secretary of Defense Dick Cheney in announcing Dugan's relief. "And as a general matter of policy I don't think we want to be demeaning the contributions of other services."[3]

This was no case of ambush journalism. "What is remarkable about the Dugan case," noted *Defense Media Review,* "is that the editors of the *Los Angeles Times* and *The Washington Post* took pains to contact Dugan to ensure they were presenting Dugan's views accurately. . . . In the end, Dugan gave them the go-ahead."[4]

Although it may have seemed to some that he had taken leave of his senses, General Dugan, a most distinguished fighter pilot with some three hundred combat missions in Vietnam, was in fact reflecting long-established Air Force thinking. It was that doctrinal thinking, not General Dugan, that was schizophrenic.

"At the heart of warfare lies doctrine," General Curtis E. LeMay had said. "It represents the central beliefs for waging war. . . . Doctrine is of the mind, a network of faith and knowledge reinforced by experience which lays the pattern for the utilization of men, equipment, and tactics. It is the building material for strategy. It is fundamental to sound judgement."[5]

LeMay was correct in believing that "doctrine is of the mind." The problem was that from almost the beginning of its existence there have been not one but several minds over the Air Force's proper wartime role. The resulting schizophrenic disputes over what constitutes this proper role were a more virulent form of the earlier controversy within the Navy over whether "Sea Power" writ large could in itself be war-winning, or whether sea power's "true value," as

Corbett said, "lies in its influence on the operations of armies."

What made the arguments so virulent was that the whole *raison d'être* of a separate Air Force rested on the independent application of air power to achieve objectives apart from those sought by armies and navies. But even after such a separate Air Force was established in 1947, the controversy continued. Obviously separate status was not the real issue.

And neither was air power's crucial role on the battlefield. As General Elwood R. Quesada's IX Tactical Air Command proved in Europe in World War II—and as was validated by the Fifth Air Force in Korea, the Seventh Air Force in Vietnam (and the Ninth Air Force in the Gulf)—there is no argument that tactical Air Force fighters and fighter bombers are critical not only to battlefield success but to battlefield survival as well.

Air supremacy is an absolute precondition for successful ground operations. And once the ground battle is joined, close air support to neutralize enemy artillery and destroy enemy troop concentrations, and aerial interdiction of enemy lines of communications and supply are also crucial.

And there is also no question of air power's strategic role. As in World War II, Korea, and Vietnam (and in the Gulf as well), aerial attack of strategic targets in the enemy's homeland by bombers and fighter-bombers to disrupt his command and control facilities and destroy his capability to wage war is an important part of breaking the enemy's will to resist.

But these are not enough to satisfy the air power advocates. For them the real issue is the Orwellian argument that while all the armed forces are equal, some are more equal than others. The Army, Navy, and Marine Corps concede that they are joint services, relying on cooperation with each other to achieve

national military objectives. And so does most of the
Air Force as well. But there are those within its ranks,
as General Dugan's remarks made clear, who have the
conceit that air power can win wars all by itself.

Command of the Air

This vanity is not new. The roots are especially deep,
stretching back to the period just after the First World
War. Appalled by the carnage in the trenches during
that conflict, Italian general Giulio Douhet believed
that air power offered a better and more humane way
to wage war. Incongruous as it may sound, he believed
that by bombing of cities a civilian population could
be terrorized into compelling their government's surrender, thereby ending a war with *minimum* casualties.

In his 1921 classic *The Command of the Air,* Douhet argued that aircraft had altered the fundamental
character of war. Douhet believed that air power had
little significance as "auxiliaries" to armies and navies. Air forces had to be independent of ground and
naval forces, and armed, structured, and deployed for
the decisive strategic role.

"In Douhet's thinking," wrote Richard H. Kohn
and Joseph P. Harahan in the editors' introduction to
the 1983 Office of Air Force History reprint of Douhet's work, "airpower became the use of space off the
surface of the earth to decide war on the surface of the
earth." The first effort of air forces, Douhet wrote,
was "to conquer the command of the air—that is, to
put the enemy in a position where he is unable to fly,
while preserving for one's self the ability to do
so. . . ."

"For Douhet," noted Kohn and Harahan, "aircraft
were only useful as instruments of the offense. By
bombing cities and factories instead of military forces

. . . the enemy could be defeated through shattering the civilian will to continue resistance.'' Thus the idea that air power alone would decide wars was born. A translation of *The Command of the Air* was available at the U.S. Army Air Service (as the Air Force was then known) Tactical School as early as 1923, and extracts of Douhet's work were circulated at the school (after 1926 part of the newly redesignated Army Air corps) in the early 1930s.[6]

American airmen undoubtedly shared Douhet's belief in an independent air force, but they were repelled by his idea of winning wars through terror bombing of innocent civilians. ''While translations of Douhet were available at the Tactical School, great controversy exists over how much they were used, if at all,'' notes Air Force major Mark Clodfelter, professor of Air Studies at the Air University.

''At the Tactical School, a uniquely American idea of strategic bombing evolved from ideas articulated by [Brigadier General] Billy Mitchell. Rather than focusing on destroying civilian will through terror bombing, American theorists at the Tactical School (such as Haywood Hansel, Lee George, Ken Walker, and Laurence Kutner) stressed destroying an enemy's *war-making capacity* through *precision* raids against his *vital centers*.

''Such bombing would, in turn, destroy the will of the civilian populace, because besides destroying the enemy's war-making capability, the raids would destroy the industries and transportation net essential to the normal functioning of everyday life. Yet the civilian populace was *not* to be targeted; American theorists believed that they could destroy civilian morale without having to kill women and children.''[7]

These Army Air Corps views were reflected in a 1936 Army Command and General Staff School manual. ''An air raid which involves . . . the wholesale destruction of noncombatants can not be justified or condoned [and will] be condemned by the civilized world," it stated. "Air raiding among civilized nations will have to be confined to military or semi-military objectives and thus will constitute one of the important supporting units in the conduct of a war."[8]

Strategic Bombing in World War II

With high-explosive and incendiary bombing (but not chemical bombing, which he had also called for), Douhet's theories were put to the test during World War II. In Europe, not only the Axis Powers but Great Britain as well deliberately targeted civilian populations in an attempt to break the enemy's will to resist.[9]

But "Army Air Force officers, especially General [Carl A.] Spaatz, consistently expressed moral revulsion at the wholesale slaughter of noncombatants which terror bombing of cities obviously entailed." Our allies had no such compunctions. Under the leadership of "Bomber Harris" (the Royal Air Force's air chief marshal Sir Arthur Harris), an air offensive "aimed primarily at the homes of the German people" began in March 1942.

This campaign "reached one of its climaxes in the fire raids on Hamburg at the end of July 1943, when in four days the RAF killed about 42,000 people, more than had died in the whole 'Blitz' against Britain. . . . The terror bombing of Germany reached its final dreadful climax in the Dresden raids of February 13–14, 1945, which killed some 35,000 people."[10]

Collateral damage caused by U.S. "precision" bombing of industrial targets added to the toll. "The allied bombing offensive killed some 305,000 Germans and injured about 780,000."[11] The effect on German war production remains arguable, but clearly the bombing had not, as Douhet preached, "shatter[ed] the civilian will to continue resistance."

In fact, it may have precisely the opposite effect. "[T]here were indications of the tendency to push the enemy people more deeply into the arms of Hitler's government, on which they became more dependent as other bonds of community were blasted away."[12]

But if the results of the battlefield test of Douhet's theories on the decisiveness of strategic bombing were mixed in the war with Nazi Germany, they appeared to have been validated in the war against imperial Japan. As historian Russell F. Weigley reports, in a departure from their previous restraint on terror bombing in Europe, in 1945 the Army Air Force (AAF) "opened against Japan a terroristic city-bombing campaign which was to surpass even what the RAF had done. . . .

"In the spring of 1945 it was not yet evident how little the British campaign of terror bombing had contributed to the defeat of Germany. . . . In any event, the AAF gave wide discretion in the determination of bombing strategy for Japan to Major General Curtis E. LeMay's XXI Bomber Command." After an inconclusive campaign against Japanese war industries, "LeMay moved toward making cities the primary targets":

> On March 9 [1945], he sent 334 B-29s, carrying some 2,000 tons of bombs on an incendiary-bomb raid against Tokyo. In loss of life this was the most destructive air raid in history, without exception; it killed 83,793 people, while injuring 40,918, destroying about a quarter of Tokyo's buildings, leaving more than a million homeless.

> LeMay followed up with similar raids: against Nagoya on March 11, with a heavier weight of bombs than had fallen on Tokyo; against Osaka, Kobe, and Nagoya

again. . . . Thousands fled their homes, dislocating war industry more than the terror bombing of Germany had ever done, swelling the ranks of an eventual eight and a half million refugees of the American aerial campaign, and spreading fear throughout the land.

The hope of both AAF and Navy leaders that Japan could be brought to surrender without invasion was probably decisive in producing Washington's endorsement of LeMay's bombing methods. In that, it seemed merely a logical extension of policy to employ the two atomic bombs, which killed from 70,000 to 80,000 at Hiroshima and 35,000 at Nagasaki. . . .[13]

But even though those raids precipitated the surrender of Japan in August 1945, critics were not yet convinced that strategic bombing was the be-all and end-all. Tactical air power more than held its own. As Kohn and Harahan point out, "Tactical aviation altered the nature of land and naval warfare and so contributed to the outcome of World War II that a few historians have suggested that its influence outweighed that of the strategic bombing campaigns against Germany and Japan."[14]

The Strategy of Massive Retaliation

But the perceived success of strategic bombing against Germany and Japan, as well as the advent of the atomic age, seemed to have validated the claims of the air power advocates. An independent Air Force could no longer be denied. Even before the creation of the Air Force, the primary role of strategic bombing was acknowledged.

On March 21, 1946, the Army Air Force's Strategic Air Command (SAC) was created as a "specified" command with responsibility for delivery of America's nuclear munitions. When the Army Air Force became the separate U.S. Air Force in July 1947, SAC retained that special relationship, becoming at once an integral part of the Air Force and an independent specified command reporting directly to the secretary of defense.

By then under the command of General Curtis E. LeMay (who would command SAC from October 1948 to June 1957), SAC played only a secondary role in the Korean war. Several of its B-29 bombardment groups were loaned to the Far East Air Force's Bomber Command for both air support of tactical operations and strategic bombing of enemy hydroelectric plants, irrigation dams, and other war-related facilities. But while strategic bombing contributed to the enemy's eventual signing of the armistice agreement in 1953, it was not, as its advocates claimed, decisive in and of itself. Even such massive bombing as the 1,403-plane raid on the North Korean capital of Pyongyang on August 29, 1952, failed to break the enemy's will to resist.

Tactical air operations, on the other hand, played a major role in defeating the enemy armed forces. The U.S. Fifth Air Force, including Navy, Marine, and allied aircraft, almost completely dominated the airspace over the battlefield. They flew 66,997 counter-air sorties and shot down 950 enemy planes.

From the beginning of U.S. involvement in the war on June 26, 1950, to the start of the Korean Armistice on July 27, 1953, the U.S. and allied air forces destroyed 1,317 tanks, 882,920 vehicles, 967 locomotives, 10,407 freight cars, 1,153 bridges, 118,231 buildings, 65 tunnels, 8,663 gun positions, 8,839 bunkers, 16 oil-storage tanks, and 593 barges and boats, and killed 184,808 enemy troops.[15]

But despite these successes, it was the Strategic Air Command that would dominate the Air Force after the Korean war. In January 1954, Secretary of State John Foster Dulles announced a "strategy of massive retaliation," wherein primary reliance for the security of the United States would be placed on strategic nuclear weapons: "a maximum deterrent at a bearable cost."[16]

For almost the next two decades the "bomber types" of the Strategic Air Command would dominate the Air Force, and for a while the rest of the armed forces as well. Their arrogance was overweening. General Maxwell D. Taylor, Army chief of staff in the late 1950s, recalled a proposal that while SAC's nuclear forces deterred major war, "the Army be converted into essentially a home guard-civil defense force and that the major responsibility for limited wars be assigned to the Navy and the Marine Corps."[17]

But the next war would not be the nuclear holocaust that SAC had prophesied. As I have written elsewhere, "Faced with U.S. nuclear superiority . . . both the Soviets and the Chinese began to develop and expand their own nuclear capabilities . . . a long-term effort that would take years to accomplish. In the meantime, a counter-strategy to U.S. nuclear superiority had to be devised. The Soviets found such a strategy in 'Wars of National Liberation.' Announced by [Soviet] Premier Nikita Khrushchev in January 1961 on the eve of President John Kennedy's inauguration, it was essentially a low cost effort using surrogate forces in order to avoid a direct confrontation with the United States."[18]

The Air War in Vietnam

The test of this "new kind of warfare" would come in Vietnam. While "counterinsurgency," at least in principle, occupied the attention of the other services, the Air Force's primary concentration was on tactical and strategic air operations. First was the tactical air war in South Vietnam under the command of COMUS-MACV (commander, U.S. Military Assistance Command, Vietnam) in Saigon and his deputy, the commander of the Seventh Air Force. Involved was close air support of Army and Marine forces, interdiction of enemy supply lines, an intratheater airlift within Indochina. Also involved was coordination of the Military Airlift Command intertheater airlift between Vietnam and the United States and targeting and coordination of SAC B-52 bombing strikes in support of ground operations.

Next was the strategic air war, under the command of CINCPAC (commander in chief, Pacific Command) in Honolulu and, in the case of B-52 operations, CINCSAC (commander in chief, Strategic Air Command), at the Offutt Air Force Base near Omaha, Nebraska. Foremost were the air campaigns against North Vietnam, including the Rolling Thunder air campaign, beginning in 1965, and the 1972 Linebacker air campaigns. Then there was interdiction of the Ho Chi Minh Trail in southern Laos from 1965 to 1973 and air support for the Royal Laotian Army in northern Laos from December 1964 to February 1973.

Other activities included air operations in Cambodia from March 1969 to August 1973; special air commando missions; and defoliation, search-and-rescue, and advisory operations.[19]

As in the Korean war, tactical air operations in South Vietnam proved crucial to battlefield success. Because of the enormous firepower that air power provided, the U.S. military, as noted earlier, never lost a major battle there. At the U.S. Army's 1st Cavalry Division's Battle of Ia Drang in November 1965, for example, not only U.S. Seventh Air Force tactical fighters but also SAC B-52 bombers helped thwart North Vietnamese Army (NVA) attempts to overrun South Vietnam.

Then there was Operation Niagara in 1968, in support of the besieged Marine fire base at Khe Sanh, where 24,000 tactical air sorties and 2,700 B-52 sorties dropped over 110,000 tons of bombs. And during the NVA 1972 Eastertide offensive, U.S. tactical air sorties and B-52 strikes played a major role in turning back the multidivision NVA attack, destroying most of the NVA's heavy tanks and artillery and inflicting some 100,000 casualties.

And in hundreds of smaller battles in between, tactical air support played a critical role. With veteran Air Force fighter pilots serving as forward air controllers attached to ground infantry, armor, and cavalry battalions, close air support was more effective than it had ever been in previous wars. And Air Force tactical airlift kept isolated outposts provisioned and reinforced, even under enemy attack.

But also as in the Korean war, strategic bombing was another matter. For one thing, SAC domination of the Air Force had imposed its toll. As Air Force colonel Jacksel M. Broughton, a veteran fighter pilot of the Korean and Vietnam wars, noted, "We had ignored the basics of tactical aviation ever since the end of Korea in favor of atomic weapons delivery."[20]

After the Korean War the Air Force was dominated by the Strategic Air Command whose mission it was to execute the national strategy of Massive Retaliation. . . . Most of the emphasis, even in TAC [Tactical Air Command] was on delivery of nuclear weapons. All that we learned in Korea about close air support, air interdiction and air-to-air combat was forgotten. . . . When the Vietnam War started we simply had to relearn the basics, and we paid a terrible price in doing so. . . .

During the 1965–1968 *Rolling Thunder* air campaign, the bombing of the North was carried out not by bombers of the Strategic Air Command but by fighter bombers of the Tactical Air Command. . . . Ironically during this time SAC's B-52 bombers were being used in support of ground operations in the south. . . .

The senior leadership was SAC-dominated—what we called "SACumcized." For example, at PACF [Pacific Air Command] they just simply could not understand the basic fighter-bomber tactic of high-speed, low-level pop-up to a target, drop your bombs and get out of there. [For them it was] World War II-type strategic bombing all over again. They subscribed to the flawed routine of approaching Hanoi at the same time, same altitude, same heading and airspeed every day. . . .[21]

The split between SAC and TAC was only part of the problem. So was the geographic distance in command and control. "The further removed a headquarters is from the scene of combat," wrote Air Force general William W. Momyer in his analysis of the air war in Vietnam, "the greater the tendency to . . . become excessively involved in the political chessboard aspects of the war while neglecting the realities upon which success in combat depends."[22]

And so also was that "political chessboard" itself, primarily the delusion, as discussed in an earlier chapter, that the bombing of North Vietnam was mainly to "send signals," not to win the war. The attendant bombing pauses and political dithering in target selection diluted the effectiveness of the strategic air campaign.

Some 6,162,000 tons of bombs were dropped by Air Force fighter-bombers and bombers in Southeast Asia—almost triple the 2,150,000 tons dropped during World War II and far exceeding the 454,000 tons dropped during the Korean war,[23] but these figures are misleading. Many were wasted bombing holes in the jungle in an ineffective interdiction campaign, and less than 1,000,000 tons were dropped on North Vietnam itself.

In any event, the will of the North Vietnamese people to continue the war was not broken. The closest it came was during the "Christmas bombing" of 1972, the Linebacker II air attacks on Hanoi and Haiphong in December 1972. During the intensive air campaign, 729 B-52 sorties as well as 2,123 fighter-bomber sorties were flown, most of them at night. Noteworthy was the use of laser-guided "smart bombs" to take out the Hanoi power plant and radio station.

But it was no terror bombing, although false charges were made that the "Christmas bombing" involved "carpet bombing" of Hanoi—that is, the deliberate targeting of civlian areas, as in Dresden in World War II. "American antiwar activists visiting the city during the attack urged the mayor to claim a death toll of 10,000," reported Stanley Karnow. "He refused, saying that his government's credibility was at stake. The official North Vietnamese figures for fatalities . . . was 1,318 in Hanoi."[24]

"The 11-day campaign came to a close on the 29th of December 1972," wrote General Momyer, "when the North Vietnamese responded to the potential threat of continued air attacks to the economic, political, social, and military life of their country. It was apparent that airpower was the decisive factor leading to the peace agreement of 15 January 1973."[25]

The Post-Vietnam Reassessment

More so than the other services, the Air Force came out of the Vietnam war with a chip on its shoulder, convinced that given the opportunity it could have won that war by itself. As Momyer, a four-star general who commanded the Seventh Air Force in Vietnam from July 1966 to August 1968 and the Tactical Air Command from 1968 to 1973, noted in his 1978 evaluation,

> The development of air strategy in World War II, Korea and Vietnam was a repetitious process. In each case, planners first perceived airpower as a subordinate part of a joint strategy that would employ an extensive ground campaign to end the war on favorable terms. On the other hand, airmen came increasingly to believe that airpower, in its own right, could produce decisive results. The validity of such a view was suggested by results of the Allies' combined bomber offensive in Europe and by the surrender of Japan in the 1940s. Additional evidence came from the skies over Hanoi in December 1972. . . .[26]

The Air Force, said Dr. Earl H. Tilford, Jr., a veteran Air Force officer and former editor of the *Air University Review,*

> made a conscious effort "to put Vietnam behind it" just as two decades before it had put Korea behind it when Secretary of the Air Force Thomas K. Finletter had declared that the Korean War was a unique, never-to-be-repeated diversion from the true course of strategic air power.
>   As was the case in the mid-1950s, the post-Vietnam U.S. Air Force returned its attention to preparing to counter the Soviet threat. . . . Thus, the Air Force, to a greater extent than the Army, failed to learn from the Vietnam War—except, of course, in matters relating to air tactics. . . . From the top to the bottom, Air Force

officers preferred to focus on Linebacker Two as a reaffirmation of traditional doctrines and strategies. . . .

Study of the Vietnam War . . . was slighted at the Air War College. . . . From 1974 through 1979, the Air War College . . . devoted only 2.5 hours of study to the Vietnam war in a case study . . . focused on the role of airpower in Linebacker One and Two.[27]

But there were bright spots as well. "I believe," said Air Force chief of staff General Lew Allen, Jr., in 1982, "that a continuing study of military history, combat leadership, the principles of war, and, particularly, the application of airpower, is necessary for us to meet the challenges that lie ahead." This was the genesis of Project Warrior, "to improve the warfighting spirit and perspective of Air Force people [and] to encourage an improved understanding of the theory and practice of war."[28]

Also in 1982, the Air Force signed a memorandum of agreement with the U.S. Navy for closer cooperation in training and operations. And as will be discussed in greater detail in the chapter on AirLand Battle doctrine, in April 1983 a memorandum of understanding was signed with the U.S. Army. This formalized a July 1975 agreement between TAC and the Army's Training and Doctrine Command to work together to enhance joint employment of Army and Air Force tactical forces.

In May 1984 a memorandum of agreement was signed with the Army on joint force development. "In focusing upon battlefield operations—and particularly the extended battlefield—rather than doctrinal abstractions, the Army and Air Force were taking hard critical looks at concepts and doctrines of most-likely theater war and reevaluating them in the light of fighting to win."[29]

Yet another bright spot was the reemphasis on

fundamentals at the Air University at Maxwell Air Force Base, Alabama, in the late 1970s, sparked by its commander, Lieutenant General Raymond B. Furlong. Among other things, with the help of Air Force lieutenant colonel David MacIsaac, who had earlier performed a similar service at the Navy War College, the study of Clausewitz's *On War* was integrated into the curriculum of the Air War College in 1978. These initiatives continued with the creation of the Air University Center for Aerospace Doctrine, Research, and Education (CADRE) in January 1983.

And the Air Force Academy at Colorado Springs, Colorado, also played a role. In October 1990, for example, a military history symposium was held titled "Vietnam 1964–1973: An American Dilemma." The capstone of the symposium was Air Force major Mark Clodfelter's analysis of Linebacker II. An instructor in the History Department of the Academy (now on the faculty of the Air University), Clodfelter summerized the findings of his 1989 critical examination of that campaign, *The Limits of Air Power: The American Bombing of North Vietnam* (New York: The Free Press, 1989), a work now required reading at the Air War College:

"Had the North Vietnamese reverted to guerrilla warfare in the summer of 1972 [after the failure of their disastrous Eastertide offensive] as was their pattern . . . the Linebacker campaigns would have had a meager effect on their warfighting capability," Clodfelter argued.

"In all likelihood, the desire to preserve the North Vietnamese Army helped induce the Hanoi leadership to sign an agreement in January 1973." Other factors included President Richard Nixon's 1972 trips to Peking and Moscow, which caused the Soviet Union and China to forgo further support for North Vietnam in order to achieve warmer relations with the United

States; the widening Sino-Soviet split; Soviet refusals to ship supplies through the minefields in Haiphong Harbor; and, because of Nixon's diplomacy, the elimination of the Soviet and Chinese threat of intervention in the war.

"To Nixon and many of the war's air commanders," Clodfelter concluded, "Linebacker II was the decisive element of American military power that ended a long and frustrating conflict. Yet the results . . . were largely fortuitous, owing at least as much to Hanoi's decision to wage conventional war and Nixon's superpower diplomacy as they did to Nixon the Mad Bomber."[30]

Vietnam Redux

But Clodfelter's reasoned, scholarly analysis was no match for the emotions of those who fought the war. "The most popular and most widely accepted Vietnam myth is that Linebacker Two 'won' the war," notes Tilford. "The our-hands-were-tied thesis has dominated thinking about Vietnam in the Air Force because it blames the final outcome on a pernicious press, the antics of antiwar activists . . . and, perhaps, most disturbingly, on 'interference' by politicians who restrained the military."[31]

That latter point surfaced in an August 24, 1990, *The New York Times* interview with Central Command's air chief, Air Force lieutenant general Charles A. Horner, commander of the U.S. Ninth Air Force. "Many of us here who are in this position now were in Vietnam, and that war left a profound impact on our feelings about how our nation ought to conduct its business," he said. "We will carry out any particular policy but as individuals we think that war is a very serious business and it should not be dragged out in an effort to achieve some political objective."[32]

In words that must have seemed particularly apt in the opening days of the Persian Gulf crisis, General Momyer had warned in 1978 that as he looked to the future:

> The increasing complexity of international politics . . . will entice us again toward parcelling our air forces for the winning of battles rather than unifying and focusing them for the winning of wars.
>
> [W]e are reluctant to act decisively. We prefer to make smaller decisions, win battles, and hope that the enemy will lose heart. And our airpower will permit us to win most battles. But that way leads to a series of Khe Sanhs and eventually in a free society to war-weariness and dissent. As an alternative to this approach, airpower offers the possibility of an early LINE-BACKER II campaign. . . .
>
> Airpower can be strategically decisive if its application is intense, continuous, and focused on the enemy's vital systems. In short, airpower can win battles or it can win wars. All commanders since Pyrrhus have been tempted at one time or another to confuse the two, but few distinctions in war are more important. The future airman's right to insist that such distinction be made is, I believe, one of the things our airmen purchased so dear in Vietnam.[33]

Although General Dugan claimed otherwise ("I would not argue that air power alone can be decisive," he said), Momyer's reaffirmation of not so much Dou-het's but Army Air Service/Army Air Corps Tactical School principles that air power could in fact be decisive clearly echo in Dugan's remarks to the press. As John M. Broder observed in his September 16, 1990, *Los Angeles Times* interview with Dugan, "Most Air Force officers believe to this day that if they had been allowed to bomb North Vietnam without limits the U.S. would have won the war."[34]

And that belief echoes in official Air Force doctrine as well. "As a critical element in the interdependent land-naval-aerospace team, aerospace power can be the decisive force in warfare," states AFM (Air Force Manual) 1–1, *Basic Aerospace Doctrine of the United States Air Force,* dated March 16, 1984. Accordingly, the Air Force's first mission is "to neutralize or destroy an enemy's war-sustaining capabilities or will to fight [through] attacks . . . directed against an enemy's key military, political, and economic power base."[35]

General Dugan's relief notwithstanding, Operation Desert Storm would give the Air Force the chance to do just that in its air campaign against Iraq.

NOTES

1. Michael J. Dugan, quoted in John M. Broder's "U.S. War Plan in Iraq: 'Decapitate' Leadership," *The Los Angeles Times* (September 16, 1990), pp. A1, A6–7.

2. Michael J. Dugan, quoted in David C. Morrison's "Overestimating Air Power," *National Journal* (September 29, 1990), p. 2366.

3. Dick Cheney, "News Conference by Defense Secretary Dick Cheney," *The Reuters Transcript Report* (September 17, 1990), pp. 1–2.

4. Stephen Aubin, "Dugan's Miscalculation: Who Is Really to Blame?" *Defense Media Review,* vol. IV, no. 5 (September 30, 1990), pp. 1–2.

5. Curtis E. LeMay, quoted in AFM 1–1: *Basic Aerospace Doctrine of the United States Air Force* (Washington, D.C.: U.S. Air Force, 1984), introduction.

6. Giulio Douhet, *The Command of the Air,* trans. Dino Ferrari and ed. Richard H. Kohn and Joseph P. Harahan (Washington, D.C.: U.S. Government Printing Office, 1983), pp. viii–ix.

7. Major Mark Clodfelter, USAF, letter to the author (August 15, 1991). Emphasis in originals.

8. *The Principles of Strategy for an Independent Corps or Army in a Theater of Operations* (Fort Leavenworth, Kan.: The Command and General Staff School Press, 1936), p. 18.

9. The definitive work on World War II strategic bombing is the 132-volume *U.S. Strategic Bombing Survey* (Washington, D.C.: United States Government Printing Office, 1945–46). More manageable is the 10-volume extract *Strategic Bombing in World War II,* ed. David MacIsaac. (New York: Garland Publishing, 1976).

10. Russell F. Weigley, *The American Way of War: A History of United States Military Strategy and Policy* (New York: Macmillan Publishing Company, 1973), pp. 354–56.

11. Ibid., p. 359.

12. Ibid., pp. 355–56.

13. Ibid., pp. 363–65.

14. Kohn and Harahan in Douhet, *Command of the Air,* p. ix.

15. Harry G. Summers, Jr., *Korean War Almanac* (New York: Facts on File, 1990), pp. 67–69, 115–17.

16. John Foster Dulles, *Department of State Bulletin,* vol. XXX (January 12, 1954), pp. 107–10.

17. Maxwell D. Taylor, ". . . . But Not for a Pentagon Feud," *The Washington Post* (March 10, 1980), p. A27.

18. Harry G. Summers, Jr., *On Strategy: A Critical Analysis of the Vietnam War* (New York: Dell Publishing, 1984), p. 108.

19. Harry G. Summers, Jr., *Vietnam War Almanac* (New York: Facts on File, 1985), pp. 73–74.

20. Jack Broughton, *Going Downtown: The War Against Hanoi and Washington* (New York: Orion Books, 1988), pp. 63, 104.

21. Jacksel M. Broughton, "Curbs on Power Base," *Vietnam* (Winter 1988), pp. 32–33.

22. William W. Momyer, *Airpower in Three Wars* (Washington, D.C.: U.S. Government Printing Office, 1978), p. 337.

23. *The United States Air Forces in Southeast Asia,*

1961–1973, ed. Carl Berger, Appendix IV (Washington, D.C.: U.S. Government Printing Office, 1977), p. 366.

24. Stanley Karnow, *Vietnam: A History* (New York: The Viking Press, 1983), p. 653.

25. Momyer, *Airpower in Three Wars*, pp. 240–43.

26. Ibid., p. 34.

27. Earl H. Tilford, Jr., *Setup: What the Air Force Did in Vietnam and Why* (Maxwell Air Force Base, Ala.: Air University Press, 1991), pp. 283–84, 294.

28. Robert Frank Futrell, *Ideas, Concepts, Doctrine: Basic Thinking in the United States Air Force 1961–1984*, vol. II (Maxwell Air Force Base, Ala.: Air University Press, 1989), pp. 742–43.

29. Ibid., pp. 743–44.

30. Mark Clodfelter, "Nixon and the Air Weapon," *Fourteenth Military History Symposium*. U.S. Air Force Academy, Colorado Springs, Colo. (October 17–19, 1990).

31. Tilford, *Setup*, p. 289.

32. Charles A. Horner, quoted in Michael R. Gordon's "Generals Favor 'No Holds Barred' By U.S. if Iraq Attacks the Saudis," *New York Times*, August 25, 1990, p. 1.

33. Momyer, *Airpower in Three Wars*, p. 339.

34. John M. Broder, "U.S. War Plan in Iraq. . . ," *The Los Angeles Times* (September 16, 1990), p. A6.

35. AFM 1–1, *Basic Aerospace Doctrine of the United States Air Force* (Washington, D.C.: Department of the Air Force, March 16, 1984), pp. 1-3, 3-2.

7

Strategic Military Doctrine

As Clausewitz wrote, "No one starts a war—or rather, no one in his right mind ought to do so—without first being clear in his mind what he intends to achieve by that war, and how he intends to conduct it."

War may be different today than in Clausewitz's time, but the need for well-defined objectives and a consistent strategy is still essential.

Secretary of Defense Casper W. Weinberger,
November 28, 1984[1]

The Atomic Revolution

By 1984, the secretary of defense himself was quoting the great nineteenth-century Prussian military philosopher Carl von Clausewitz on the fundamentals of strategic military doctrine. But a generation earlier Clausewitzian theory and doctrine, along with all conventional war theory and doctrine, had been dismissed as antiquated and irrelevant in the atomic age.

And so had the Army itself. In July 1947, when its traditional title as the "War Department" was abandoned in favor of the less bellicose "Department of the Army," part of the Army's soul went with it. The

Army's primacy as the nation's decisive battlefield force had been seemingly eclipsed by the atomic "revolution" almost two years earlier.

More than a name change was involved. The Army's very *raison d'être* was in question. As Temple University's Russell F. Weigley saw it, "The atomic bomb . . . represented a strategic revolution. The atomic explosions at Hiroshima and Nagasaki ended Clausewitz's 'the use of combats' [in the Howard-Paret translation, "the use of engagements for the object of the war"[2]] as a viable inclusive definition of strategy.

"A strategy of annihilation could now be so complete that a use of combats encompassing atomic weapons could no longer serve 'for the object of the War,' unless the object of war was to transform the enemy's country into a desert. . . . To shift the American definition of strategy from the use of combats for the objects of wars to the use of military force for the deterrence of wars . . . amounted to a revolution in the history of American military policy."[3]

The Korean War

But the "revolution" was stillborn. If the North Koreans had been deterred from invading South Korea in June 1950 for fear the United States would drop an atomic bomb on Pyongyang, the revolution would have been confirmed. But they were not, even though the United States had a near monopoly on such weapons.[4]

Instead, a bloody conventional war ensued. Acting as the executive agent for the U.N. Security Council, the United States (and the U.S. Army, which acted as the Joint Chiefs of Staff's executive agent) shouldered most of the burden of waging war in Korea, first against the North Korean Army and then against the

Chinese Communist Forces (CCF), who intervened in November 1950.[5]

The war itself was very much a "use of combats" in the classic sense. And tough combat it was. As Clay Blair pointed out in *The Forgotten War*, "the first year of the Korean War was a ghastly ordeal for the United States Army. For various reasons, it was not prepared mentally, physically, or otherwise for war."[6]

One reason is that it had bought the notion that conventional war was obsolete in the nuclear age. Armies were for occupation of defeated Germany and Japan, not for fighting, and they were trained and equipped accordingly. For another, President Harry Truman and his feckless defense secretary, Louis Johnson, had cut defense spending to irresponsibly low levels.

For example, in the 24th Infantry Division's 78th Heavy Tank Battalion in Japan, equipped with one company of M24 light Chaffee tanks armed with an ineffectual 75mm main gun, spare parts were almost impossible to obtain. Among the items on back order because of Johnson's "cut the fat and not the muscle" campaign was a starter solenoid for the company's tank retriever.

When the unit went into battle in July 1950 the part was still missing, and the only way the retriever would be started was by towing. When an attempt was made to retrieve a damaged tank under enemy fire the driver was killed and the retriever stalled. Unable to get it restarted, the crew, including the company commander, Lieutenant Leonard E. Gewin, had to bail out through the turret, and all were killed in the attempt.[7]

It was a story repeated time and again in the opening days of the war: radios gone dead, antitank bazookas ineffective against enemy armor, and worn-out rifles and machine guns. The terrible memory of this "hollow army" would influence Army thinking until the very eve of the Persian Gulf war.

The most vivid account of this ordeal, T. R. Fehrenbach's *This Kind of War: A Study in Unpreparedness,* had and continues to have an enormous impact within the Army. A Korean war veteran, Fehrenbach detailed the Army's failure of spirit after World War II as well as its material shortcomings. The book was required reading in the 2nd Armored Division at Fort Hood prior to the Vietnam war, was excerpted time and again—especially his chapter "Proud Legions"— and bootleg copies were distributed among concerned Army officers.

For a time right after the Vietnam war, copies of this chapter were reprinted by the office of the Army's chief of staff in the Pentagon and issued to all newly appointed general officers. For some years it has been on the Army Command and General Staff College's required reading list and used as a teaching text by the History Department at the U.S. Military Academy. Reprinted by the Army's chief of military history in 1989, it has now been reissued by Macmillan for public sale.

The reason for its popularity is that it went to the heart of the issue most plaguing the Army—its role on the modern battlefield. As Fehrenbach noted:

> Americans in 1950 rediscovered something that since Hiroshima they had forgotten: you may fly over a land forever; you may bomb it, atomize it, pulverize it and wipe it clean of life—but if you desire to defend it, protect it, and keep it for civilization, you must do this on the ground the way the Roman legions did, by putting your young men into the mud.[8]

"Americans had learned, and learned well," he said. "The tragedy of American arms . . . is that

having an imperfect sense of history Americans sometimes forget as quickly as they learn.[9]

Massive Retaliation

And that was particularly true of the Korean war. The
ink was barely dry on the Korean Armistice Agreement of 1953, which ended the fighting, than the
conventional-war lessons of Korea were killed aborning. And the assassin was none other than one of the
Army's World War II heroes, General of the Army
Dwight D. Eisenhower, who assumed the presidency
just as the Korean war came to an end. As Colonel
A. J. Bacevich, then an international affairs fellow
with the Council on Foreign Relations (and as of this
writing commands the 11th Armored Cavalry Regiment in the Persian Gulf), explained:

> Eisenhower and his advisors believed that air power was
> the key to deterrence. Thus, the Air Force, less than a
> decade after achieving independent status, was exalted
> to primacy among the Services. . . .
>
> As the Air Force's importance grew . . . that of the Army
> declined. In Ike's view of defense in the atomic age the
> role of his old Service did not loom large. Some thought
> was given to the Army having to occupy an enemy's
> homeland once it had been devastated by a hail of
> nuclear bombs. . . . But the notion of the Army perform-
> ing major combat missions along the lines of World War
> II or Korea was the very antithesis of Eisenhower's
> thinking.[10]

"Eisenhower understood full well how his policies
were affecting his old Service," said Bacevich. "As
he observed to [JCS chairman] Admiral [Arthur W.]
Radford in 1956, 'the lack of a doctrine that assigns

the Army a definite and permanent mission has left some of them somewhat unsatisfied and even bewildered. Their role is rather hazy to many of them.' "[11]

The Vietnam War

Into this doctrinal vacuum came the Vietnam war. As I have detailed elsewhere (*On Strategy: A Critical Analysis of the Vietnam War* [New York: Dell Publishing, 1984]), counterinsurgency doctrine struck the Army with particular force. One reason was its timeliness. "Need[ing] a newly defined *raison d'être,* [the Army] joined with the civilian strategists in creating the strategy of limited war and flexible response," noted Professor Weigley. "The Army seized upon the idea of limited war as a means of keeping itself alive in the massive retaliation era of the 1950s, and the Army consequently adjusted its tactics and weapons to the prospects of limited war."[12]

But this Faustian bargain was at the price of a further piece of the Army's soul. Gone was the emphasis on the Army's traditional mission: "the defeat of an enemy by application of military power directly or indirectly against the armed forces which support his political structure."[13]

Now "military intellectuals were advancing the notion that the U.S. Army was the arm of the government best equipped to carry out the entire range of activities associated with 'nation building.' "[14] For the Army, counterinsurgency appeared to provide a whole new mission—civil affairs activities, establishment of schools and public health systems, assistance to police, and other sorts of "civic action."

The one thing the Army did not "intend to achieve" was victory. Testifying before the Senate in 1966, General Maxwell D. Taylor said the United States was not trying to "defeat" North Vietnam, only "to cause them to mend their ways." General Taylor likened the concept of defeating the enemy to "Appomattox or something of that sort."[15] The analogy was more apt than he knew. The war would indeed end with an "Appomattox." Unfortunately, it would not be the United States accepting the sword of surrender.

But while the enemy was fighting war the old-fashioned way—to win—the United States was chasing the counterinsurgency chimera. "The fundamental purpose of U.S. military forces," said the 1968 edition of FM 100-5, the Army's basic doctrinal manual, "is to preserve, restore, or create an environment of order and stability within which the instrumentalities of government can function effectively under a code of laws."[16]

In addition to what today would be called a "politically correct" restatement of the Army mission, this edition of FM 100-5 also dropped the familiar phrase "The ultimate objective of all military operations is the destruction of the enemy's armed forces *and his will to fight,*"[17] reducing it merely to "defeat of the enemy's armed forces." The doctrine, intentionally or not, had been tailored to fit the existing battlefield situation.

"Destruction of the enemy's armed forces" was not the problem in Vietnam. After their uprising during the Tet offensive of 1968, the Viet Cong guerrillas ceased to be an effective fighting force. And during the 1972 Eastertide offensive, the North Vietnamese Army (NVA) was defeated as well.

But the United States was never able to break the enemy's will to resist. After the U.S. withdrawal in January 1973 in accordance with the Paris Peace Accords, the NVA, with the considerable help of the Soviet Union, regenerated itself into a force of more than twenty divisions well equipped with tanks, missiles, and heavy artillery.

Two years after the U.S. withdrawal this formidable force, using conventional military doctrine, crushed their South Vietnamese opponents in a massive crossborder blitzkrieg bearing more resemblance to the Nazi juggernaut that crushed France in 1940 than to the black-pajama guerrillas of popular imagination.

As the North Vietnamese commander, General Van Tien Dung, reported in his account of that final campaign, at the initial Battle at Ban Me Thuot in the Central Highlands on March 10, 1975, "the ratio was 5.5 of our troops for each enemy soldier. As for tanks and armored vehicles the ratio was 1.2 to 1. In heavy artillery, the ratio was 2.1 to 1." Overall "the enemy has 5 divisions against our 15, excluding the [5-division] strategic reserve forces. Thus we cannot fail to win victory."

The NVA General Staff charged with planning the maneuvers of General Dung's four Army corps worked beside a large poster that read, "Lightning speed, more lightning speed; boldness, more boldness." Meanwhile, "cadres of the front-line staff had to admit somewhat ruefully that they could not draw maps quickly enough to catch up with the advance of our forces."[18]

Dung's comments echoed the words of General George S. Patton, Jr., thirty years earlier as he raced his U.S. Third Army across Europe. But such sentiments were out of fashion in the American Army during the Vietnam war. They were not forgotten, however, and a decade and a half after the fall of Saigon, the VII and XVIII corps of the U.S. Third Army would once again be on the move with boldness and lightning speed, racing across the sands of the Kuwaiti Theater of Operations.

The Postwar Renaissance

It took almost thirty years for the Army to descend from the height of its World War II glory in 1945 to the depths of its Vietnam despair in 1975. But before it hit bottom, the trip back had already begun. Fittingly, it was lead by veterans of that last great conflict, beginning with General Creighton W. Abrams, Jr., one of Patton's most famous tank commanders, whose 37th Tank Battalion spearheaded Patton's drive across Europe and that raised the siege of Bastogne during the 1944 Battle of the Bulge.

Succeeding General William C. Westmoreland as COMUSMACV (commander, U.S. Military Assistance Command Vietnam—i.e., the senior U.S. military commander in Vietnam) in 1968, Abrams planned and supervised the Army's withdrawal from Vietnam, culminating in the departure of the last Army ground combat unit in Vietnam, the 3rd Battalion, 21st Infantry, in August 1972.

Two months later, in October 1972, Abrams once again succeeded Westmoreland, this time as Army chief of staff. Refusing to give in to a "Vietnam syndrome," Abrams set out to put the Army back on its feet. As we have seen earlier, with his "Astarita Group" he set out to define the Army's postwar roles and missions, and with his "total force" concept he began the rejuvenation of the Army's Reserve components. As will be seen, with his formation of the Training and Doctrine Command (TRADOC) he set in motion the Army's formulation of its own warfighting doctrine. But most of all, he gave the Army back its soul.

Sadly, General Abrams died in office in October 1974 before his plans could be fully realized. But the stage had been set. "I was fortunate to have a solid foundation on which to build," said General Fred C.

Weyand, Army chief of staff at the time of the fall of Saigon. "It had been laid by my predecessor as Army Chief of Staff, General Creighton Abrams, who turned the Army away from its Vietnam troubles and re-oriented it to its vital security interests in Europe and Northeast Asia. . . . Most importantly, he gave the Army a sense of mission and a sense of self-worth."[19]

Also a World War II veteran, having served as an intelligence officer on the staff of General Joseph "Vinegar Joe" Stilwell in the China-Burma-India Theater, General Weyand later commanded the 1st Battalion, 7th Infantry, in the Korean war. He took the U.S. 25th Infantry Division into battle in Vietnam and commanded the corps-level II Field Force Vietnam during the 1968 Tet offensive. General Weyand was America's last commander in Vietnam, succeeding General Abrams on COMUSMACV in 1972.

Concerned that the Vietnam war not be ignored, as had been the case with the Korean war, he encouraged criticism from within by a series of articles on the war and on the role of military force in the postwar world that were widely distributed within the Army.[20]

Intellectual ferment within the Army took place on several levels. Most important were those at the Army chief of staff-Army War College level, which concerned itself primarily with strategic issues and education, and those at the TRADOC-Command and General Staff College level, which focused on warfighting doctrine and training. From there, the post-Vietnam renaissance soon permeated the entire Army.

On War

Among the many events that took place in the interactions among the Army chief of staff and his Deputy chief of staff for Military Operations and Plans (ODCSOPS) and the Army War College at Carlisle

Barracks, Pennsylvania, three in particular had a significant effect on future battlefield operations.

First was the rediscovery of the importance of the theories and philosophies of Carl von Clausewitz and the integration of his *On War* into the Army War College curriculum. This would set the tone for subsequent strategic, operational, and tactical doctrine. Second was coming to grips with Vietnam through a Clausewitzian analysis of the war and the publication of *On Strategy: The Vietnam War in Context*. Third was the publication of the Army's strategic Field Manual 100-1 *The Army*.

Ironically, the Army War College was the last of the three service war colleges to integrate Clausewitz into its curriculum, even though *On War* dealt primarily with land strategy. Still caught up in the management and "touchy-feely" issues that characterized the Vietnam era, it was not until Major General Jack N. Merritt was brought in from the Artillery School in 1980 to revitalize the curriculum that the Army War College became serious about warfighting and military strategy.

There was a realization that there was a need to move army thinking from a postwar to a prewar mindset. A similar transition had taken place in the early 1930s as the military put World War I behind it and began preparing for the conflict then brewing in Europe. A wealth of strategic thinking from that era was unearthed by Colonel Ralph L. Allen, then an Army War college instructor, from the files of the U.S. Army Military History Institute and distributed among key faculty members.

Under the leadership of Colonel Donald E. Lunday, then chairman of the Army War College's Department of Military Strategy, Planning and Operations, campaign planning was reintroduced into the core curriculum. The Advanced Warfighting Studies

Program (AWSP) was created by Colonel Dwight L. "Hooper" Adams and Lieutenant Colonel Clayton Newell akin to the SAMS (School for Advanced Military Studies) program at the Command and General Staff College discussed in Chapter 9.

In the meantime, Army War College faculty members, including Chaplain (Colonel) Charles Kreite and Colonel Wallace Franz, an Army Reserve officer, had been talking at the Air War College with Air Force lieutenant colonel David MacIsaac, who had been instrumental in getting *On War* incorporated into both the Naval War College and Air War College curricula. MacIsaac, who had received his doctorate in history while studying under legendary professor Ted Ropp at Duke University, had taught Clausewitzian theory at the Air Force Academy, the Navy War College, and the Air War College.

MacIsaac's arguments were particularly persuasive, and in 1981, upon the recommendation of General Merritt, Army chief of staff General Edward C. Meyer approved the adoption of the 1976 Howard-Paret translation of *On War* for use by the Army War College. It was a far-reaching decision.

Americans have never been a philosophically turned people, and the military was no exception. Most military officers, as with most Americans, were Uptonians and Jominians when it came to war, even though they had never heard of Brevet Major General Emory Upton and his *The Military Policy of the United States* or Baron Antoine de Jomini and his *The Art of War*.[21]

But they agreed with Upton that the military and politics were, as a 1936 Command and General Staff College manual put it, "diametrically and fundamentally things apart."

"Strategy begins where politics ends," the manual emphasized. There is always "the tendency for statesmen to meddle with the conduct of operations" and "an inherent temptation for a government to indulge in petty economies which may prove ruinous to the conduct of a campaign." The commander "must not allow himself to be paralyzed by such interference."[22] It could have been talking, it seemed, about both the Korean and Vietnam wars.

And Jomini had an even deeper influence. His notion that war could be reduced to mathematical and geometric formulas went back to the Civil War, where it was said that generals on both sides went to war with a sword in one hand and Jomini's *The Art of War* in the other. As early as 1869, in an address to the U.S. Military Academy, General William Tecumseh Sherman noted that "there exist many good men who honestly believe that one may, by the aid of modern science, sit in comfort and ease in his office chair, and with little blocks of wood to represent men, or even with figures and algebraic symbols, master the great game of war.

"I think this an insidious and most dangerous mistake," he said.[23] What he would have said about the ultimate Jominians, Defense Secretary Robert S. McNamara and his "Whiz Kids," who raised quantification to an obscene level, is probably unprintable.

Clausewitz refuted both of those fallacies. To those who complained about political interference in war, he reminded them that war is a political act:

The only source of war is politics—the intercourse of governments and peoples. . . . Subordinating the political point of view to the military would be absurd, for it is policy that creates war. Policy is the guiding intelligence, and war only the instrument, not vice versa. No other possibility exists, then, than to subordinate the military point of view to the political.

No major proposal required for war can be worked

out in ignorance of political factors; and when people talk as they often do, about harmful political influence on the management of war, they are not really saying what they mean. The quarrel should be with the policy itself [Assistant Secretary of Defense John Mc-Naughton's "slow squeeze" strategy for the conduct of the Vietnam war was a prime example], not with its influence.[24]

Clausewitz took on Jomini directly when he emphasized that "absolute, so-called mathematical factors never find a firm basis in military calculations. From the start there is an interplay of possibilities, probabilities, good luck and bad that weaves its way throughout the length and breadth of its tapestry."

And he seemed to have anticipated the "Whiz Kids" when he scoffed,

They aim at fixed values; but in war everything is uncertain, and calculations have to be made with variable quantities. They direct the inquiry exclusively toward physical quantities, whereas all military action is intertwined with psychological forces and effects. They consider only unilateral action, whereas war consists of a continuous interaction of opposites. . . . Military activity is never directed against material force alone; it is always aimed simultaneously at the moral forces which give it life, and the two cannot be separated.[25]

Having drawn his theories from the French Revolutionary War, Clausewitz was peculiarly in tune with the American military, which had come into existence in the wake of the American Revolutionary War. His subordination of the military to political control and his insistence that war was a "remarkable trinity" of the people, the government, and the army[26] fit the American way of war almost exactly.

What gave Clausewitzian theory its timelessness was that he had not intended "a sort of manual for action" but instead an "analytical investigation . . . meant to educate the mind of the future commander, or, more accurately, to guide him in his self-education, not to accompany him to the battlefield." It was never intended "to construct an algebraic formula for use on the battlefield," but "to provide a thinking man with a frame of reference."[27]

And it did precisely that. Clausewitzian theories provided a frame of reference for the Army's post-Vietnam strategic doctrines and its operational and tactical doctrines as well.

On Strategy

It also provided a lens for an examination of the Vietnam war. Concerned that the Army would end up blaming the press and politicans for the loss of the Vietnam war rather than facing the Army's own short-comings, General Walter T. Kerwin, Jr., then vice chief of staff of the Army—another World War II veteran who had been wounded in action, while serving as an artillery officer with the 3rd Infantry Division in Italy—ordered the Army War College to make a critical analysis of that conflict and prepare a readable summary for internal and possibly public use.

Having earlier worked with General Weyand in his analysis of the Vietnam war ("Vietnam Myths and American Military Realities," *CDR'S CALL* [July–August 1976]), in the summer of 1979 I was reassigned from the Army General Staff to the Army War College at Carlisle Barracks, Pennsylvania, to oversee that project.

There was no dearth of material. An earlier attempt to contract the study to civilian consultants had resulted in eight volumes of raw data. In addition, the

Center of Military History had compiled an excellent series of monographs on various aspects of the war. The problem was how to pull all this information together and bring it into focus.

Listening to Colonel Franz's long conversations with the Air War College's David MacIsaac on the relevancy of *On War* to modern war, I turned in desperation to Clausewitz. If he was as good as they said he was, he ought to have the answers.

And he did. Reading the Howard-Paret translation for the first time with the Vietnam war in mind, it all fell into place. The United States had not lost the war because of the press or the politicians or because of wily Oriental stratagems. It lost it because of a failure to appreciate and apply basic military fundamentals. Using Clausewitzian theories and the classic principles of war, *On Strategy: The Vietnam War in Context* provided a concise 137-page critical analysis of the Vietnam war.

The book was not without its critics, especially among the counterinsurgency crowd, who had perpetuated the notion that the war was lost because their nostrums had been ignored. But the Army's war plans director in the Pentagon, Major General John Segal, and his boss, Lieutenant General Glenn K. Otis, the DCSOPS (Deputy Chief of Staff for Plans and Operations), were adamant that the book be published, and they escalated the argument to the chief of staff level. On the same day that he approved *On War* to be integrated into the Army War College curriculum, Army chief of staff General Edward C. Meyer ordered the publication and distribution of *On Strategy*.

It was to have an impact far beyond its original expectations. It was first printed in April 1981, and General Meyer distributed copies over his imprimatur to all Army general officers, active and retired. Representative Newt Gingrich (R., Ga.) of the Congressional Military Reform Caucus sent copies to all members of the U.S. House and Senate. It was to spread to Australia and to Korea, where it was used as a student text in their war and staff colleges.

Because of its impact a civilian version, *On Strategy: A Critical Analysis of the Vietnam War*, was published in hard copy by Presido Press in 1982 and in paperback by Dell Publishing in 1984. Praised across the political spectrum, labeled "a classic" by CBS newsman Dan Rather and by *Newsweek* magazine, it was adopted by many colleges and universities, including Harvard, Stanford, and Georgetown, as a teaching text on the Vietnam war.

But its greatest impact was within the military itself. As intended, it became a teaching text at the Army War College and Army Command and General Staff College. But it quickly spread to the other services as well and was soon adopted by the Air and Naval War colleges, the National Defense University, and the Air, Navy, and Marine Corps Command and Staff colleges. For over a decade it has been required reading throughout the armed forces, and it was the one book that most field-grade officers in the Persian Gulf, regardless of service, had read.

As General Merritt had said in his foreword, "By incorporating this book into our course of instruction . . . the Army has taken a major step in improving its ability to implement, through force of arms, the national policies of the United States when called upon to do so."[28] One would like to believe that was true. But if nothing else, it drove a stake through the heart of any nascent "Vietnam syndrome" within the armed forces and allowed them to look to the future rather than dwell on the past.

FM 100-1, *The Army*

Clausewitzian theory was formally incorporated into Army doctrine with the publication of FM (Field Manual) 100-1, *The Army* in August 1981. Previously Army strategic and tactical doctrine had been published in one volume: FM 100-5, *Field Service Regulations: Operations*. As will be discussed in greater detail below, the 1976 edition of FM 100-5, *Operations* dropped strategic doctrine and concentrated exclusively on warfighting.

In 1978, the Army War College was assigned to prepare a new manual, FM 100-1, *The Army,* which was to be the source book for strategic doctrine. Rewritten in 1981 to reflect the changes under way within the Army, it clearly stated the Clausewitzian emphasis on the "remarkable trinity":

> The scope and intensity of modern warfare are . . . defined and limited by political purposes and military goals. The interactions of military operations, political judgements, and national will serve to further define, and sometimes limit, the achievable objectives of a conflict and, thus, to determine its duration and the conditions for its termination.[29]

FM 100-1 also reflected the Army's renewed confidence in itself and its primacy on the battlefield; those characteristics had disappeared over a generation earlier, at the beginning of the atomic age. "[T]he fundamental truth is that *only ground forces* possess the power to exercise direct, continuing and comprehensive control over land, its resources, and its people."

It went on to say that "Land forces thus perform important, and largely unique, functions besides denial and destruction: *landpower can make permanent the otherwise transitory advantages achieved by air and naval forces*.[30]

The June 1986 revision was even more direct: "The Army is the decisive component of military force by virtue of its ability to control the land areas essential to people and nations. People live on land. Ultimately, the control of land determines the destiny of peoples and nations."[31]

Another important contribution of FM 100-1 was the revitalization of the principles of war. Drawn in large measure from the works of British Major General J. F. C. Fuller during the First World War, they were first adopted by the U.S. Army in 1921. Having degenerated into a kind of checklist that could be more misleading than helpful, they had been dropped from the 1976 version of FM 100-5, *Operations,* and there was some initial hesitancy in incorporating them into the manual.

They were included in FM 100-1 (and later in the 1982 and 1986 editions of FM 100-5, *Operations,* as well) when Colonel (now Major General) Charles A. Hines proposed that they be introduced in a new light, in the Clausewitzian sense as a series of "military planning interrogatories—a set of questions that should be considered if military strategy is to best serve the national interest."[32] As will be seen in Part III of this book, "The Remarkable War," they provide a useful framework for analysis.

NOTES

1. Caspar W. Weinberger, *The Uses of Military Power* (Washington, D.C.: OASD-PA (Press Release 609-84) November 28, 1984), p. 5. See also Carl von Clausewitz, *On War,* ed. and trans. Michael Howard and Peter Paret (Princeton, N.J.: Princeton University Press, 1976), p. 579.

2. Carl von Clausewitz, *On War,* trans. and ed. Michael Howard and Peter Paret (Princeton, N.J.: Princeton University Press, 1976), p. 128.

3. Russell F. Weigley, *The American Way of War: A History of United States Military Strategy and Policy* (New York: Macmillan Publishing Company, 1973), pp. 365, 367–68.

4. For a discussion of nuclear weapons and the Korean war see Roger Dingman, "Atomic Diplomacy during the Korean War" and Rosemary Foot, "Nuclear Coersion and the Ending of the Korean War," *International Security* (Winter 1988/89), pp. 50–112.

5. For an overview of the Korean war see Harry G. Summers, Jr., *The Korean War Almanac* (New York: Facts on File, 1990). The "executive agent" system is explained on p. 109.

6. Clay Blair, *The Forgotten War: America in Korea 1950–1953* (New York: Times Books, 1987), p. ix.

7. The author served as a corporal and then as a sergeant with the 24th Infantry Division's A Company, 78th Heavy Tank Battalion (later Heavy Tank Company, 21st Infantry Regiment) and L Company, 21st Infantry Regiment, from December 1948 to June 1951, including a year in front-line combat in Korea.

8. T. R. Fehrenbach, *This Kind of War: A Study in Unpreparedness* (New York: Macmillan Publishing Company, 1963), p. 427.

9. Ibid., p. 443.

10. A. J. Bacevich, *The Pentomic Era: The U.S. Army Between Korea and Vietnam* (Washington, D.C.: National Defense University Press, 1986), pp. 15–16.

11. Ibid., p. 145. Significantly, this was the Army into which the senior Army leaders of the Persian Gulf war were commissioned: Desert Storm commander General H. Norman Schwarzkopf in 1956, Army chief of staff General Carl E. Vuono in 1957, and chairman of the Joint Chiefs of Staff General Colin L. Powell in 1958.

12. Weigley, *The American Way of War*, pp. 418, 466.

13. Field Manual (FM) 100–5, *Field Service Regulations: Operations* (Washington, D.C.: Department of the Army, 1954), p. 5.

14. Douglas S. Blaufarb, *The Counterinsurgency Era:*

U.S. Doctrine and Performance 1950 to the Present (New York: The Free Press, 1977), p. 287.

15. Maxwell D. Taylor, 89th Cong. 2nd sess., Senate Committee on Foreign Relations "To Amend Further the Foreign Assistance Act of 1961 As Amended," *Vietnam Hearings* (1966) pp. 440–60.

16. Field Manual (FM) 100–5, *Operations of Army Forces in the Field* (Washington, D.C.: Department of the Army, 1968), p. 1–6.

17. Ibid., p. 5–1.

18. Van Tien Dung, *Great Spring Victory,* trans. and published by *Foreign Broadcast Information Service.* vol. 1, FBIS-APA-76-110 (June 7, 1976); vol. II, FBIS-APA-76-131 (July 7, 1976), pp. I–18, II–56, II–76.

19. Fred C. Weyand, "Troops to Equal Any," *Vietnam* (Summer 1988), p. 25.

20. Fred C. Weyand, "Serving the People: The Basic Case for the United States Army," *CDRS CALL* (May–June 1976); "Vietnam Myths and American Military Realities," *CDRS CALL* (July–August 1976); and "Serving the People: The Need for Military Power," *Military Review,* vol. LVI, no. 12 (December 1976). I was then serving on General Weyand's staff, and he insisted that the byline on the latter two articles include my name as coauthor, even though my contribution was limited to polishing his ideas and formulations.

21. See Brevet Major General Emory Upton's *The Military Policy of the United States* (originally published in 1904) and Baron Antoine de Jomini's *The Art of War* (originally published in 1862), both republished in the 1960s by Greenwood Press as part of the West Point Military Library series.

22. *The Principles of Strategy for an Independent Corps or Army in a Theater of Operations* (Fort Leavenworth, Kan.: The Command and General Staff School Press, 1936), pp. 19–20.

23. William Tecumseh Sherman, *Address to the Graduating Class of the United States Military Academy* (New York: D. Van Nostrand, Publisher, 1869), p. 8.

24. Clausewitz, *On War,* pp. 607–8.

25. Ibid., pp. 86, 136–37. The most trenchant critique of

Robert McNamara's quantified approach to war is Gregory Palmer's *The McNamara Strategy and the Vietnam War: Program Budgeting in the Pentagon, 1960–1968* (Westport, Conn.: Greenwood Press, 1968).

26. Ibid., p. 89.

27. Ibid., p. 141.

28. Jack N. Merritt in Harry G. Summers, Jr., *On Strategy: The Vietnam War in Context* (Washington, D.C.: U.S. Government Printing Office, 1982), pp. ix–x.

29. Field Manual 100-1, *The Army* (Washington, D.C.: Department of the Army, 1981), p. 7.

30. Ibid., p. 8. Emphasis in original.

31. FM 100-1, *The Army* (Washington, D.C.: Department of the Army, 1986), p. 8.

32. FM 100-1, *The Army* (1981 ed.), pp. 13–18.

8

AirLand Battle Doctrine

> AirLand Battle doctrine . . . enlarges the battle-
> field area, stressing unified air and ground oper-
> ations throughout the theater. It distinguishes
> the operational level of war . . . from the tactical
> level. It recognizes the non-quantifiable ele-
> ments of combat power, especially maneuver
> which is as important as firepower. . . . Most
> importantly, it emphasizes the human element.
>
> FM 100-5, *Operations* (1982)[1]

Training and Doctrine Command

First proclaimed in 1982, AirLand Battle doctrine was
a long time in coming. Thirty-seven years before its
debut, it appeared that the atomic ''revolution'' had
forced the Army out of its traditional warfighting role.
And the Vietnam war seemed to have written finis to
its limited-war role as well.

But in the most remarkable postwar recovery of all
the armed forces, the Army, like the phoenix, rose
from the ashes to recapture its soul and reassert its
battlefield primacy.

While strategic doctrine was being formulated at

the Army War College, the Army's battlefield doctrine
and its warfighting techniques were undergoing major
revisions at the Training and Doctrine Command
(TRADOC) at Fort Monroe, Virginia, and at the Command and General Staff College (CGSC) at Fort Leavenworth, Kansas.

Created by Army chief of staff General Creighton
Abrams in 1973, TRADOC was under the initial command of General William E. DePuy, who had commanded the 1st Infantry Division in Vietnam. Like
Abrams a World War II veteran, DePuy's service with
the 90th Infantry Division in that war would shape his
vision of the future direction of the Army.[2]

DePuy's first priority at TRADOC had been to
upgrade the Army's training programs; however, the
Arab-Israeli "Yom Kippur" war of October 1973
caused a reordering of those priorities. The intensity
and lethality of that war "powerfully demonstrated to
DePuy that there was no time to lose in addressing
doctrinal issues first. . . . TRADOC therefore embarked on a program to reorient and restructure the
whole body of Army doctrine from top to bottom."[3]

DePuy's emphasis on "how to fight" would have a
major impact on future U.S. combat operations.
Among the innovations he and his successors at TRA-
DOC spawned, three in particular stand out. First was
FM 100-5, *Operations,* and the revolution in Army
warfighting doctrine, especially the inclusion of the
operational level of war and the emphasis on maneuver
warfare. Second was the revolution in education and
training, including opposing-forces maneuvers at the
National Training center and Combat Training Centers. Finally, interrelated with the first two innovations, was the coordination that developed between
TRADOC and the Air Force's Tactical Air Command
(TAC) on joint air-ground operations.

FM 100-5, *Operations*

The 1976 version of FM 100-5 was very much a stop-gap measure that reflected the realities of the time. Ironically, it was the 1973 Yom Kippur war in the Middle East that would begin the process of revitalization resulting in the Army's success in its own Middle East war almost two decades later:

> Neither defeated nor victorious [in Vietnam]; misunderstood and unappreciated at home; rent by racial, drug, and disciplinary problems; short of experienced leaders; and in the throes of major personnel policy changes associated with the end of conscription, the Army, like its sister services, was not combat ready.

> When compared to the requirements of modern mid-intensity warfare as illustrated in the 1973 October War, the condition of the U.S. Army . . . spurred TRADOC's officers to address the Army's doctrine.

> First and most obvious was the need to retrain the Army in tactics and techniques appropriate to the new battlefield . . . focused squarely and without apology on "how to fight."[4]

Criticized severely because of its defensive and mechanistic orientation on weapons rather than soldiers, the 1976 version of FM 100-5 "nevertheless . . . made the officer corps as a whole think about doctrine. . . . DePuy wrought a revolution in post-World War II American military thinking. The subsequent editions of FM 100-5 that appeared in 1982 and 1986 . . . were evolutionary, however much they may have differed in substance."[5]

And differ they did. First officially mentioned in the 1976 edition, AirLand Battle became the centerpiece of the 1982 and 1986 revisions of FM 100-5. And this was not the only change. Moving away from the systems-oriented "battle calculus" built around firepower models and force ratios, the new manuals stressed the human dimension of warfare and the need for leadership to deal with the fluidity of the modern battlefield.[6]

The principles of war, and their application to classic and modern theory, once again became the foundation of Army doctrine. Maneuver became the "dynamic element of combat." And most importantly, by direction of General Glenn K. Otis, then TRADOC commander, the 1982 edition of FM 100-5 reintroduced the concept of "operational art"—the intermediate level of war between military strategy and tactics—back into Army warfighting doctrine. AirLand Battle *was* the operational level. And with it came thinking about maneuver of corps and armies and the need for campaign planning, skills that would later prove crucial.

AirLand Battle doctrine defined the battlefield in broad terms. It consisted not only of fighting along the line of contact—now called *close operations*—but also included *deep operations* "directed against enemy forces not in contact [to] create the conditions for future victory" and *rear operations*—"rearward of elements in contact designed to assure freedom of maneuver and continuity of operations, including continuity of sustainment and command and control."[7]

Demonstrating a pronounced sense of history, the 1982 and 1986 editions of FM 100-5 repeated, among other things, Clausewitz's maxims on warfare and used, as Clausewitz had done, historical examples such as Grant's Vicksburg campaign and the 1914 Battle of Tannenberg to illuminate theoretical concepts.

"Significantly," as historian John L. Romjue noted, "the 'air-land war' changed in definition from its 1976 meaning of cooperation and mutual support between the land and air arms. AirLand Battle in 1982 referred to simultaneous battles on the forward line and deep in the enemy's rear echelons, in close concert by airpower and ground forces."

The conceit of the nuclear theorists that the atomic bomb had rendered all past military history and theory irrelevant was finally put to rest. "AirLand Battle was a return to the tried and true principles of experience in war."[8]

Training

Among those "tried and true principles" was training. As the May 1986 version of FM 100-5, *Operations*, pointed out, "Clausewitz stated the purpose of peacetime armies very clearly. He said: 'The whole of military activity must relate directly or indirectly to the engagement. The end for which a soldier is recruited, clothed, armed and trained, the whole object of his sleeping, eating, drinking, and marching *is simply that he should fight at the right place and the right time*.'[9]

"Training is the cornerstone of success," the manual went on to say. "It is a full-time job for commanders in peacetime." By 1986 that fact was axiomatic, but ten years earlier, when the 1976 manual said, "The Army's need to prepare for battle overrides every other aspect of unit missions," it was a revolutionary statement. The idea that "*The commander's first concern* must be to order all the activities of his unit to meet his primary obligation . . . *produce a unit ready to fight and win now*"[10] flew in the face of decades of neglect.

In the pre-Vietnam and Vietnam-era Army the emphasis was on maintenance and management, not training. The scourge of the commander was the

CMMI (command material maintenance inspection), when hordes of inspectors armed with clipboards would descend unexpectedly on your motor pool and arms room. You could ignore training with impunity, but fail your maintenance inspection and your career was over.

"I feel like I have blood on my hands," I told my brigade commander in the 2nd Armored Division at Fort Hood in 1965. As the battalion S3 (operations officer) of the 2nd Battalion, 50th Infantry, training was my responsibility. But there was no time for training. Our soldiers were kept busy in the motor pool ensuring that their armored personnel carriers could pass a surprise CMMI. Yet we were shipping the soldiers off one by one into combat in Vietnam as individual infantry replacements.

But with the establishment of TRADOC in 1973, such perversions came to an end. Not only did DePuy dictate that training assume the primary position, he also took steps to ensure that such would be the case. Promotion of soldiers would rest in their proficiency in common skills—marksmanship, map reading, and the like—as measured by hands-on training, and by competitive written MOS (military occupational specialty) tests to measure their specific job proficiency.

For platoon, company, and battalion commanders, the litmus test was the Army Training and Evaluation Program (ARTEP), designed to match closely the realities of the modern battlefield. Created by Brigadier General (later General) Paul F. Gorman, an infantry platoon leader in the Korean war and infantry battalion commander in Vietnam, the ARTEP listed the critical tactical tasks that any given combat unit must be able to perform:

For each task, the ARTEP specified the conditions under which a task must be performed and the standards of performance that must be achieved for the task to be successful in combat. The ARTEP delineated tasks for all echelons from the squad through the battalion task force . . . [and] provided the field commander with a single source for focusing his unit's collective training and measuring its capabilities. . . . ARTEP became a powerful stimulus to the adoption of new fighting techniques.[11]

In his critique of TRADOC's early days, Major Paul H. Herbert could have been talking about training initiatives when he observed that DePuy's emphasis on FM 100-5 "played an important part in the U.S. Army's post-Vietnam history precisely because it was unambiguous, and that was because DePuy overcame the bureaucracy, however controversial his methods. . . . Having decided what the Army had to do, he used the manuals and schools to tell the Army to do it and ARTEP and other devices to check to be sure that the Army complied."[12]

Although DePuy's 1976 edition of FM 100-5 did not survive, his emphasis on training expanded and flourished. The opening of the National Training Center (NTC) at Fort Irwin, California, in the Mohave Desert in January 1982 provided an even more effective tool than the ARTEP to measure combat-readiness.

Maneuvering against an Air Force red flag aggressor squadron and an Army opposing force (OPFOR) unit that re-created a Soviet motor rifle regiment by using Soviet equipment, doctrine, and tactics, the NTC provided the most realistic battlefield scenario possible in peacetime.

Using MILES (multiple laser engagement system) devices that register "hits" on equipment and personnel alike, not only do individuals know when they have been disabled by "enemy" fire, but so, too, do the umpires in the control centers who later debrief the units on what they did right and wrong.[13]

Later duplicated as Combat Training Centers (CTCs) at the Hohenfels Training Center in West Germany and (for light infantry) at Fort Chaffee, Arkansas), the NTC/CTCs developed combat skills to a degree never before possible. Adding to those skills was the widespread use of simulators, which gave tank crews, for example, an opportunity to hone their precision gunnery techniques, "firing" thousands of rounds of "ammunition" under realistic field conditions.

It is noteworthy that every one of the U.S. Army tank battalions, armored cavalry squadrons, and mechanized infantry battalions that led the blitzkrieg against Iraq had had several rotations through the combat training centers at Fort Irwin or at Hohenfels prior to their deployment to the Gulf.

That training was especially fortuitous, for at the NTC/CTCs they had maneuvered against OPFOR units simulating Soviet tactics and equipment. When they went into real combat in the Persian Gulf they were confronting Iraqi units using the selfsame Soviet tactics and equipment, literally fighting battles they had rehearsed for almost a decade. "Soldiers do in combat," preached the late general Bruce C. Clarke, a distinguished World War II combat leader and one of the Army's premier trainers, "what they are in the habit of doing in training." The Persian Gulf war would prove him correct.

TRADOC and the Tactical Air Command

Establishing collaboration with the Air Force was among the initial missions that General Abrams gave General DePuy when TRADOC was formed in 1973.

Assisted by the close proximity of their respective headquarters at Fort Monroe and Langley Air Force Base, both in Virginia, DePuy and [Air Force] General Robert J. Dixon, the TAC [Tactical Air Command] commander, brought their two commands into close cooperation, if not complete doctrinal harmony. The Air Force never challenged the basic ground doctrine of FM 100-5. . . . More important, TRADOC-TAC cooperation sprang from a realization, greatly enhanced by the 1973 October War, of the mutual interdependence of the two services.[14]

In July 1975, the Air Land Force Application (ALFA) agency was formed by direction of TAC and TRADOC to "develop, coordinate, integrate, and manage programs . . . regarding concepts, tactics, techniques, and procedures for the conduct of joint warfighting."[15] Gradually the air-ground synchronization essential to AirLand Battle was beginning to take shape.

Inspired by Army Major General John H. Cushman, commander of the CGSC (Command and General Staff College) and CAC (Combined Arms Center) at Fort Leavenworth, who had written about air-ground integration as early as 1965, "officers at Fort Leavenworth began to use the term 'air-land' and 'air-land battle' to express this idea."

On April 10, 1975, Cushman briefed General DePuy and General Dixon on his concept of air/land operations, which argued that purely air or ground battles would be the exception, "and would take second priority to articulating the doctrine and equipping, training and fielding the forces necessary for the air-land fight." But he was ahead of his time. "Neither service was yet willing to go that far because [it] could require significant redefinition of service roles and apportionment of assets:

By rejecting Cushman's air-land battle concept, Generals DePuy and Dixon agreed on a safer, more productive approach: tacit acceptance of two arenas of battle, one on the ground and one in the air, each the primary province of a respective service, and explicit acknowledgement that the two arenas are mutually interdependent, leading to procedural, but not doctrinal collaboration.[16]

"The name AirLand Battle implied that there was cooperation and agreement between the Army and the Air Force," noted Air Force historian Robert Frank Futrell, "but in fact the doctrine was a unilateral development of the Army." He went on to quote an unnamed Air Force officer who said, "When we say we agree with the air-land battle concept, what we are saying is that we agree that the concept is a good concept for the Army."[17]

But that would soon change. In April 1983, Army chief of staff General Edward C. Meyer and Air Force chief of staff General Charles A. Gabriel signed a memorandum of understanding (MOU) that, among other things, committed the Army and Air Force to cooperate in "joint tactical training and field exercises based on AirLand Battle doctrine."

Although it "did not mean that the Air Force was adopting completely the Army's AirLand Battle concept, senior Air Force officers concluded that the services working together under the MOU would improve the effectiveness of joint operations and help to iron out doctrinal differences between the Army and the Air Force." The next year, on May 22, 1984, General Gabriel and Army chief of staff General John A. Wickham, Jr., signed a memorandum of agreement (MOA) that included thirty-one initiatives bearing on the air-land combat team.

Not only were such familiar areas as battlefield

interdiction, close air support, and intratheater airlift included, but also such items as rotary-wing support for special operations forces, night combat, J-STARS (joint surveillance target acquisition radar systems), and "programs essential to the joint conduct of airland combat operations."

At the time this agreement was seen as "the initial step in the establishment of a long-term, dynamic process whose objective will continue to be the fielding of the most . . . effective airland combat force."[18] Six years later that objective would be realized on the battlefields of the Persian Gulf.

NOTES

1. FM (Field Manual) 100-5, *Operations* (Washington, D.C.: Department of the Army, 1982) p. 7-1.

2. Paul H. Herbert, *Deciding What Has to Be Done: General William E. DePuy and the 1976 edition of FM 100-5, Operations (Leavenworth Papers No. 16)* (Fort Leavenworth, Kan.: Combat Studies Institute, 1988), p. 22.

3. Ibid., pp. 25, 36.

4. Ibid., p. 101.

5. Ibid., p. 106.

6. John L. Romjue, *From Active Defense to AirLand Battle: The Development of Army Doctrine 1973–1982* (Fort Monroe, Va.: U.S. Army Training and Doctrine Command, 1984), p. 70. See also FM 100-5, *Operations* (Washington, D.C.: Department of the Army, 1982) and its successor FM 100-5, *Operations* (Washington, D.C.: Department of the Army, 1986).

7. "Fundamentals of AirLand Battle Operations," FM 100-5, *Operations* (1986), pp. 19–21.

8. Romjue, *From Active Defense to AirLand Battle,* pp. 72–73.

9. FM 100-5, *Operations* (1986), p. 6. Emphasis in original. See also Carl von Clausewitz, *On War,* trans. and ed.

Michael Howard and Peter Paret (Princeton, N.J.: Princeton University Press, 1976), p. 95.

10. FM 100-5, *Operations* (1976), pp. 1-5. Emphasis in original.

11. Herbert, *Deciding What Has to Be Done*, pp. 38–39.

12. Ibid., pp. 104–5.

13. For a description of what a National Training Center rotation entailed, see Daniel P. Bolger, *Dragons at War: 2-34th Infantry in the Mohave* (Novato, Calif.: Presidio Press, 1986). Although its designation had changed in the interim, this unit would deploy to the Persian Gulf with the 24th Infantry Division.

14. Herbert, *Deciding What Has to Be Done*, pp. 68–69.

15. *Air Land Force Application (ALFA) Agency* (Langley AFB/Fort Monroe, VA: TAC Regulation 20-2/TRADOC Regulation 10-4, 23 September 1988).

16. Herbert, *Deciding What Has to Be Done*, pp. 70–72.

17. Robert Frank Futrell, *Ideas, Concepts, Doctrine: Basic Thinking in the United States Air Force: Volume II, 1961–1984* (Maxwell Air Force Base, Ala.: Air University Press, 1989), p. 551.

18. Ibid., pp. 551, 554–55.

III

THE REMARKABLE WAR

Theory will have fulfilled its main task when it is used to analyze the constituent elements of war, to distinguish precisely what at first sight seems fused, to explain in full the properties of the means employed and to show their probable effects, to define clearly the nature of the ends in view, and to illuminate all phases of warfare in a thorough critical inquiry. Theory then becomes a guide to anyone who wants to learn about war from books.

Carl von Clausewitz, *On War*,
Book Two, chap. 2, p. 141

9

Tactics, Grand Tactics, and Strategy

> As I report to you, air attacks are under way
> against military targets in Iraq. . . . I've told the
> American people before that this will not be
> another Vietnam. And I repeat this here tonight.
> Our troops will have the best possible support
> in the entire world, and they will not be asked to
> fight with one hand tied behind their back.
>
> President George H. Bush,
> address to the nation
> (January 16, 1991)[1]

A Sea Change in the Strategic Environment

President Bush's promise that "our troops . . . will
not be asked to fight with one hand tied behind their
back" may just have been, as *The Economist* noted,
"an effort to exorcise the demons of the past."[2] But
whether President Bush realized it or not, his words
put a finish to the almost half-century fallacy that the
atomic age has rendered obsolete the Clausewitzian
dictum that strategy is "the use of engagements [i.e.,
battles] for the purpose of war."[3]

As Saddam Hussein was in the process of discov-
ering, "battles" were once again the method by which

war would be waged. With the end of the Cold War just over a year earlier, a sea change had taken place in the strategic environment. Not only was the confrontation with the Soviet Union at an end, so was America's national policy of containment. And with it went the shackles that had forced the U.S. military to fight both the Korean and Vietnam wars "with one hand tied behind their back."

As a national policy, containment has well served the national interests of the United States. As George F. Kennan had prophesied in his 1946 "Long Telegram" from Moscow and in his later "X" article in *Foreign Affairs* magazine,[4] containing Communist expansion and allowing the contradictions inherent in Marxist-Leninist dogma to destroy it from within proved to be the best long-term way to achieve victory in the Cold War.

Although it had taken some forty-three years to work its will, when communism disintegrated in the wake of the fall of the Berlin Wall in November 1989, "containment" was vindicated as the correct Cold War political policy for the United States.

For the military, however, "containment" has the unintended effect of "asking it to fight with one hand tied behind its back." As will be discussed in detail in Chapter 11, "The Offensive," it caused the military to shift from the strategic *offensive* to the strategic *defensive* and forced the surrender of battlefield initiative to the enemy.

Not only that, as will be seen in Chapter 12, "Mass, Economy of Force, and Maneuver," it also caused confusion as to where and how American combat power should be focused. "Only if statesmen look to certain military moves and actions to produce effects that are foreign to their nature do political decisions influence operations for the worse," said Clausewitz.[5] That's what happened in Vietnam. We set out to deter the enemy, but ended up deterring ourselves instead. As former secretary of state Dean Rusk noted:

> Our conduct of the war and especially the bombing of North Vietnam were influenced by the possibility of Chinese intervention. . . . With our policy of graduated response, at no time did we present Beijing and Moscow with a major change in the war that forced them to decide whether or not to intervene. . . .

> An American offensive against North Vietnam would likely have triggered Hanoi's mutual security pact with China and brought Beijing in. We . . . tried to avoid threatening the Chinese or leaving our intentions unclear, as had been done by General MacArthur's advance to the Yalu. The possibility of Chinese intervention definitely influenced how we fought the war.[6]

Grand Tactics and Operational Art

But this time America's hands were no longer tied. Unlike North Korea's Kim Il Sung and North Vietnam's Ho Chi Minh, Saddam Hussein was not shielded by the skirts of China and the Soviet Union. American military strategy had come full circle, and in many important respects was back to World War II again. Like Adolf Hitler, to whom he had been compared, Saddam Hussein was to feel the full fury of America's conventional military might.

Gradualism and stalemate were out the window. "Prior to ordering our forces into battle," said President Bush, "I instructed our military commanders to take every necessary step to prevail as quickly as possible and with the greatest degree of protection possible for American and allied servicemen and women.

"No president can easily commit our sons and daughters to war," he concluded. "They are the nation's finest. Ours is a volunteer force—magnificently trained, highly motivated. The troops know why they're there."[7]

And that was more than just rhetoric. Because of the renaissance in military thinking in the 1970s and 1980s, our soldiers, sailors, airmen, marines, and coast guardsmen were the best-trained and best-prepared military force that the United States had ever committed to action.

But as the Vietnam war in particular had made clear, no matter how well the troops performed at the tactical level on the battlefield, it was all for naught if the strategies and "grand tactics" were faulty. While "strategies"—the ends for which wars are waged—are largely political, "grand tactics" and "tactics" are the exclusive province of the military. As was seen in Part II, this was the military's main focus during the interwar years between Vietnam and the war in the Gulf.

"Grand tactics," now called "operational art," drew special attention. Traditionally the Army had seen combat in two dimensions, the tactical or battlefield level and the strategic or national level. The theater level had generally been ignored. This led to a major gap in thinking about war. For example, at the tactical level there are five forms of attack: envelopment, turning movement, infiltration, penetration, and frontal attack.

What had not been clear is that at a higher level of command—now called the operational level—these forms of attack could be used in combination with each other. As would happen in the Gulf, one element might launch a penetration to pin the enemy down and pave the way for an envelopment or turning movement by other elements of the same command.

Such operational-level thinking—"the employment of military forces to attain strategic goals in a theater of war or theater of operations through the design, organization, and conduct of campaigns and major operations"[8]—was the hallmark of the service's post-Vietnam renaissance: the Navy's Maritime Strategy, the Marine Corps' Amphibious Warfare Doctrine, the Air Force's Aerospace Doctrine, and most importantly the Army's AirLand Battle doctrine, developed, as was seen earlier, in close coordination with the Air Force's Tactical Command.

AirLand Battle Doctrine

It was the AirLand Battle doctrine that would prove to be the blueprint for victory in the Persian Gulf war. As General Crosbie E. Saint, the commander of the U.S. Army in Europe and the Seventh Army, noted in his reflections on the Gulf war:

> Looking back, we should have known from the outset that the Iraqis were probably a pretty good tactical army, but not playing in our league. After all, Saddam spent his time talking about "the Mother of all battles," clearly a tactical event, while we were talking about the campaign, an operational set of sequenced events.

> One of our greatest successes which deserves further publicity was the return on investment we got from educational changes made in our schools to stress the operational art and warfighting thought in general.

> In a similar vein, the operational aspects of AirLand Battle doctrine had gone through the ten year assimilation process that is normally associated with getting soldiers comfortable with new ideas. Had this war occurred back in the late 70's or early 80's the training we

associated with the "active defense" [the 1976 edition of FM 100-5] wouldn't have helped much.[9]

The Human Dimension

Among the "educational changes" referred to by General Saint was the creation of the "second-year program" at the Army Command and General Staff College at Fort Leavenworth, Kansas. A return to pre-World War II practice—then major Dwight D. Eisenhower was a two-year student at Leavenworth—the program, formally called the School for Advanced Military Studies (SAMS), was established in 1983.

The brainchild of Army lieutenant colonel (now Brigadier General) Huba Wass de Czege, one of the prime movers behind the 1982 edition of FM 100-5, the program was established "as a highly selective course aimed at teaching the operational level of war to students who volunteered to stay on for a second year of instruction at the Command and General Staff College."

As envisioned by Wass de Czege, SAMS "would produce a small group of officers who could 'seed the Army . . . [and] plan large-unit operations.' " That vision became a reality during the Persian Gulf war.

"Besides the SAMS graduates in Saudi Arabia with their assigned units," reported the *Army Times*, "four SAMS graduates were temporarily assigned to Headquarters, U.S. Central Command, as part of the J-5 plans division." Nicknamed the "Jedi Knights" (after the heroic figures in the *Star Wars* movies), "the group worked very closely with the commander in chief [General Schwarzkopf], the J-5 and component commanders in developing and analyzing courses of action and the ground concept of operations for Operation Desert Storm."[10]

It was yet another example that wars are fought

and won by men and women, not by machines. As FM 100-5 prophesied in 1986, "The human dimension of war will be decisive in the campaigns and battles of the future just at it has been in the past." While modern technology did wonders in the Persian Gulf war, those machines would have been just so much useless junk without the dedicated and courageous men and women who kept them in operation under arduous and often dangerous conditions.

"Suvorov was right," said General Saint. " 'Easy training, hard combat; hard training, easy combat.' . . . The small unit leadership performed very well: from movement, taking care of their soldiers, maintenance, to the firefight—all were superb. We attribute this proficiency in large measure to the quality of NCOES [Noncommissioned Office Educational System—i.e., training schools for sergeants] as well as dedicated training time for the teams to train under their warfighting leadership."[11]

Framework for Analysis

"Successful *strategy* achieves national and alliance political aims at the lowest possible cost in lives and treasure," stated the 1986 edition of FM 100-5, which served as the blueprint for Operation Desert Storm. "*Operational art* translates those aims into effective military operations and campaigns. Sound *tactics* win the battles and engagements which produce successful campaigns and operations.

"While the principles of war apply equally to strategy, operational art, and tactics, they apply differently to each level of war."[12] Using those nine classic principles of war, the remainder of Part III will make a critical analysis of the Persian Gulf war, primarily at the strategic level, but with some attention to the level of operational art as well.

As we discussed earlier, the principles of war are now seen as military planning interrogatories rather than as a mechanical checklist. As applicable at the squad tactical level as they are at the presidential strategic level, the principles pose three fundamental questions: "What are we trying to do?," "How are we going to do it?," and "Who will command and control it?"

The chapter "The Objective" addresses the first question. The next three chapters—"The Offensive"; "Mass, Economy of Force, and Maneuver"; and "Security, Surprise, and Simplicity"—address the second question. The final question is addressed in the chapter "Unity of Command and Coalition Warfare."

NOTES

1. George H. Bush, statement by the president, the White House, office of the press secretary (January 16, 1991).

2. "American Survey: The Home Front," *The Economist,* vol. 318, no. 7690 (January 19, 1991), p. 25.

3. Carl von Clausewitz, *On War,* trans. and ed. Michael Howard and Peter Paret (Princeton, N.J.: Princeton University Press, 1976), p. 177.

4. George Kennan, *Memoirs: 1925–1950* (Boston: Little, Brown & Company, 1967), pp. 271–97, 354–67.

5. Clausewitz, *On War,* p. 608.

6. Dean Rusk, *As I Saw It* (New York: W. W. Norton & Company, 1990), pp. 456–57.

7. George H. Bush, statement by the president, the White House, office of the press secretary (January 16, 1991).

8. FM (Field Manual) 100-5, *Operations* (Washington, D.C.: Department of the Army, 1986), p. 10.

9. Crosbie E. Saint, "Thoughts on the Victory in Desert Storm," CINCUSAREUR Heidelberg, Germany, to CINCEUR, Vaihingen, Germany (March 26, 1991).

10. Sean D. Naylor, "Revenge of the 'Jedi': Brotherhood of Planners Plotted Storm Win," *Army Times* (April 22, 1991), pp. 12–14.

11. Saint, "Thoughts on the Victory in Desert Storm." "Suvorov" (Count Alexander Vasilievich Suvorov [1729–1800]) was a field marshal in the Russian Army during the Napoleonic wars.

12. FM 100-5 (1986), p. 9. Emphasis added. The principles of war are contained in Appendix A, pp. 173–77.

10

The Objective

Our objectives are clear. Saddam Hussein's forces will leave Kuwait. The legitimate government of Kuwait will be restored to its rightful place and Kuwait once again will be free. Iraq will eventually comply with all relevant United Nations resolutions. . . .

President George H. Bush,
address to the nation
(January 16, 1991)[1]

War Is a Political Act

"Our objectives are clear," said President Bush. And so they were. It was proof positive that the primary lesson of the Vietnam war had been learned: the critical importance of the *objective,* the first principle of war.

It is first because all else flows from it. At the tactical and operational levels of war it defines the mission to be achieved. And at the strategic level—with strategy roughly defined as the use of means to achieve ends—the objective, by defining the ends to be attained, is literally half of the strategic equation.

"The political object is a goal, war is the means of reaching it," said Clausewitz, "and means can never be considered in isolation from their purpose."[2]

And it has yet another crucial function. The objective determines the war's value, and it is this value against which the costs of war are assessed by the public in determining their support for the war—costs measured in terms of taxes and, more importantly, by risks to the lives of their sons and daughters.

Failure to appreciate the criticality of the objective was one of the main reasons for our failure in Vietnam. As the Roman philosopher and statesman Lucius Annaeus Seneca had said almost two thousand years ago, "If you don't know the port to which you are sailing, all winds are foul." And so they were.

One of the reasons we failed to see the importance of the objective, especially in its strategic political sense, was that war was still seen in an Uptonian sense as something separate and apart from the political process. It was not a new failing.

"The general definition which for many decades has been acceptable," said General of the Army Douglas MacArthur during the "Great Debate" in the Senate in 1951 after his relief from command in the Korean war, "was that war was an ultimate process of politics; that when all of the political means failed, we then go to force."[3] And MacArthur was not alone in his views.

Even earlier, in the closing days of World War II, then Army chief of staff General George Marshall vetoed sending American troops into Czechoslovakia to head off the advancing Soviet Army. "Personally and aside from the logistical, tactical and strategical implications," he said, "I would be loath to hazard American lives for purely political purposes." But as the renowned military theorist Bernard Brodie caustically commented, "To avoid hazarding American lives is bound to be commendable, but if it was not done for 'purely political purposes,' what then was that or any other war all about?"[4]

This Uptonian mind-set was directly opposed to the Clausewitzian tenet that "war should never be thought of as *something autonomous* but always as an *instrument of policy*.[5] As General MacArthur later acknowledged, Clausewitz had the better of the argument. During the 1951 Senate hearings he was confronted with a statement he had made in 1932, while serving as Army chief of staff:

> The national strategy of any war, that is, the selection of national objectives and the determination of the general means and methods to be applied in obtaining them, as well as development of the broad policies applicable to the prosecution of the war, are decisions that must be made by the head of state, acting in conformity with the expressed will of the Government.

MacArthur was unruffled by the attack. "As I look back, Senator, on my rather youthful days then," he said, "I am surprised and amazed how wise I was."[6] But that wisdom fell on deaf ears, especially those of Senator Lyndon B. Johnson of Texas, a member of that Senate panel. Thirteen years later, as head of state, the one thing Johnson failed to do was decide on "the selection of national objectives and the determination of the general means and methods to be applied in obtaining them."

War's Very Object Is Victory

Earlier, in his address to a joint session of the Congress on April 19, 1951, General MacArthur had emphasized that "once war is forced upon us, there is no alternative than to apply every available means to

bring it to a swift end. War's very object is victory—
not prolonged indecision. In war, indeed, there can be
no substitute for victory."[7] And MacArthur was absolutely right. The only question that remained to be
decided was precisely what constitutes "victory."

It has been said that Americans don't fight wars,
they fight moral crusades, and MacArthur was no
exception. The paradigm of war for most Americans
even today, including those born long after the event,
is defined by the messianic terms of World War II—
total victory, total destruction of the enemy's armed
forces, the enemy's unconditional surrender, and the
trial and execution of his leaders. As General MacArthur (who had achieved just such a victory over Japan)
told the Senate, "I believe if you do not [seek such a
victory], if you hit soft, if you practice appeasement
in the use of force, you are doomed to disaster."[8]

But in the history of warfare, World War II was an
anomaly. On January 24, 1943, at a press conference
following the Casablanca conference, President
Franklin D. Roosevelt and Prime Minister Winston
Churchill of Britain demanded the unconditional surrender of Germany, Italy, and Japan. "This demand
specified something new in international law," noted
the University of Cologne's professor Andreas Hillgruber, " 'total and political capitulation' . . . it rejected outright the concept of an accord as in the
'normal European wars' of the past."

The reason for the demand of unconditional surrender was that "Roosevelt refused under any circumstances to countenance a repetition of the stalemate
with which World War I had ended, when Germany
claimed that Woodrow Wilson's Fourteen Points established its absolute right to erect a lasting new
order."[9]

But except for World War II, most wars, including
most American wars, have been limited wars. As

Clausewitz observed, "In war many roads lead to success, and . . . they do not all involve the opponent's outright defeat."[10] During the "Great Debate" Senator Brian McMahon of Connecticut observed that "in the course of our history I believe there have been a number of instances in which we accomplished our objectives without what might be called a final and complete defeat of the enemy, such as was visited upon Germany. Certainly in the War of 1812 we fought the British on the sea and on our own mainland [but] we didn't insist on a military victory over England as essential. . . . Now, in the Spanish-American War when we accomplished the liberation of Cuba, we didn't proceed to Madrid to capture Madrid. . . . We negotiated a treaty after accomplishing our objectives. . . ."[11]

And MacArthur's protestations notwithstanding, that's what we did in Korea as well. Our objectives there had been clearly spelled out. Initially it was the restoration of the *status quo ante bellum,* as called for by the June 25 and 27, 1950, resolutions of the U.N. Security Council.

With the Soviet delegate, Yakov Malik, absent (he had been boycotting the United Nations since the previous January over the question of the admission of Communist China to the United Nations) and unable to cast a veto, the United States, as it would again some forty years later, was able to get U.N. Security Council authorization for its military actions to repel aggression.[12]

But as Clausewitz had prophesied, "The original political objects can greatly alter during the course of the war and may finally change entirely since *they are influenced by events and their probable consequences.*"[13] And that's what happened in Korea. "After the Inchon landing [in September 1950], General MacArthur called on these North Koreans to turn in their arms and cease their effort," Secretary of State

Dean Acheson told the Senate; "that they refused to do, and they retired into the North, and what General MacArthur's military mission was was to pursue them and round them up . . . and as I said many times, we had the highest hopes that when you did that the whole of Korea would be unified. That did not come to pass, because the Chinese intervened."[14]

Once again the political objective changed, this time back to restoration of the *status quo ante bellum*. And at the very time the "Great Debate" was being held in the Senate, those objectives were achieved in Korea by the defeat of the Chinese Communist Forces (CCF) "Fifth Step Fifth Phase Offensive."

On April 22, 1951, the CCF 27-division, 250,000-man force attacked the U.N. lines along a forty-mile front, only to be repulsed by the Eighth U.S. Army and its allies with terrible losses. Two months later peace negotiations began, concluding with the 1953 Korean Armistice Agreement, which left South Korea essentially as it had been before the war. It was a victory by definition, for the U.S. objective of restoring the *status quo ante bellum* had been achieved.

Confusion in Vietnam

But because it did not fit the total-victory model of World War II, the Korean war was seen by many Americans as a defeat or, at best, a draw, even though peace there has lasted almost forty years. The result was that the Korean war model, the only model that could have given at least a prospect of victory in Vietnam, was never seriously considered.[15]

Indeed, as was seen earlier, presidential adviser and former chairman of the Joint Chiefs of Staff General Maxwell Taylor himself had ruled out victory as an objective in the war. Instead there was a confusing mishmash of contradictory goals. In an examination of the *official* justifications most often cited for America's involvement in Indochina from 1948 through 1967, University of Nebraska professor Hugh M. Arnold found some *twenty-two* separate rationales, many mutually exclusive, for America's military presence in Southeast Asia.[16]

That confusion led to the most damning statistic of the Vietnam war. In a 1974 survey of Army generals who had commanded in Vietnam, Brigadier General Douglas Kinnard, later the Army's chief of military history, found that "almost 70 percent of the Army generals who managed the war were uncertain of its objectives." That fact, Kinnard went on to say, "mirrors a deep-seated strategic failure: the inability of policy-makers to frame tangible, obtainable goals."[17]

And that included the Joint Chiefs of Staff as well. When Clark Clifford took over as secretary of defense following the 1968 Tet offensive, he found that four years after American forces had been committed to battle in Vietnam the Joint Chiefs of Staff still had no concept of victory and no plan to bring the war to a satisfactory conclusion.[18]

The lack of an objective had caused a lack of focus from the White House to the Pentagon to the battlefield in Vietnam. All this was not lost on the American people. The subliminal message of President Johnson's failure to articulate his objectives clearly, and his failure to mobilize the military's reserve forces, as had been the case in every other American war, was that the war was of little consequence.

With the value never established—one of the primary functions of the objective—the American public eventually concluded that the costs were exorbitant. The surprising thing is that it took them three years—1964 to 1967—to do so.

According to statistical analysis by John Mueller of Rochester University, the crossover point came in the summer of 1967, months before the enemy's 1968 Tet offensive, which supposedly marked the turning point of the war. It was based not on the rantings of the antiwar movement but on a pragmatic cost-benefit analysis.

No peaceniks, the American people's attitude was "Either win the damn thing or get the hell out." When the government seemed unable to do either, public support for the war went into a precipitous decline.[19] As Clausewitz had predicted, "Once the expenditure of effort exceeds the political object, the object must be renounced. . . ."[20]

Although the United States never officially admitted it, that's exactly what it did when President Richard M. Nixon began to withdraw U.S. ground forces from Vietnam in 1969. At last the United States had an objective, albeit one disguised as a platitude. "Peace with honor" was in reality a subterfuge for getting out of Vietnam as decorously and as quickly as possible.

As with the Korean war, the conflict ended through diplomatic negotiations, this time with the so-called Paris Peace Accords of 1973. But unlike Korea, American guarantees to uphold the peace were only empty words. When the twenty-plus divisions of the North Vietnamese Army's crossborder blitzkrieg swept south in the spring of 1975, the United States callously abandoned its erstwhile ally to its fate. Its shabby objective of "peace with honor" had proven to be a mockery.

The Post-Vietnam Renaissance

Fortunately for the nation, the military did not blame the civilian leaders for the failures of Vietnam. Instead they followed the course charted by Navy lieutenant commander Dudley W. Knox almost sixty years earlier. "Who is to blame," he asked rhetorically, for "the disastrous results that must follow a failure in Washington to hold similar views about fundamentals?

"Surely not the civilians of the government who have long since learned to regard professional advice with suspicion," Knox wrote in the March–April 1915 edition of the *U.S. Naval Institute Proceedings*. "It is we ourselves who are at fault and we can fairly blame neither Congress, our form of government, the un-military characteristics of the people nor any civilian official."[21]

When he began the revolution in post-Vietnam military thinking at the Navy War College in 1972, Admiral Stansfield Turner wasted no time looking for scapegoats. Instead he concentrated his energies on getting the Navy's intellectual house in order. The "back to basics" movement he pioneered, especially in military and naval theory and doctrine, swept the armed forces. Among the many fallouts from this reexamination of fundamentals was a new appreciation of the importance of the strategic dimension of the principle of the objective.

"Not until the political purpose has been determined and defined by the President and the Congress can strategic and tactical objectives be clearly defined and developed," said the August 1981 edition of FM 100-1, *The Army*,[22] which reintroduced the strategic dimension of the *objective* into Army thinking.

While the military could dictate tactical and operational-level doctrinal changes within its own ranks, changes at the strategic level involved civilian political leaders who could not be told what to do but had to be educated and subtly convinced.

It was not an easy task, but it was one that had to be accomplished. As Clausewitz emphasized, political control of the military rests on "the natural and unavoidable assumption that policy knows the instrument it means to use."[23] As the Vietnam war had shown, that assumption required a staggering leap of faith, but by the early 1980s there was evidence that the message on the importance of the objective was getting through.

"Policies formed without a clear understanding of what we hope to achieve would . . . earn us the scorn of our troops, who would have an understandable opposition to being *used*—in every sense of the word," said Secretary of Defense Caspar W. Weinberger in a November 1984 address to the National Press Club.

Weinberger went on to lay out a series of major tests to be applied when weighing the use of U.S. combat forces abroad. "If we *do* decide to commit forces to combat overseas," he said, "we should have clearly defined political and military objectives. And we should know precisely how our forces can accomplish those clearly defined objectives. And we should have and send the forces needed to do just that."[24]

Earlier that same year, the March 16, 1984, version of AFM (Air Force Manual) 1-1, *Basic Aerospace Doctrine of the United States Air Force* (which would remain in force through the Persian Gulf war), emphasized that "the most basic principle for success in any military operation is a clear and concise statement of a realistic *objective*. . . . The ultimate military objective of war is to neutralize or destroy the enemy's armed forces and his will to fight. However, the intimate bond that ties war to politics cannot be ignored. War is a means to achieve a political objective and must never be considered apart from the political end."[25]

And the Army agreed. Amplifying the 1981 edition quoted earlier, the 1986 version of FM 100-1, *The Army,* which also would remain in effect through the

Gulf war, emphasized the political dimensions of the principle of the objective:

> A nation at war must apply the force necessary to attain the political purpose for which the war is being fought. When the potential purpose is the total defeat of the adversary, then the strategic military objective will be the destruction of the enemy's will to resist, including the unconditional surrender of his armed forces. Strategic objectives cannot be clearly identified and developed, however, until the political purpose has been determined by the President. . . .[26]

The Persian Gulf War

And President Bush did just that. On August 2, 1990, the very day of the Iraqi invasion of Kuwait, he issued Executive Order 12722, declaring a national emergency "to address the threat to the national security and foreign policy of the United States posed by the invasion of Kuwait by Iraq."

Also on August 2, the United States voted to approve U.N. Security Council Resolution 660, which condemned the aggression and demanded an immediate Iraqi withdrawal. Other actions continued apace. As General Colin L. Powell, the chairman of the Joint Chiefs of Staff, later reported to the Senate:

> On August 6, four days after 140,000 Iraqi soldiers brutally invaded Kuwait and appeared to be driving onward toward Saudi Arabia, Secretary (of Defense Dick) Cheney met with Saudi King Fahd to assess the situation and brief the king on what support the United States could provide. Subsequently, King Fahd requested U.S. assistance to protect and defend his country and, on August 7, at the direction of the president, U.S. forces began deploying to the region.

All initial and subsequent U.S. military deployments have been undertaken in support of U.S. national security objectives as clearly laid out by the president.[27]

These objectives were spelled out by President Bush in an address to the nation on August 8, 1990. "Four simple principles guide our policy," he said. "First, we seek the immediate, unconditional and complete withdrawal of all Iraqi forces from Kuwait. Second, Kuwait's legitimate government must be restored to replace the puppet regime. And third, my administration, as had been the case with every president from President Roosevelt to President Reagan, is committed to the security and stability of the Persian Gulf. And fourth, I am determined to protect the lives of American citizens abroad."

Bush went on to say that "immediately after the Iraqi invasion, I ordered an embargo of all trade with Iraq and together with many other nations, announced sanctions. . . . The Soviet Union and China ended all arms sales to Iraq, and this past Monday [August 6, 1990], the United Nations Security Council approved for the first time in 23 years mandatory sanctions [i.e., Resolution 661] under Chapter VII of the United Nations charter."[28]

Mobilization

The president accompanied his words with action. As he spoke, carrier battle groups led by the USS *Independence* and USS *Eisenhower* were already on station in the Gulf area. En route were units of the Army's 82nd Airborne Division, a Navy maritime prepositioning squadron, and F-15s from the Air Force's 1st Tactical Fighter Wing. Other forces quickly followed.

"Marine Corps units were married with their heavy

equipment prepositioned at Guam and Diego Garcia,'' said General Powell in a later review of U.S. military actions. ''Additional Naval forces were introduced . . . [and] heavier ground forces began to be airlifted as their tanks and combat equipment began the long trek by sea. . . . In order to move forces as quickly and efficiently as possible, 38 ships from the Ready Reserve Fleet were activated and, for the first time in history, we activated a portion of the Civil Reserve Air Fleet.''[29]

Following the August 17, 1990, activation of the Civil Reserve Air Fleet (more about this in Chapter 12, ''Mass, Economy of Force, and Maneuver''), President Bush literally put his political future at risk to demonstrate forcefully the value he placed on resisting Iraqi aggression. On August 22, 1990, he continued his mobilization of the country for war with Executive Order 12727, which ordered 40,000 reservists to active duty ''to augment the active armed forces of the United States for the effective conduct of operational missions in and around the Arabian Peninsula.''[30] Not only were they ordered to active duty, many were also immediately dispatched to the war zone.

On January 18, 1991, to ''provide additional authority . . . to the continuing threat posed by Iraq's invasion of Kuwait,'' Bush issued Executive Order 12743, authorizing a Reserves call-up for up to twenty-four consecutive months.[31] Many more Reserve units and individuals were dispatched to the Gulf. It was the largest mobilization since the Korean war forty years earlier.

At their peak strength these Army and Air National Guard and Army, Navy, Air Force, Marine, and Coast Guard Reserve men and women constituted 228,561 personnel, including some 106,000 in the Desert Storm area of operations. A total of 143,211 were Army Reserve members, 34,693 Air Force, 30,548 Marine

Corps, 19,119 Navy, and 990 Coast Guard. Most were organized into 798 Reserve component units from communities all across the country. Now the entire nation was involved.[32]

General Abrams's total-force concepts discussed earlier had been validated. The very thing President Johnson feared—that "many more families and virtually every town and city would be affected by a call-up with a much different class cross-section and much more political impact than draft calls"[33]—proved to be President Bush's greatest asset in building and maintaining public support for his actions.

As General Crosbie E. Saint, commander of the U.S. Army in Europe and the Seventh Army noted, "The early decision to call up the reserves, while probably motivated by necessity, turned out to be a major catalyst in consolidating American public opinion firmly behind our strategy in the gulf. The size of the call up meant that everyone had players from their state. The moral ascendancy that U.S. troops had when they knew their country was behind them cannot be discounted."[34]

Objectives Attained

Even though the means of their attainment changed from reliance on economic sanctions to the use of offensive military action, the national objectives of the United States remained constant throughout the course of the war: "First, the immediate and unconditional withdrawal of all Iraqi forces from Kuwait. Second, the restoration of Kuwait's legitimate government. Third, security and stability for the Gulf. . . . [F]ourth, the protection of American citizens abroad."[35]

As the doctrinal manuals prescribed, Central Command's military campaign plans at the operational level of war were designed specifically to achieve those strategic objectives. And that's what they did. As General Schwarzkopf later explained, "We were driving into their [Republican Guard's] flank now, with two corps completely intact, and they were in a complete rout. And I reported that situation to General Powell. And he and I discussed, have we accomplished our military objectives? . . . And the answer was 'Yes.' There was no question about the fact that the campaign objectives that we established for ourselves were accomplished. The enemy was being kicked out of Kuwait . . . we had destroyed the Republican Guard as an effective fighting force."[36]

"Kuwait is liberated," President Bush told the American people in a nationwide television address on February 27, 1991. "Iraq's army is defeated. Our military objectives are met. . . .

"After consulting with Secretary of Defense Cheney, chairman of the Joint Chiefs of Staff Powell and our coalition partners, I am pleased to announce that at midnight tonight EST, exactly 100 hours since ground operations commenced and six weeks since the start of Operation Desert Storm, all United States and coalition forces will suspend offensive combat operations. . . ."[37]

NOTES

1. George H. Bush, statement by the president, the White House, office of the press secretary (January 16, 1991).

2. Carl von Clausewitz, *On War,* trans. and ed. Michael Howard and Peter Paret (Princeton, N.J.: Princeton University Press, 1976), p. 87.

3. 82nd Cong., 1st sess., Senate Joint Committee on Armed Services and Foreign Relations, *Military Situation in*

the Far East, vol. I (Washington, D.C.: U.S. Government Printing Office, 1951), p. 45.

4. Bernard Brodie, *War and Politics* (New York: Macmillan Publishing Company, 1983), pp. 43–44.

5. Clausewitz, *On War,* p. 88.

6. *Military Situation in the Far East,* vol. I, p. 105.

7. Douglas MacArthur, *Reminiscences* (New York: McGraw-Hill Book Company, 1964), p. 404.

8. *Military Situation in the Far East,* vol. I, p. 40.

9. Andreas Hillgruber, "Unconditional Surrender," in *The Historical Encyclopedia of World War II,* ed. Marcel Baudot et al. (New York: Facts on File, 1980), pp. 461–62.

10. Clausewitz, *On War,* p. 94.

11. *Military Situation in the Far East,* vol. I, pp. 960–61.

12. For an account of U.N. actions during the Korean war see Trygve Lie, *In the Cause of Peace: Seven Years with the United Nations* (New York: The Macmillan Company, 1954).

13. Clausewitz, *On War,* p. 92.

14. *Military Situation in the Far East,* vol. III, pp. 1734–35, 2247–2258.

15. For a discussion of alternate strategies in Vietnam see Bruce Palmer, Jr., *The Twenty-five-Year War: America's Military Role in Vietnam* (Lexington, Ky.: The University Press of Kentucky, 1984), pp. 105–6.

16. Hugh M. Arnold, "Official Justifications for America's Role in Indochina, 1948–1967," *Asian Affairs* (September–October 1975), p. 31.

17. Douglas Kinnard, *The War Managers* (Hanover, N.H.: University Press of New England, 1977), p. 25.

18. Clark Clifford in Michael Maclear, *The Ten Thousand Day War: Vietnam 1945–1975* (New York: St. Martin's Press, 1981), p. 216.

19. See chart "Popular Support for Vietnam War and Two Presidents" in John Mueller's "A Summary of Public Opinion and the Vietnam War" in the appendix to *Vietnam as History,* ed. Peter Braestrup (Washington, D.C.: University Press of America, 1984). For a more detailed discussion see John Mueller, *War, Presidents and Public Opinion* (New York: John Wiley & Sons, 1973).

20. Clausewitz, *On War*, p. 92.

21. Dudley W. Knox, "The Role of Doctrine in Naval Warfare," *U.S. Naval Institute Proceedings*, vol. 41, no. 2 (March–April 1915), pp. 353–354.

22. FM 100-1, *The Army* (Washington, D.C.: Department of the Army, 1981), p. 14.

23. Clausewitz, *On War*, p. 607.

24. Caspar W. Weinberger, *The Uses of Military Power* (Washington, D.C.: Office of the Assistant Secretary of Defense for Public Affairs (press release 609-84) November 28, 1984), pp. 3, 6.

25. AFM 1-1, *Basic Aerospace Doctrine of the United States Air Force* (Washington, D.C.: Department of the Air Force, 1984), pp. 2–5.

26. FM 100-1, *The Army* (Washington, D.C.: Department of the Army, 1986), pp. 14–15.

27. Colin L. Powell, "Operation Desert Shield: The Chairman's Review," *Defense Issues*, vol. 5, no. 44 (December 3, 1990), pp. 1–2.

28. George Bush, "America Will Stand By Her Friends," *Defense Issues*, vol. 5, no. 32 (August 8, 1990), p. 1.

29. Powell, "Operation Desert Shield: The Chairman's Review," p. 1.

30. George Bush, the White House (August 22, 1990), repr. in *Federal Register* (August 27, 1990).

31. George Bush, the White House (January 18, 1991), repr. in *Federal Register* (January 23, 1991).

32. Statistics on reserve forces were provided by Major Doug Hart, USAF, Reserve component desk officer, officer of the assistant secretary of defense for public affairs Directorate for Defense Information (June 19, 1991).

33. Lewis Sorley, "Creighton Abrams and Active-Reserve Integration in Wartime," *Parameters: U.S. Army War College Quarterly*, vol. XXI, no. 2 (Summer 1991), pp. 37–39.

34. Crosbie E. Saint, "Thoughts on the Victory in Desert Storm," Message 260800Z Mar 91, CINCUSAREUR, Heidelberg, Germany (March 26, 1991).

35. George Bush, "Why We Are in the Gulf," *Newsweek* (November 26, 1990), p. 28.

36. H. Norman Schwarzkopf, interview with David Frost in Roger Cohen and Claudio Gatti, *In the Eye of the Storm* (New York: Farrar, Straus, & Giroux, 1991), pp. 270–71.

37. George Bush, address to the nation, United Press International (February 27, 1991).

11

The Offensive

Our strategy to go after this Army is very, very simple. First we're going to cut it off, and then we're going to kill it.

General Colin L. Powell, USA,
chairman of the Joint Chiefs of Staff,
news conference (January 23, 1991)[1]

National Policy and the Strategic Offensive

Of the seven principles of war that address the fundamental question "How are we going to do it?" the *offensive*—"seize, retain and exploit the initiative"[2]—is the most important. And until the very eve of the Persian Gulf war it was almost the most impotent. Although still very much alive at the operational and tactical levels of conflict, at the strategic level it had been in suspended animation for over forty years.

To make matters worse, this fact was generally unrecognized. With the World War II paradigm of war in mind, most Americans, military as well as civilian, took it for granted that defeat of the enemy on the battlefield through offensive military action was the way that wars were decided. They did not realize that when the Chinese intervened in the Korean war in November 1950, that ceased to be true for the United States. From that point on, America's wars could not be decided by victory on the battlefield. Instead, conflict termination would be through bargaining at the negotiating table.

The reason, as discussed earlier, was that after the Chinese intervention President Truman dropped "rollback and liberation" as U.S. national military policy and adopted instead a policy of containment—a decision later endorsed by Eisenhower in the 1956 Hungarian uprising and by every subsequent American president. Since military strategy exists to achieve the ends of national policy, it must of necessity be consonant with that policy. In changing national policy, President Truman unwittingly changed U.S. military strategy as well.

The Strategic Defensive

From the strategic offensive it went to the strategic defensive. Instead of defeating the Chinese and North Korean armies in the field so as to break the enemy's will to resist (the traditional mission of offensive military action), the mission changed to one of deterrence and defense.

As then assistant secretary of state Dean Rusk explained to the Senate during the 1951 "Great Debate" on the Korean war, "What we are trying to do is maintain peace and security without a general war." But that guidance wasn't very helpful.

"My whole effort since Red China came in there has been to get some definition, military definition, of what I should do," complained MacArthur, in words

General Westmoreland could have repeated almost verbatim fifteen years later in Vietnam. Commenting on Rusk's new mission statement, MacArthur said:

> That policy seems to me to introduce a new concept into military operations . . . the concept that when you use force you can limit that force. . . .
>
> It seems to me the worst possible concept, militarily, that we would simply stay there, resisting aggression, so called. . . . The very term of "resisting aggression," it seems to me [means] that you destroy the potentialities of the aggressor to continually hit you. . . .
>
> When you say, merely, "we are going to continue to fight aggression," that is not what the enemy is fighting for. The enemy is fighting for a very definite purpose— to destroy our forces in Korea.[3]

Limited war was hardly a new concept. "Most wars, it can be argued, have been limited," wrote military historian Dave R. Palmer in his 1978 analysis of the Vietnam war. "One can dig back in history to say that the final Punic War—when Rome defeated Carthage, slaughtered the population, razed the city, plowed under the ruins and sowed the furrows with salt—was not in any way limited. . . . But it is hard to find other examples; in some manner or other a limiting factor was always present."[4]

And neither was the concept of the strategic defense that MacArthur complained about. One of the eight books that comprise Carl von Clausewitz's *On War* is devoted exclusively to the defense. He could have been addressing MacArthur's complaints directly when some 120 years earlier he asked rhetorically, "What is the concept of defense?" "The parrying of a blow." "What is its characteristic feature?" "Awaiting the blow." "What is the object of the defense?" "Preservation."[5]

In the American military the permeations of the strategic defense had been laid out in 1894 at the School of Application for Infantry and Cavalry at Fort Leavenworth, Kansas, the predecessor of the Army Command and General Staff College.

A translation of Colmar, Baron von der Goltz's *The Conduct of War* explained them in detail. While most military theorists saw war in two dimensions, offensive and defensive, von der Goltz pointed out that there were actually four dimensions. First was the strategic offense combined with the tactical offense. "Destruction of the enemy, conquest of his territory" was the result. Then there was the strategic offense combined with the tactical defense. "General situation favorable for victory," was the result, "which, however, is without results because the fighting power of the enemy is not impaired."

Turning to the defensive dimension, first was the strategic defense combined with the tactical defense, which resulted in "complete absence of a decision." Finally there was the strategic defense combined with the tactical offense. There the results were "victory on the field of battle without general results for the campaign or war."[6] The latter would become our Cold War military strategy, with results exactly as von der Goltz had predicted more than half a century earlier.

Reflecting the harsh realities of the time, the 1939 and 1941 editions of the Army's operational doctrinal manuals mentioned the "strategically defensive mission" in their discussion of the principle of the offensive. In fact, General MacArthur himself, first at Bataan and Corregidor and then in Australia, had spent the first months of World War II on the strategic defensive.

But then in the hubris surrounding our overwhelming victories in that war, the strategic defense dropped out of the doctrinal manuals, never to return. One reason was that once the United States became a great power, the defense seemed beneath its dignity. "While it may sometimes be necessary to adopt a defensive posture," states the current edition of FM 100-1, "this should only be a temporary condition until the necessary means are available to resume offensive operations."

At the strategic level, that "temporary condition" was to last for over forty years, from November 1950 to January 1991. But because it was never officially acknowledged, the portents of that posture were never clear, either to the military or to their civilian superiors.

What drove this change, pure and simple, was that the United States had been unnerved by the Chinese intervention, and further frightened by fear of the Soviet Union and its nucelar arsenal. That's what really kept us from attacking the Chinese sanctuaries in Korea. But the United States could hardly admit such a thing.

Taking Council of Our Fears

And that's why we could never squarely face the fact that throughout the Cold War when it came to China, the Soviet Union, or their client states, we were on the strategic defensive. As Clausewitz explained:

> That sort of fraudulence is [rooted] in the nature of the case. The counterweights that weaken the elemental force of war, and particularly the attack, are primarily located in the political relations and intentions of the government, which are concealed from the rest of the world, the people at home, the army, and in some cases even from the commander.

For instance no one can and will admit that his decision to stop . . . was motivated by fear that his strength would run out, or that he might make new enemies or that his own allies might become too strong. That sort of thing is long kept confidential, possibly forever. . . .[7]

In his autobiography, former secretary of state Dean Rusk gave an insight into this defensive mindset. "One military memorandum discussed American ground forces invading North Vietnam and opined that such an invasion in the eye of the memo writer would not 'bring in the Chinese.' But the memo continued, asserting, 'But if they do come in, that will mean nuclear war.' In the memorandum the clause looked like fine print. But such a sentence pops off the page at an American president."[8]

We had violated Confederate general Thomas J. "Stonewall" Jackson's famous admonition "Never take council of your fears."[9] He didn't mean to disregard the dangers of war—the possibility of nuclear war ought to "pop off the page."

His caution was not to be so paralyzed by such fears that you cause yourself to be even more imperiled. But we had done just that, using euphemisms such as "deterrence" to cover up the fact that we had opted for the strategic defensive.

Thus a whole generation of military officers failed to perceive what von der Goltz had made clear before the turn of the century: No matter how fine an army, no matter how well they were led, no matter how bravely they might fight—the best result obtainable on the strategic defensive is *stalemate*.

That's exactly what had happened in both the Korean and Vietnam wars. In Korea the battlefield was stalemated in 1951 with the defeat of the CCF spring offensive. The negotiators took over, and two years later the war ended with the Korean Armistice of 1953. In Vietnam, the war was stalemated with the defeat of the VC and North Vietnamese Army's (NVA) 1968 Tet offensive. Again the negotiators took over, and five years later the war ended (for the United States, at least) with the 1973 Paris Peace Accords.

In both wars the enemy was quick to take advantage of the long hiatus between the stalemating of the battlefield and the final diplomatic settlement. In the "outpost battles" in Korea from 1951 to 1953, the United States suffered 63,200 casualties, including 12,300 killed in action. The effect on U.S. public opinion was so severe that two of the more famous of these outposts, Old Baldy and Pork Chop Hill, were abandoned to the enemy rather than suffer the casualties necessary to retain them under allied control.[10]

The same thing happened in Vietnam. Again the enemy sought to inflict maximum casualties during the negotiations so as to influence American public opinion. In May 1969, a year after talks first began in Paris, the Battle of Hamburger Hill dominated the American press. Normally the NVA would have retreated back into their Laotian sanctuaries, but this time they chose to stand and fight. American public outrage over what appeared to be a senseless loss of American lives led to emphasis on "Vietnamization" rather than further combat actions.[11]

As Clausewitz said, the essence of the defense is waiting. But waiting is not the strong suit for action-oriented Americans. In both Korea and Vietnam, as the battlefield stalemated, front-line morale plummeted and discipline began to deteriorate. At home public support rapidly faded away, driven both by frustration and by the enemy's cynical exploitation of American POWs as hostages to the negotiating process.

The Paper Tiger

America paid a terrible price for its failure to understand and explain the ramifications of its defensive military strategy. Not only did the Korean war end in what many Americans saw as a defeat rather than the logical consequences of our chosen strategy, in Vietnam the frustrations of the strategic defensive caused them to give up on the war entirely.

Abroad the consequences were even more severe. The Asian diplomat quoted earlier had summed it up perfectly. "America was regarded as a paper tiger," he said in a March 1991 interview. His country "had . . . figured that the United States would lack the will to fight."[12] And it was not an unreasonable assumption.

The United States could be brave enough against Grenada or Libya or Panama, where no confrontation with the Soviet Union was involved. But the very fact that those "pissant countries," as Lyndon Johnson would have called them, would dare challenge the United States ought to have given us pause. As American military authority ebbed, it was becoming increasingly necessary to use U.S. military power to protect American interests abroad.

But even that option seemed to be ruled out when a Soviet client state was involved. Among the roots of the Persian Gulf war was the U.S. reaction to the June 16, 1976, assassination of Francis C. Meloy, the U.S. Ambassador to Lebanon. Although the murderers were known, says a 1990 investigative report, "the U.S. government engaged in a deliberate cover-up of the real facts in order to avoid public or congressional pressure to retaliate against those responsible for the murderers.

"Unfortunately the U.S. failure to retaliate against the killers laid the groundwork for the subsequent deaths of other Americans in Lebanon during the 1980s as terrorists—emboldened by American timidity in the face of repeated attacks—grew even more aggressive."[13]

The Correlation of Forces

PLO terrorists were not the only ones who were emboldened. Iraq's Saddam Hussein surely noted that when terrorists blew up the Marine barracks in Beirut in 1983, killing 241 American servicemen, the United States supinely withdrew, taking no military action for fear of offending Syria, a Soviet client state. And when Syrian-backed terrorists, reportedly at the Soviet KGB's behest, kidnapped top CIA agent William Buckley in 1985 and tortured him to death, the United States primly averted its eyes.

An even stronger signal was sent on July 31, 1989, when Middle East terrorists flaunted their murder of Marine colonel William Higgins, an official emissary of the United States, by releasing a grisly videotape of his corpse hanging from a rope.

In other times such an outrage would have been considered an act of war—it was the murder of a Mongolian emissary in 1218, for example, that sent Genghis Khan rampaging across Asia and Europe and led to the sack of Baghdad by his grandson in 1258. But in the United States there was little public outrage at this atrocity, and the reaction of George Bush, no Genghis Khan, was to throw a barbecue on the White House lawn.

No wonder that not quite a year later, on July 25, 1990, Saddam Hussein would pay scant attention to the feeble remonstrations of April Glaspie, the U.S. ambassador to Iraq, about his military buildup on the Kuwaiti border.[14]

Her remarks would later be compared to Dean

Acheson's January 1950 National Press Club speech that excluded Korea from the U.S. Asian defense perimeter and supposedly gave the green light to North Korean aggression. Critics would charge that Glaspie's comment "We have no opinion on the Arab-Arab conflicts like your border disagreement with Kuwait" and President Bush's later conciliatory message "We believe that differences are best resolved by peaceful means and not by threats involving military force or conflict"[15] likewise gave the go-ahead to Iraqi aggression.

But it was not these messages that convinced Saddam Hussein of America's pusillanimity. He had long since taken the measure of America's resolve and found it wanting. President Bush could have given him a nuclear ultimatum and he probably would have laughed it off. Believing he was still under the protection of the Soviet Union, he thought he could ignore U.S. pleas with impunity. And in the unlikely event it did intervene, the Vietnam war proved that the United States lacked the will to win.

But since that war the world correlation of forces had come full circle. In his confrontation with the United States, Saddam Hussein would find himself not playing the role of Ho Chi Minh as intended, but instead would be cast in the role of the South's Nguyen Van Thieu. In October 1972, Thieu had "commented bitterly that compared to the United States, South Vietnam was no more than a dot. Its loss would mean little to America, he said, which had its strategies to pursue with Moscow and Peking."[16]

As events would prove, with the end of the Cold War, Iraq, too, was only a dot on the map compared to the USSR. Its loss would mean little to the Soviet Union, which had its strategies to pursue with Washington and the West. That fact was confirmed on August 2, 1990, when the Soviet Union, instead of vetoing U.N. Security Council Resolution 660 condemning Iraqi aggression, voted instead in favor of it.

Operation Desert Shield

Containment of the Soviet Union had given way to cooperation with it. As it had forty years earlier, when *containment* replaced *rollback and liberation,* military strategy reacted to this change in national policy. Once again the *offensive* was an American strategic military option.

But from necessity as well as from conviction, President Bush decided not to exercise that option immediately. "At my direction," he told the nation on August 8, 1990, "elements of the 82nd Airborne Division, as well as key elements of the United States Air Force, are arriving today to take up defensive positions in Saudi Arabia. . . . The mission of our troops is wholly defensive. . . . They will not initiate hostilities, but they will defend themselves, the kingdom of Saudi Arabia and other friends in the Persian Gulf."[17]

As naval historian Norman Friedman noted, "the U.S. buildup was code-named Desert Shield to emphasize that it shielded Saudi Arabia from further attack."[18] And for a while it was a thin shield indeed. Although there were those who called for immediate air attacks on Iraq, President Bush wisely rejected these irresponsible calls for premature offensive action.

The Navy carriers on station and the Air Force's 1st Tactical Fighter Wing could defend Saudi airspace, but their offensive-strike capability was limited. Not only that, such early air attacks might well have precipitated a retaliatory Iraqi ground attack that the United States was not yet prepared to meet.

While the 82nd Airborne Division had been airlifted into place to show the flag, they were no match for the Iraqi armored divisions that had just overrun Kuwait in a matter of hours and were now poised on the Kuwait-Saudi border. This was a precarious period for the United States.

At his press conference at the end of the war, General Schwarzkopf commented that one thing about the press he was delighted with was that "in the very, very early stages of this operation, when we were over here building up and we didn't have much on the ground, you were all giving us credit for a whole lot more over here. And as a result that gave me quite a feeling of confidence that we might not be attacked quite as quickly as I thought we were going to be attacked."[19]

It would be weeks before the first American armored and mechanized forces—the U.S.-based 24th Infantry Division, 1st Cavalry Division with a brigade from the 2nd Armored Division, and the 3rd Armored Cavalry Regiment—would finally arrive in-country. Initially arrayed behind the Saudi Task Force inland from the Persian Gulf, they provided sufficient combat power to defend Saudi Arabia from ground attack, even though they still did not have the power necessary for offensive action.

Of necessity, the majority of the American military in the Gulf were on the strategic, operational, and tactical defensive. This time it would prove to be, as FM 100-1's discussion of the principle of the offensive stated, "a temporary condition until the necessary means are available [for] offensive actions."

Sanctions

But while the military dimension of U.S. national power was on the defensive, the diplomatic and economic dimensions were very much on the offensive. As will be seen in Chapter 14, "Unity of Command

and Coalition Warfare,'' the diplomatic campaign to build an effective political coalition against Saddam Hussein was an integral part of U.S. strategy.

As so was its campaign to put pressure on him through imposition of economic sanctions. On August 6, 1990, the U.N. Security Council voted 13–0 (Cuba and Yemen abstaining) in favor of Resolution 661, which imposed a trade and financial embargo on Iraq. This was to become the initial cornerstone of U.S. national strategy. ''These sanctions, now enshrined in international law, have the potential to deny Iraq the fruits of aggression,'' said President Bush on August 8, ''while sharply limiting its ability to either import or export anything of value, especially oil.''[20]

While the rest of the military was on the defensive, the Navy and Coast Guard immediately went on the operational and tactical offensive to create and enforce a naval blockade against Iraq. Interceptions began on August 17, 1990, with the USS *John I. Hall* stopping the Iraqi tanker *Al Fao* in the Red Sea and the intercept of the Iraqi tankers *Al Abid* and *Al Byaa* in the Persian Gulf by the USS *England*.[21] This blockade would continue throughout the war and into the subsequent cease-fire.

As General Schwarzkopf noted in his speech at the U.S. Naval Academy on May 23, 1991:

> More than 200 ships from 13 nations conducted over 10,000 flawless intercepts, which formed a steel wall around the waters leading to Iraq. And these operations continue today. Thanks to these superb efforts not one cargo hold, not one crate, not even one pallet of seaborne contraband even touched Saddam Hussein's shores. The result: Iraq lost 90% of its imports, 100% of its exports, and had its gross national product cut in half.[22]

One of the major points of contention was whether economic sanctions alone could have achieved U.S. political objectives in the Gulf. Among those advocating such a position, according to Bob Woodward's insider's account of the crisis, was General Colin L. Powell, the chairman of the Joint Chiefs of Staff.[23]

When Woodward's book was published in May 1991, many found this revelation surprising. Paradoxical as it may sound, however, the professional military have always traditionally been opposed to the use of force. And the "Vietnam syndrome" had nothing to do with it. "The military man normally opposes reckless, aggressive, belligerent action," noted Harvard professor Samuel Huntington in his 1967 landmark work on the military and the state. They believed that "generally war should not be resorted to except as a final recourse, and only when the outcome is a virtual certainty. . . . Thus, the military man rarely favors war."[24]

And the Persian Gulf war was no exception. While "chicken hawks" (self-appointed "military experts" who themselves had assiduously avoided military service) clamored for war, senior military officers cautioned patience. Appearing before the Senate Armed Services Committee on November 28, 1990, two former chairmen of the Joint Chiefs of Staff, Air Force general David C. Jones and Navy admiral William J. Crowe, Jr., both argued that sanctions be given additional time to work.[25]

And so did Marine commandant General Alfred Gray. "I keep saying, what's the hurry here? Time is on our side . . . not Saddam's," Gray said on November 21, 1990. "We ought to let this [economic embargo] unfold and stay behind it."[26]

The Strategic Offensive

But according to postwar accounts by both *The Washington Post*'s Bob Woodward and *The New York Times*'s Thomas L. Friedman and Patrick E. Tyler, the Bush administration had begun planning for a shift to the strategic offensive soon after the crisis began.[27]

Woodward recounts how in early October 1990, General Powell presented President Bush with two courses of action. One was to build up for offensive action. The second was to give sanctions time to work, an option Powell privately favored. "There is a case here for the containment or strangulation policy," he reportedly said. "It may take a year, it may take two years, but it will work someday." The president was noncommittal. "I don't think there's time politically for that strategy."[28]

"There was a sense of drift," a senior administration official told Friedman and Tyler. "Saddam Hussein seemed to have the initiative. We felt we had to do something to get it back."[29] Central Command (CENTCOM) in Riyadh was given forty-eight hours' notice to present an offensive campaign plan to the president.

Briefed by Schwarzkopf's chief of staff, Marine major general Robert B. Johnson, it reportedly began with a reminder that "Central Command had deployed its forces in accordance with the president's deter-and-defend mission." Although they had not had a lot of time to think it through, Johnson said, if ordered to attack now, this is how it would be done.

According to Woodward's account, the plan was broken into four phases. The first three phases were the "deep battle" portion, calling for an all-out campaign against Iraq:

Phase One would be an air attack on Iraqi command, control and communications, attempting to sever Saddam in Baghdad from his forces in Kuwait and southern Iraq. Simultaneously, airpower would destroy the Iraqi Air Force and air defense system [as well as] Iraqi chemical, biological and nuclear weapons facilities.

Phase Two would be a massive, continuous air bombardment of Iraqi supply and munitions bases, transportation facilities and roads, designed to cut off the Iraqi forces from their supplies.

Phase Three would be an air attack on the entrenched Iraqi ground forces of 430,000 men and the Republican Guard.

The fourth phase, the ground attack or "close battle" portion, consisted of a Marine amphibious landing on the Kuwaiti coast and an Army frontal attack directly into the Iraqi defensive positions. Given the number of allied ground forces available, this "straight up the middle" approach was virtually the only one immediately available.

President Bush, said Woodward, had internalized the lessons of Vietnam—"send enough forces to do the job and don't tie the hands of the commanders." As Secretary Cheney had said, "The President belongs to what I call the 'Don't screw around' school of military strategy." The fourth phase was unacceptable, and General Powell was sent to the Gulf to find out what was needed for an effective ground campaign.

"I want the VII Corps," Schwarzkopf reportedly told Powell on October 21, 1990. "If the President is serious about offense . . . he is going to have to send the VII Corps."[30] As will be seen in the following chapter, "Mass, Economy of Force, and Maneuver," that request, and its subsequent approval, had an enormous significance for the conduct of the war.

On October 30 the president was briefed on the new plan. "In the two-hour meeting," reported Friedman and Tyler, "Mr. Bush made two fundamental decisions: first, to set in motion the machinery for a mid-winter war against the Iraqi Army and, second, to win a United Nations mandate for that war."[31]

On November 8, 1990, President Bush publicly announced that U.S. military strategy in the Gulf would undergo a fundamental change. Except for blockade forces, the military would remain for now on the operational and tactical defensive. But almost forty years to the day since it had been abandoned, President Bush put the American military back on the strategic offensive:

> In three months, the U.S. troop contribution to the multinational force in Saudi Arabia has gone from 10,000 to 230,000 as part of Operation Desert Shield. General Schwarzkopf reports that our forces, in conjunction with other coalition forces, now have the capability to defend successfully against any further Iraqi aggression.
>
> After consultation with King Fahd and our other allies, I have today directed the Secretary of Defense to increase the size of U.S. forces committed to Desert Shield to ensure that the coalition has an adequate offensive military option should that be necessary to achieve our common goals.[32]

Operation Desert Storm

As von der Goltz had predicted almost a century earlier, the strategic offense combined with the tactical defense had produced a "general situation favorable for victory, which, however, is without results because the fighting power of the enemy is not impaired.'' But by early January 1991, all that was about to change.

On November 29, 1990, with U.N. Security Council Resolution 678, President Bush had received his U.N. mandate for the prosecution of the war. On a vote of 12–2 (Cuba and Yemen against and China abstaining), the Security Council authorized U.N. members to use ''all necessary means'' to enforce previous U.N. Security Council resolutions if Iraq had not left Kuwait by January 15, 1991. And on January 12, 1991, the Congress of the United States, by a vote of 52–47 in the Senate and 250–183 in the House, gave the president authorization to use military force against Iraq.

The only thing missing were the heavy Army forces necessary for a ground attack. Lack of available shipping had delayed the move of VII Corps' armored divisions from Germany, and they would not be completely in position in Saudi Arabia by the U.N. deadline. On December 19, 1990, Lieutenant General Calvin A. H. Waller, the deputy commander of U.S. forces in the Gulf, had set off a minor crisis when he publicly acknowledged that fact.[33]

But the air assets were in place, and sufficient ground forces were now deployed so they could turn back any Iraqi ground counterattack. At 9:01 P.M. on January 16, 1991, President Bush announced to the American people that ''just two hours ago, allied air forces began an attack on military targets in Iraq and Kuwait. These attacks continue as I speak. Ground forces are not engaged.''[34]

Coordinated by CENTAF (Center Command Air Force), the allied air war was a spectacular success, realizing all of the objectives that CENTCOM had set for it. Although there were those in the Air Force who shared the hope of former Air Force chief of staff General Michael Dugan that a sufficiently intense stra-

tegic air campaign would win the war, the air war was
in fact an integral part of the overall CENTCOM
campaign plan. And this was exactly as intended. As
General Powell had told the House Armed Services
Committee the month before:

> Many experts and others in this town believe that [our
> objectives] can be accomplished by surgical air strikes
> or sustained air campaigns without the use of other
> forces, particularly ground forces. The fundamental flaw
> in such strategies is that they leave the initiative in
> Saddam's hands. . . .

> General Schwarzkopf, the Joint Chiefs of Staff and I . . .
> recommended and the President approved a force
> buildup capable of . . . making the Iraqis face the
> consequences of a combined air, land and sea campaign
> from a powerful coalition force. . . .[35]

Even though the bombing had inflicted severe damage, the Iraqis were able, as General Powell had predicted, to hunker down and maintain the strategic
initiative. On February 18, 1991, Iraqi foreign minister
Tariq Aziz arranged a "peace plan" with the Soviet
Union that would have allowed them three weeks to
withdraw from Kuwait and permitted them to avoid
the ignominy of surrender. But President Bush was
having none of it.

Acting to regain the initiative, at noon on February
22, 1990, he issued a twenty-four-hour ultimatum for
Iraq to begin withdrawing from Kuwait. As *The New
York Times* noted, "the hasty withdrawal . . . would
be a humiliating defeat for Baghdad, which could even
lead to the downfall of President Saddam Hussein."[36]
To no one's surprise, the ultimatum was rejected.

But Bush had not been bluffing. At 4:00 A.M.
February 24 Gulf Time (8:00 P.M. February 23 Eastern

Standard Time), the ground war began. One hundred hours later, it was all over. " 'Seven months ago, America and the world drew a line in the sand,' said President Bush. 'We declared that the aggression against Kuwait would not stand, and tonight America and the world have kept their word.'[37]

"The President's declaration came," noted *The Washington Post,* "after U.S. and British armored forces, in the largest tank battle since World War II, crushed most of the Republican Guard divisions . . . completing the virtual destruction of the half-million-man Iraqi army of occupation."[38] The offensive was once again the American way of war. Patton would have been proud.

NOTES

1. Colin L. Powell, "The Right Stuff," *U.S. News & World Report* (February 4, 1991), p. 26. See also Andrew Rosenthal, "Pentagon Is Confident on War. . . ," *The New York Times* (January 24, 1991), p. 1.

2. FM 100-1, *The Army* (Washington, D.C.: Department of the Army, 1986), p. 15.

3. 82nd Cong., 1st sess., Senate Joint Committee on Armed Services and Foreign Relations, *Military Situation in the Far East* (Washington, D.C.: U.S. Government Printing Office, 1951), pp. 30–31, 39–40, 68.

4. Dave R. Palmer, *Summons of the Trumpet: US-Vietnam in Perspective* (Novato, Calif.: Presidio Press, 1978), p. xix.

5. Carl von Clausewitz, *On War,* trans. and ed. Michael Howard and Peter Paret (Princeton, N.J.: Princeton University Press, 1976), p. 357.

6. Colmar, Baron von der Goltz, *The Conduct of War: A Brief Study of Its Most Important Principles and Forms,* trans. 1st Lt. Joseph T. Dickman, 3rd Cavalry, assistant instructor in the art of war, U.S. Infantry and Cavalry

School (Kansas City, Mo.: The Franklin Hudson Publishing Company, 1896), p. 32.

7. Clausewitz, *On War,* p. 388.

8. Dean Rusk, *As I Saw It* (New York: W. W. Norton & Company, 1990), p. 457.

9. Thomas J. Jackson in Douglas Southall Freeman, *Lee's Lieutenants,* vol. I (New York: Charles Scribner's Sons, 1942), pp. 469–70.

10. Harry G. Summers, Jr., "Outpost Battles," *Korean War Almanac* (New York: Facts on File, 1990), p. 208.

11. Harry G. Summers, Jr., "Hamburger Hill," *Vietnam War Almanac* (New York: Facts on File, 1985), pp. 184–85.

12. Quoted in Michael Breen. "North Korea in Gulf 'shock,' " *Washington Times* (March 12, 1991), p. A1.

13. Neil C. Livingstone and David Halevy, *Inside the PLO* (New York: William Morrow & Company, 1990), pp. 96, 99.

14. Bob Woodward, *The Commanders* (New York: Simon & Schuster, 1991), pp. 211–12.

15. Elaine Sciolino, "Envoy's Testimony on Iraq Is Assailed," *The New York Times* (July 13, 1991), p. 1.

16. Arnold R. Isaacs, *Without Honor: Defeat in Vietnam and Cambodia* (Baltimore: The Johns Hopkins University Press, 1983), p. 44.

17. George Bush, "Address to the Nation: America Will Stand By Her Friends," *Defense Issues,* vol. 5, no. 32 (August 8, 1990), p. 1.

18. Norman Friedman, *Desert Victory: The War for Kuwait* (Annapolis, Md.: Naval Institute Press, 1991), p. 106.

19. H. Norman Schwarzkopf, "Schwarzkopf Answers Reporters' Questions," *The Washington Post* (February 28, 1991), p. A36.

20. Bush, "Address to the Nation" (August 8, 1990).

21. Friedman, *Desert Victory,* pp. 102–3.

22. H. Norman Schwarzkopf, "A Tribute to the Navy-Marine Corps Team," *U.S. Naval Institute Proceedings,* vol. 118, no. 8, p. 44.

23. Woodward, *The Commanders,* pp. 41–42, 299–303.

24. Samuel P. Huntington, *The Soldier and the State*

(Cambridge, Mass.: The Belknap Press of Harvard University, 1967), pp. 68–70.

25. 101st Cong., 2nd sess., Senate Hearings Before the Committee on Armed Services. *Crisis in the Persian Gulf Region: U.S. Policy Options and Implications* (Washington, D.C.: U.S. Government Printing Office, 1990), pp. 182–257.

26. R. Jeffrey Smith and George Lardner, Jr., "Iraq Sanctions Seem Working Slowly," *The Washington Post* (November 24, 1990), p. 1.

27. Woodward, *The Commanders,* and Thomas L. Friedman and Patrick E. Tyler, "From the First, U.S. Resolve to Fight," *The New York Times* (March 3, 1991), p. 1.

28. Woodward, *The Commanders,* pp. 41–42.

29. Friedman and Tyler, "From the First," p. 1.

30. Woodward, *The Commanders,* pp. 304–10.

31. Friedman and Tyler, "From the First," p. 1.

32. George Bush, the White House (Washington, D.C., November 8, 1990).

33. Barton Gellman, "Officials Dispute General on Gulf Forces' Readiness," *The Washington Post* (December 21, 1990), p. 32.

34. George Bush, the White House (Washington, D.C., January 16, 1991).

35. 101st Cong., 2nd sess., House Hearings Before the Committee on Armed Services, *Crisis in the Persian Gulf: Sanctions, Diplomacy, and War* (Washington, D.C., U.S. Government Printing Office, 1990), p. 541.

36. Michael R. Gordon, "The Seven-Day Strategy," *The New York Times* (February 23, 1991), p. 1.

37. Rick Atkinson and Steve Coll, "Bush Orders Cease-Fire," *The Washington Post* (February 28, 1991), p. 1.

38. Ibid.

12

Mass, Economy of Force, and Maneuver

[F]uture wars will probably be fought under nonlinear circumstances. . . . The Middle East represents the clearest possible example of that probability. Given the distance to the Persian Gulf and the relative shortage of strategic life it is axiomatic . . . there could be no continuous fronts stretching from the Alps to the sea or across the waist of Korea. . . .

The generation of officers now in command, seasoned in the airmobile environment of Vietnam, is especially well suited for such operations. Accustomed to open flanks, to operating on the basis of ambiguous intelligence, seeking the enemy and not the terrain, concentrating rapidly, and adapting constantly to the flow of events—these leaders have maneuver in their bones.

General William E. DePuy, USA (Ret.),
"FM 100-5 Revisited" (November 1980)[1]

Political-Military Stalemate

The interrelated principles of mass, economy of force, and maneuver regulate military action and thus play a major role in answering the fundamental question "How are we going to do it?" Mass and economy of force are reciprocals: The former says "concentrate combat power at the decisive time and place"; the latter, "allocate minimum essential combat power to secondary efforts." At the strategic level, maneuver— "place the enemy in a position of disadvantage through the flexible application of combat power"— has mainly to do with strategic mobility, the means of getting there, a critical consideration in view of the geographic reality that the United States is physically separated from most world crisis areas by the Atlantic and Pacific oceans.[2]

Given the dexterity of their application at the strategic, operational, and tactical levels during the Persian Gulf war, it is hard to believe that a decade earlier, critics were complaining that the U.S. military lacked the flexibility necessary for such actions and would be unable to maneuver rapidly enough to react to changing world and battlefield conditions.

They proved dead wrong. One reason is that they labored under a serious error in logic—*post hoc ergo propter hoc,* "after this, therefore because of it." They took the military performance in the Korean and Vietnam wars as evidence that the military did not understand maneuver warfare.

"Let the critics relax," said General DePuy in his remarkably prescient article extracted above, written ten years before the Persian Gulf war. The U.S. Army "is not by its character, preference or record of historic performance an attrition-minded, defensive-minded fighting organization," DePuy pointed out. "The brilliant landing at Inchon, the march to the Yalu and the Ridgway counteroffensive were more typical of the American view of how to fight a war than the political-military stalemate along the 38th Parallel."[3]

"Political-military stalemate" was the real explanation for the apparent inability to apply mass, economy of force, and maneuver during the Korean and Vietnam wars. As was discussed in the previous chapter, "stalemate" was the best result possible, given the restrictions inherent in our chosen defensive strategy.

Mass and Economy of Force

But the main reason they were wrong is that mass and economy of force in particular underwent major political changes on the very eve of the Persian Gulf war, changes so profound that they dictated the very outcome of the war. In the past we had opted to contain rather than confront the Soviet Union, whom we considered to be our main Cold War adversary. While that strategy proved correct in the long run, it had a paralyzing effect in the short term, confusing our choice of where to mass and where to use an economy of force.

As former secretary of state and national security adviser Henry Kissinger pointed out:

> We had entered the Korean War because we were afraid that to fail to do so would produce a much greater danger in Europe in the near future. But then the very reluctance to face an all-out onslaught in Europe severely circumscribed the risks we were prepared to run to prevail in Korea. . . .
>
> Ten years later we encountered the same dilemmas in Vietnam. Once more we became involved because we considered the warfare in Indochina the manifestation of a coordinated global Communist strategy. Again we sought to limit our risks because the very global challenge of which Indochina seemed to be a part also made Vietnam appear as an unprofitable place for a showdown.[4]

Because it was feared that Korea was merely a diversion and that the main Soviet attack would actually come in Europe, the United States massed in Europe and used an economy of force to fight the shooting war in Korea. It was in effect a replay of its World War II "Europe First" strategy, another irritant in the Truman-MacArthur controversy. By 1952, troop strength in Europe had increased to 260,800, slightly more than the 238,600 soldiers in combat in Korea.[5]

While we massed our troops in Vietnam, drawing down in Europe to what many believed to be dangerously low levels, we never concentrated our full attention on Vietnam until it was too late.

In their insiders' account of the Vietnam-era Defense Department, for example, Pentagon "whiz kids" Alain C. Enthoven and K. Wayne Smith devoted only about fifty pages of their three-hundred-page book to Vietnam. The rest concentrated on what at the time were more pressing matters—NATO strategy, nuclear strategy, and long-forgotten major defense programs such as the B-70 bomber, the Skybolt missile, and the advanced Tactical Fighter or TFX.[6]

With minute exceptions, noted Robert W. Komer, who initiated the successful CORDS (Civil Operations and Revolutionary Development Support) program in Vietnam, "not a senior level official above the rank of office director or colonel in any US agency dealt full-time with Vietnam before 1969."[7]

This was reflected throughout the military. Although hard to believe in retrospect, during the crucial early years of the war, Vietnam was very much a back-burner affair. In 1967–68, then major Colin L. Powell and I were classmates at the Army Command and General Staff College at Fort Leavenworth, Kansas, the Army's premier midlevel school. When we arrived, not one course was being taught on Vietnam, even though the war there had been going on for almost three years. Concentration was still on the Fulda Gap and battle with the conventional armies of the Soviet Union on the plains of Central Europe.[8]

The Soviet Enabler

Ironically, it was the Soviet Union that enabled the United States finally to apply the strategic principles of mass and economy of force for the first time in over a generation. As seen in the previous chapter, the end of the Cold War and the consequent end of the U.S. policy of containment enabled the United States to shift back to the strategic military offensive, a strategy that had been abandoned forty years earlier in November 1950, when Communist China, at Soviet urging, intervened in the Korean war.

In both the Korean and Vietnam wars the Soviet Union (and, to a lesser degree, Communist China) had been the main arms suppliers to our enemies. But when on August 6, 1990, the Soviet Union and China voted in favor of U.N. Security Council Resolution 661 to impose an embargo on Iraq, the strategic environment underwent a profound reorientation.

Not only was Iraq cut off from supply of arms, equipment, and spare parts for their existing weaponry, but also, most critically, they were severed from the protection formerly provided by the nuclear shield of the Soviet Union. The primary constraint on the full application of conventional American military power had been lifted.

No longer did we need to fear, as we had in both the Korean and Vietnam wars, that direct attacks on a Soviet ally might bring the Soviet Union into the war against us and, as many feared at the time, touch off a nuclear conflagration. It was that fear that had stayed General MacArthur's hand in attacking Chinese airfields and assembly areas in Manchuria during the

Korean War and had foiled General Westmoreland's plans for an Inchon-like ground attack on the North Vietnamese coast to cut the enemy supply lines to their forces in the south.

It was a new ball game, one where the United States held the decisive advantage. "Before the [Iraqi] invasion in August," said President Bush on November 8, 1991, giving a nod to the shift in the world correlation of forces that had freed his hand, "we had succeeded in the struggle for freedom in Eastern Europe." He then announced that he had "directed the Secretary of Defense to increase the size of U.S. forces committed to Desert Shield to ensure that the coalition has an adequate offensive military option should that be necessary to achieve our common goals."[9]

Included in Europe was the Army's VII Corps, which for almost four decades had bolstered NATO defenses against Soviet attack. Now it was off to the Gulf, where its heavily armored forces would eventually lead the main attack. VII Corps' deployment could only mean that a tacit agreement had been reached with the Soviet Union, for Soviet hostility would have kept VII Corps locked in place, as it had during the Korean and Vietnam wars.

That agreement became clear when the USSR voted on November 29, 1990, in favor of U.N. Security Council Resolution 678, authorizing U.N. members to use "all means necessary" to enforce all previous resolutions if Iraq did not leave Kuwait by January 15, 1991. Because of this Soviet cooperation (and the cooperation of China as well, which abstained rather than exercise its U.N. Security Council veto to block the authorization for the use of force), the United States was finally able to apply the principles of mass and economy of force as doctrine intended.

Using an economy of force in Europe and elsewhere in the world, the United States was able to "concentrate combat power at the decisive place and time." By the start of the war over a half million Americans had deployed to the Persian Gulf. Most were part of the U.S. Third Army's VII and XVIII corps, comprising the 1st Armored, 1st Cavalry, and 1st Infantry divisions; brigades from the 2nd Armored and 3rd Infantry divisions; the 3rd Armored, 24th Infantry, 82nd Airborne, and 101st Air Assault divisions; III Corps Artillery; and the 2nd and 3rd Armored Cavalry regiments.

Next largest was the naval contingent, which included the U.S. Seventh Fleet, with more than 120 warships, including a number of surface and carrier battle groups and over 400 combat aircraft. Two-thirds of the Marine Corps deployed to the Gulf, including the I Marine Expeditionary Force, with the 1st and 2nd Marine divisions and the 3rd Marine Aircraft Wing as well as Marine Expeditionary brigades afloat.

The U.S. Ninth Air Force deployed some 1,200 aircraft. Its tactical fighter wings included squadrons of tank-killing A-10s, F-15s, F-16s, F111Fs, and F117A stealth fighter-bombers. Added to this aerial armada were the B-52G intercontinental bombers of the Strategic Air Command's 42nd and 93rd Bombardment wings, EF-111A electronic countermeasure aircraft; and RF-4C, TR-1A, and U-2R tactical and strategic reconnaissance planes.[10]

Strategic Maneuver

What General Powell was to call the "thunder and lightning" of Operation Desert Storm[11] was in place. And that's what the principle of maneuver is all about. "Given the global nature of U.S. interests and the dynamic character of the international scene, strategic mobility is critical," states the Army's strategic man-

ual, FM 100-1, *The Army*. And so is the means to do
it. "In order to react promptly and to concentrate and
to project power, strategic airlift and sealift are essential."[12]

The United States is one of the few nations in the
world capable of deploying and sustaining its military
half a world away. While the British could, with difficulty, deploy several battalions of soldiers and royal
marines to the Falklands, and the French could send
battalions of its Foreign Legion, marine infantry, and
paratroopers into Chad, in the Persian Gulf; as in both
the Korean and Vietnam wars the United States deployed whole fleets, numbered air forces, and entire
corps and divisions with hundreds of thousands of
troops and millions upon millions of tons of ammunition, equipment, and supplies.

In both the Korean and Vietnam wars the Navy's
Military Sea Transport Service, later the Military Sealift Command (MSC), and the Air Force's Military Air
Transport Service, later the Military Airlift Command
(MAC), provided a seven-thousand-mile lifeline from
the United States to its forces deployed abroad. America's armed forces in the field were better armed,
better equipped, and better fed, clothed, and supplied
than any military force in the history of warfare.[13]

It was a logistics effort so prodigious, so remarkable, and so seemingly effortless that it was generally
taken for granted. But strategic mobility was in fact
America's Achilles' heel.

Strategic Maneuver and the Persian Gulf

"USCENTCOM relies heavily on strategic lift to meet
its commitments in Southwest Asia," General H. Norman Schwarzkopf told the Senate Armed Services
Committee on February 8, 1990, six months before the
crisis in the Gulf erupted. "It is important to note . . .

that America's declining national sealift capability could jeopardize our future ability to deploy, employ and sustain any sizable reinforcements in response to a national contingency.

"If not reversed," he concluded, "this continuing erosion of sealift capability will reduce USCENT-COM's overall deployment flexability."[14] From the beginning, "getting there from here" had always been Central Command's prime worry. Prepositioned war reserve matériel at Diego Garcia and Guam would provide immediate relief, but strategic airlift and sea-lift were essential to any major commitment of force. And that's where TRANSCOM, the U.S. Transportation Command at Scott Air Force Base in Illinois, came into the picture.

Becoming fully operational only in October 1988, less than two years before the crisis in the Gulf, TRANSCOM incorporated under one roof MSC and MAC. TRANSCOM more than proved its worth during the Persian Gulf war.

During the Vietnam war the Air Force had refined its aerial refueling operations,[15] and in the Gulf war the KC-10 and KC-135 tankers of the Air Force's active and reserve Air Refueling wings enabled TRANSCOM to fly more than fifteen thousand eight hundred missions. More than half a million passengers and nearly half a million tons of supplies were moved by air to the combat zone.

This airlift involved not only the C-5s, C-141s, and C-130s of the active Air Force, Air National Guard, and Air Force Reserves, but for the first time in history the commercial aircraft of the Civil Reserve Air Fleet (CRAF) were mobilized, in the first days of the crisis.

Some fifty-five cargo and passenger aircraft from Federal Express, United Parcel Service, and other civilian companies were made available to MAC to move troops and supplies to the Gulf. In the course of the war CRAF aircraft would move 60 percent of the passengers and 27 percent of the airlifted cargo.[16]

And the Maritime Strategy's "sea bridge" became a reality. "It was the quickest and largest military sealift buildup since World War II," General Schwarzkopf told the graduating class at the U.S. Naval Academy on May 29, 1991, "an 8,000 mile, 250-ship haze-gray bridge, one ship every 50 miles from the shores of the United States to the shores of Saudi Arabia. And they offloaded some nine million tons of equipment and petroleum products for our forces."[17]

TRANSCOM had more than met the challenge. "It took almost two months for the first Army division [from the United States] to reach Korea," noted an Army logistician. "For Desert Shield, the 82nd Airborne Division was in Saudi Arabia in just 22 days; elements of its first ready brigade arrived within 2 days, and the entire brigade was 'in-country' within 6 days. In just two months three Army divisions, one-and-a-third Marine expeditionary forces and the equivalent of 14 Air Force wings were in place in Southeast Asia.

"Or consider that it took one full year to move 184,000 soldiers to Vietnam, yet that many were moved to Desert Shield/Storm in just 88 days. At its peak some 539,000 military people had been moved to the Persian Gulf."[18]

It was not that General Schwarzkopf was wrong in his February 1990 assessment of CENTCOM's strategic vulnerability. Our sealift capability remains in a parlous state. The saving grace was that the United States had been incredibly lucky. It had almost six months to move its military into place, along with the millions of tons of ammunition, supplies, and equipment necessary to sustain them in battle. But, as Clausewitz had noted, luck is an important part of war.[19]

Operational Mass, Economy of Force, and Maneuver

Revitalization of the principles of mass, economy of force, and maneuver at the strategic level enables their reemphasis at the operational and tactical levels as well. And reemphasize them General Schwarzkopf did with what he called his "Hail Mary" play. Discussed in more detail in the following chapter, it involved a massive shift of his forces to the extreme west. He said in his press briefing at the end of the war,

> This was absolutely an extraordinary move. I can't recall any time in the annals of military history when this number of forces have been moved over this distance to put themselves in a position to be able to attack.
>
> But what's more important—and I think it's very, very important that I make this point—and that's these logistics bases. Not only did we move the troops out there, but we literally moved thousands and thousands of tons of fuel, of ammunition, of spare parts, of water and of food, out there into this area, because we wanted to have enough supplies on hand so that if we launched this and if we got into a slugfest battle, which we very easily could have gotten into, we'd have enough supplies to last for 60 days.
>
> So it was an absolutely gigantic accomplishment, and I can't give credit enough to the logisticians and the transporters who were able to pull this off. . . . And of course, great credit goes to the commanders of these units who were able to maneuver their forces out there and put them into position.[20]

It has been said that when it comes to strategy the amateurs talk tactics while the professionals talk logistics. General Schwarzkopf was a professional.

NOTES

1. William E. DePuy, "FM 100-5 Revisited," *Army* (November 1980), p. 17.

2. FM 100-1, *The Army* (Washington, D.C.: Department of the Army, 1986), pp. 15–16.

3. DePuy, "FM 100-5 Revisited," p. 15.

4. Henry Kissinger, *White House Years* (Boston, Mass.: Little, Brown & Company, 1979), p. 64.

5. Harry G. Summers, Jr., "U.S. Armed Forces in Europe," in Lewis H. Gann, ed., *The Defense of Western Europe* (London: Croom Helm, 1987), p. 294.

6. Alain C. Enthoven and K. Wayne Smith. *How Much Is Enough: Shaping the Defense Program 1961–1969* (New York: Harper & Row, 1971).

7. Robert W. Komer, *Bureaucracy Does Its Thing: Institutional Constraints on US GVN Performance in Vietnam* (Santa Monica, Calif.: Rand Corporation, 1972), pp. 75–84.

8. The author was a student in the 1967–68 U.S. Army Command and General Staff College class and subsequently taught national strategy there from 1968 to 1971.

9. George Bush, the White House (Washington, D.C., November 8, 1990).

10. Joseph P. Englehardt, *Desert Shield and Desert Storm: A Chronology and Troop List for the 1990–1991 Persian Gulf Crisis* (Carlisle Barracks, Pa.: Strategic Studies Institute, U.S. Army War College, 1991), pp. 5–7. Also "The Forces," *U.S. Naval Institute Proceedings* (January 1991), pp. 83–84.

11. Colin L. Powell, *Triumph in the Desert,* ed. Ray Cave and Pat Ryan (New York: Random House, 1991), p. vii.

12. FM 100-1, *The Army* (1986), p. 16.

13. See Harry G. Summers, Jr., "MATS (Military Air Transport Service)" and "MSTS (Military Sea Transport Service), *Korean War Almanac* (New York: Facts on File, 1990), pp. 178–79, 191–93, and "Military Airlift Command" and "Military Sealift Command," *Vietnam War Almanac* (New York: Facts on File, 1985), pp. 248–50.

14. H. Norman Schwarzkopf, "Central Command: On

the Middle East Hot Seat,'' *Defense Issues,* vol. 5, no. 18 (February 8, 1990), p. 1.

15. Sam McGowan, ''Flying Gas Tanks,'' *Vietnam* (October 1991), pp. 10, 54, 56.

16. TRANSCOM statistics provided by Major Jim Bates, USAF, Public Affairs Office, Military Airlift Command, Scott Air Force Base, Illinois (March 12, 1991).

17. H. Norman Schwarzkopf, ''A Tribute to the Navy-Marine Corps Team,'' *U.S. Naval Institute Proceedings,* vol. 118 (August 1991), p. 44.

18. Gilbert S. Harper, ''The Logistics Challenge of Desert Storm,'' *The Retired Officer Magazine* (July 1991), pp. 31–36.

19. Carl von Clausewitz, *On War,* trans. and ed. Michael Howard and Peter Paret (Princeton, N.J.: Princeton University Press, 1976), p. 85.

20. ''Schwarzkopf: Strategy Behind Desert Storm,'' *The Washington Post* (February 28, 1991), p. A5.

13

Security, Surprise, and Simplicity

I think this is one of the most important parts of
the entire briefing. . . . As you know, very early
on, we took out the Iraqi air force . . . [and] for
all intents and purposes, we took out his ability
to see what we were doing down here in Saudi
Arabia. Once we had taken out his eyes, we did
what could best be described as the Hail Mary
play. . . . a massive movement of troops all the
way out to the west, to the extreme west, because we knew he was still fixed in this area with
the vast majority of his forces, and once the air
campaign started, he would be incapable of
moving out to counter this move, even if he
knew we made it.

General H. Norman Schwarzkopf
press briefing (February 27, 1991)[1]

Security and Surprise

At their best, the principles of war work in harmony
with each other. General Schwarzkopf's ability to take
offensive action, to *mass,* and to *maneuver* was made
possible by the application of the principles of *security*
and *surprise.*

"Three sweeping allied deceptions—two by land

and one by sea—transformed the ground war against Iraq from the 'mother of all battles' to the mother of all maneuvers,'' read a front-page analysis in *The Washington Post*. ''A series of amphibious feints by Marines afloat . . . and a staggering westward migration of two Army combat corps'' combined with a shift of ''Marine ground divisions in a leapfrogging dash . . . westward along Kuwait's southern border to its center'' was ''the first major test—and, officials said, a resounding vindication—of [an AirLand Battle] doctrine intended for use against the Soviet Union in Europe.''[2]

The allies were able to achieve operational and tactical *surprise* (''strike the enemy at a time or place, or in a manner, for which he is unprepared'') because in the main they had been able to enforce its reciprocal, operational, and tactical *security* (''never permit the enemy to acquire an unexpected advantage''). ''Security reduces friendly vulnerability to hostile acts, influence or surprise,'' says FM 100-1, *The Army*. ''Factors contributing to surprise include . . . deception operations . . . and operations security.''[3]

The most potentially damaging breach of security during the entire war was a February 17, 1991, front-page *New York Times* story by Michael R. Gordon, filed from Washington and therefore not subject to security review. It detailed the ''Hail Mary'' maneuver, complete with diagram, six days before the troops jumped off on the attack.[4] It could have been their death warrant.

But the Iraqis were still caught by surprise. Perhaps their intelligence was so poor that they were unaware of the story. Perhaps they saw it as an allied deception. But even if they had read and believed it, the allies still had the advantage of surprise. As FM 100-1 states, ''It is not essential that the enemy be taken unaware, but only that he become aware too late to react effectively." And as General Schwarzkopf said, "once the air campaign started, he would be incapable of moving out to counter [the allied shift to the west in preparation for a flank attack] even if he knew we made it."

Strategic Surprise

Even before the term became popular, surprise was considered a "force multiplier." As Clausewitz noted, "Whenever it is achieved on a grand scale, it confuses the enemy and lowers his morale; many examples, great and small, show how this in turn multiplies the results."

That's why, he said, "the principle is highly attractive in theory." But, Clausewitz went on to say, "basically surprise is a tactical device. . . . Preparation for war usually takes months. . . . It is very rare therefore that one state surpasses another, either by an attack or by preparations for war."[5]

Over a century later, in his 1938 treatise on surprise, German general Waldemar Erfurth agreed. "The history of modern war shows that the chances of strategic surprise are small indeed. The question might therefore be asked whether . . . strategic surprises are still possible at all. . . . A great time-lag between the conception of a plan and its execution is unavoidable. This time-lag must affect secrecy. . . . Strategic surprise, therefore in the 20th century [is] the most difficult military undertaking."[6]

This conventional wisdom was reflected in U.S. Army doctrine, which also agreed that strategic surprise was difficult to achieve. "Rapid advances in strategic surveillance technology," states FM 100-1, "make it increasingly more difficult to mask mobilization or movement of manpower and equipment."[7] But the conventional wisdom was wrong.

Three of our last four wars began with an enemy

surprise attack—the December 7, 1941, Japanese attack on Pearl Harbor; the June 27, 1950, North Korean attack on South Korea; and the August 2, 1990, Iraqi attack on Kuwait. Not only were we surprised by the North Korean invasion of South Korea, but also five months later we were surprised again by the Chinese intervention in the war. And in the third war, an enemy operational-level surprise attack, the Tet offensive of 1968, had major strategic implications.

Directly contradicting Erfurth's belief that strategic surprise in the twentieth century was "the most difficult military undertaking," the Israeli National Defense College's Ephraim Kam argues that "strategic surprise did not become a common strategy until recent times. . . . By the beginning of the twentieth century a combination of developments—improvements in communications, transportation and weapons systems, including the use of tanks and airpower; new bureaucratic structures and advanced procedures for systematic problem solving—had altered the nature of war. The resulting increase in opportunities for strategic surprise overshadowed a parallel significant improvement in the collection of information."[8]

If history is any guide, Kam appears to have the better of the argument. But surprise attack is not an end in itself. "If we surprise the enemy with faulty measures, we may not benefit at all," warned Clausewitz, "but instead suffer sharp reverses."[9]

That was certainly the end result of the Japanese attack on Pearl Harbor, the North Korean attack on South Korea, and the Iraqi attack on Kuwait. And it was partially true in Vietnam following the 1968 Tet offensive. In an observation "which goes to the heart of the matter," Clausewitz noted that "only the commander who imposes his will can take the enemy by surprise."[10]

A Matter of Will

In every case save one it was the American will that prevailed and the enemy will that was ultimately broken. "The worse the situation is, the better it may turn out," Clausewitz observed. The attacks on Pearl Harbor, on South Korea, and on Kuwait did not break American will. They energized it.

And on the Tet 1968 battlefield, General William C. Westmoreland's will prevailed as well. The Viet Cong guerrilla and North Vietnamese Army 1968 Tet offensive turned out to be a resounding tactical and operational defeat. But at the strategic level they scored what proved to be a decisive political victory.

To their great good fortune, they had inadvertently struck two vital American centers of gravity—what Clausewitz called "the hub of all power and movement on which everything depends." Not capable of destroying the American Army in the field, seizing U.S. territory, or occupying the U.S. capital—the traditional tangible centers of gravity—they concentrated their attention on the lesser-known intangible centers instead.

These include, Clausewitz said, "the community of interest [among alliances] . . . the personalities of the leaders and public opinion."[11] Coming as it did in the wake of assurances that there was "light at the end of the tunnel," the Tet offensive confirmed the American public's suspicion that the government did not know what it was doing. Worse, as Peter Braestrup noted in his landmark work on American reaction to that offensive, "it seems that President Johnson was to some degree 'psychologically defeated' by the . . . onslaught on the cities of Vietnam."[12]

There is an American tendency to see war in terms of guns, ships, tanks, planes, and the like. But as Clausewitz pointed out, "When we speak of destroying the enemy's forces we must emphasize that nothing obliges us to limit this idea to physical forces; the moral element must also be considered."[13]

When President Johnson's will was broken, the war was over. All that remained was getting out as gracefully as possible. But America's military involvement ended on a prophetic note.

In May 1972, in a prelude to the "Christmas bombing" that December that many claim brought North Vietnam back to the negotiating table and led to the January 1973 Paris Peace Accords, President Richard M. Nixon emphasized, "We have the power to destroy [North Vietnamese] war-making capacity. The only question is whether we have the *will* to use that power. What distinguishes me from Johnson is that I have the *will* in spades."[14]

Surprise in the Desert

And so did President George Bush almost twenty years later. The greatest strategic surprise of the Persian Gulf war was not Saddam Hussein's surprise attack on Kuwait. It was President Bush's totally unexpected reaction to that attack.

The widely shared perception, at home and abroad, was that Bush was "the wimp in the White House." That reputation had been allayed somewhat by his forceful, if belated, actions against Panama in December 1989, when Operation Just Cause deposed Panamanian strongman Manuel Noriega.

But Bush's faintheartedness in the Higgins affair some five months earlier and his attempts at appeasement on the very eve of the Iraqi attack had evidently convinced Saddam Hussein that the worst he had to fear from the United States was not bombs but bombast. And at first, according to Bob Woodward's account of behind-the-scenes activities in the earlier days of the crisis, it appeared that Hussein had figured correctly.

"We're not discussing intervention," Bush told reporters the day after the Iraqi invasion. "I'm not contemplating such action," he said in response to questions asking if he planned to send troops.[15] At the National Security Council meeting that followed the press interviews, "[JCS chairman General Colin] Powell had watched Bush carefully, and he did not think it was at all clear what the President was going to do or whether he would accept the loss of Kuwait."[16]

That soon changed. "I view very seriously our determination to reverse this aggression," President Bush told reporters on August 5, 1991. "This will not stand, this aggression against Kuwait." The U.S. decision to intervene had been made. "This angry statement was much more than Powell had expected," Woodward reports. "Powell marveled at the distance Bush had travelled in three days. To Powell, it was almost as if the president had six-shooters in both hands and he was blazing away."[17]

It proved to be an apt analogy, as Saddam Hussein found to his surprise and indignation on January 16, 1991, as bombs rained down on Baghdad. "What's striking about Saddam's indignation is its sincerity," wrote *The New Republic*'s Fred Barnes in a particularly trenchant analysis of strategic surprise. "He actually thought Bush was going to attack only Iraqi forces in Kuwait. Baghdad and the rest of Iraq would be safe, like China north of the Yalu in the Korean war.

"Saddam's problem was that he thinks the United States (and thus Bush) is feckless," Barnes said. "Saddam's biggest blunder was reckoning that Bush would not go to war." But even then, "Saddam figured Bush wouldn't be bold enough to hit military-related sites in Baghdad."[18]

He was wrong on all counts. Not only did the United States achieve strategic surprise, it achieved operational and tactical surprise as well. It was one of the greatest deception operations in the history of warfare.

The Media as Deceiver

Paradoxically, *lack* of strategic security—open media discussion of war plans, strategic intentions, and the like—have tended to facilitate strategic surprise. "This was a stupendous misreading of Bush," says Barnes. "OK, so Bush had trouble fathoming Saddam, and the Arab mind, etc. But that failure is small compared with Saddam's boneheadedness about Bush. At every juncture in the Persian Gulf war, Saddam sold Bush short. Maybe he'd read some of the wimp stories in the American press."[19]

Barnes was no doubt being facetious, but there was more truth there than he may have realized. The military tends to see the media as jeopardizing security. "This problem [of achieving strategic surprise] is compounded in an open society such as the United States, where freedom of the press is ensured," says FM 100-1.[20] But in fact it may be its greatest ally.

Newspaper accounts of Woodrow Wilson's 1916 campaign promises not to send American boys to fight in World War I and stories about U.S. pacifism must have misled imperial Germany and the Central Powers to believe that the United States would stay out of the war. And press and radio accounts of Franklin Roosevelt's similar promises during his 1940 reelection campaign, as well as stories on American isolationism, draft resistance, and antiwar protests, including running the ROTC off college campuses, encouraged Nazi Germany and imperial Japan to believe America would not fight.

In the Korean war, it was obvious that Kim Il Sung and his backers in Moscow and Peking had misread media accounts of Harry Truman's drastic cuts in the defense budget and the partisan wrangling over U.S. Asian policy.

And as Dave R. Palmer points out in his analysis of the Vietnam war, the North Vietnamese belief that the United States would not intervene was based on what appeared to be valid assumptions. In August 1964, for example, "President Johnson had announced publicly that he would not consider bombing North Vietnam or 'committing American boys to fight a war that I think ought to be fought by the boys of Asia to protect their own land.' "[21]

When the Rolling Thunder air campaign against North Vietnam began in March 1965, and U.S. ground combat troops began streaming ashore, "the leaders in Hanoi were dumbstruck. . . . Consternation and disbelief were their initial reaction."[22] And their ability to predict U.S. actions did not improve over time. In the fall of 1972, they believed from all they read and heard that President Richard Nixon was paralyzed by the antiwar movement. But as wave after wave of B-52 bombers appeared over Hanoi on December 18, 1972, they realized that once again they had been misled.

"All I know is what I read in the newspapers," may have been a great slogan for Will Rogers. But the American media provide a shaky foundation upon which to base predictions on whether the United States will react to foreign provocations.

Security and the News Media

Ironically, the news media today generally look upon the Vietnam war as the good old days, where they had total access and near total freedom of coverage.

Within the military, however, there are still lingering suspicions that the media were somehow responsible for the loss of the war.

It is a dumb notion. While the media are good at showing the cost of war—although not nearly as good as they would have you believe—that cost only has meaning in relationship to the value of the war as determined by the objectives set by the government.

Not media portrayals of the cost of war, but the government's failure to establish those objectives, and hence fix the value of the war, was the primary cause of lack of public support. In fact, although television was to claim that they brought the horrors of war into the living room, postwar analysis of TV footage revealed that less than 3 percent—seventy-six of twenty-three hundred stories from 1965 to 1970—contained scenes of heavy combat with dead or wounded shown on the screen.[23]

And they did not jeopardize security, either. As Barry Zorthian, the head of JUSPAO (the Joint U.S. Public Affairs Office in Saigon responsible for overseeing the media) observed, "In the four years (1964–1968) that I was in Vietnam with some 2,000 correspondents accredited. . . . we had only four or five cases of security violations . . . of tactical military information.

"There was only once or twice that ground rules were deliberately challenged, and the correspondent's credentials were immediately lifted."[24] Zorthian's comments were corroborated by the official Army history of the war, which acknowledged that "a system of voluntary guidelines . . . largely eliminated security problems." It was "major flaws in the administration's strategy" that poisoned the well:

Believing that the press had in most cases supported official policies in earlier American wars, especially

World War II, many members of the military expected
similar support in Vietnam. When the contradictions
engendered by President Johnson's strategy of limited
war led instead to a more critical attitude, the military
tended increasingly to blame the press for the credibility
problems they experienced, accusing television news in
particular of turning the American public against the
war.[25]

This antagonism came to a head in the 1983 Grenada
crisis, when the press was initially barred from the
battlefield. As a result of the furor, General John W.
Vessey, Jr., the chairman of the Joint Chiefs of Staff,
convened a panel, chaired by Major General Winant
Sidle, the former Chief of Information for U.S. Military Assistance Command Vietnam, to enquire into
military-media relations. Among its recommendations
was planned-for news media pooling to furnish the
media early access to an operation, with the understanding that pools would be terminated as soon as
possible and full coverage allowed. Another recommendation was the provision of military "escorts" to
"assist correspondents in covering the operations ad-
equately."[26]

The Media and the Persian Gulf War

These provisions were incorporated into CENTCOM's
*Operation Desert Shield Ground Rules/Guidelines for
News Media,* which correspondents had to agree to
abide by:

A public affairs escort may be required because of
security, safety, and mission requirements as determined
by the host commander. . . .

Prior to or upon commencement of hostilities, media
pools will be established to provide initial combat cov-

erage of U.S. forces. . . . News media personnel who are
not members of the official CENTCOM media pools will
not be permitted into forward areas. Reporters are
strongly discouraged from attempting to link up on their
own with combat units. U.S. commanders will maintain
extremely tight security throughout the operational area
and will exclude from the area of operation all unauthor-
ized individuals.[27]

These guidelines turned out to be one of the most
controversial aspects of the war. Instead of a temporary measure, as envisioned by the Sidle panel, media
pools (whose membership was determined by the media themselves) remained in effect the entire time. And
the "escorts," instead of assisting correspondents,
served in many cases to limit and deny their access.[28]

These restrictions were undeniably effective. Tight
security measures aided deception of the enemy and
facilitated operational and tactical surprise. But they
came at a price. Rear Admiral Riley D. Mixson, commander of Carrier Group 2 in the Red Sea, noted that
although the Navy flew 23 percent of the war's combat
missions, that fact was almost unknown. The reason?
"We tend to avoid the press," he said.[29]

As the Navy's chief of information, Rear Admiral
Brent Baker, pointed out, "A Gallup public opinion
poll in early 1991 showed 85% of the public had a high
level of confidence in the military as an institution
after Desert Shield/Storm, the highest public confidence rating in our history. Where did the public get
its perception of the military's professionalism? They
got it from news media reports."[30]

In its discussion of the principle of security in the
1981 edition, FM 100-1 warned that "at the *strategic
level* . . . implementation of . . . security measures
must be balanced against the need to prevent them
from severing the link between the American people

and its Army."[31] Noticeably, that caveat dropped out of the 1986 edition, which was in force during the Gulf war.

Its continued absence could permit the idea to flourish that if security worked so well this time, even more media restrictions should be applied the next time around. That could be disastrous. To the degree that it jeopardizes public support, total security may be worse than no security at all.

Simplicity

"If one has never personally experienced war," Clausewitz said, "everything looks simple; the knowledge required does not look remarkable, the strategic options are so obvious that by comparison the simplest problem of higher mathematics has an impressive scientific dignity."

But, as he went on to say, "Everything about war is very simple, but the simplest thing is difficult."[32] The trick is to take this difficulty and translate it into terms as simple as it appears on the surface. That's what the principle of simplicity ("Prepare clear, uncomplicated plans and clear, concise orders to ensure thorough understanding") is all about.

A prime example is General H. Norman Schwarzkopf's explanation of his plans and strategies for the conduct of the Persian Gulf war, reprinted as an appendix to this work. It skillfully translates the enormous difficulties and complexities of the campaign into simple terms understandable not only to military professionals but to civilian laymen as well, especially including those watching around the world whose sons' and daughters' lives had been at risk.

And the principle of simplicity serves another function as well. It is a kind of litmus test against which the other principles can be measured. As we have seen, the objective for the Persian Gulf war was sim- plicity itself compared to the contradictory objectives that obfuscated the Vietnam war. And the principles of the offensive, mass, economy of force, and maneu- ver had been freed of their Cold War convolutions and could be applied in the Gulf with a clarity not possible in Korea and Vietnam. As will be seen in the following chapter, the application of simplicity to the military chain of command would also reap major benefits on the Persian Gulf battlefield.

N O T E S

1. H. Norman Schwarzkopf, "Schwarzkopf: Strategy Behind Desert Storm," *The Washington Post* (February 28, 1991), p. A35.

2. Barton Gellman, "Deceptions Gave Allies Fast Vic- tory," *The Washington Post* (February 28, 1991), p. 1.

3. FM 100-1, *The Army* (Washington, D.C.: Department of the Army, 1986), pp. 16–17.

4. Michael R. Gordon, "Ground Strategy: Focus on Rear Line, How U.S. Intends to Cut Off Iraq's Army and 'Kill It,' " *The New York Times* (February 17, 1991), pp. 1, 6.

5. Carl von Clausewitz. *On War*, trans. and ed. Michael Howard and Peter Paret (Princeton, N.J.: Princeton Univer- sity Press, 1976), pp. 198–99.

6. Waldemar Erfurth, *Surprise*, trans. Stefan T. Possony and Daniel Vilfroy (Harrisburg, Pa.: Military Service Pub- lishing Company, 1943), pp. 31, 39–40.

7. FM 100-1, *The Army* (1986), p. 17.

8. Ephraim Kam, *Surprise Attack: The Victim's Per- spective* (Cambridge, Mass.: Harvard University Press, 1988), pp. 1–2.

9. Clausewitz, *On War*, pp. 200–201.

10. Ibid.

11. Ibid., pp. 595–96.

12. Peter Braestrup, *The Big Story: How the American Press and TV Reported and Interpreted the Crisis of Tet 68*

in Vietnam and Washington (New Haven, Conn.: Yale University Press, 1978), p. 471.

13. Clausewitz, *On War*, p. 97.

14. Henry Kissinger, *White House Years* (Boston, Mass.: Little, Brown & Company, 1979), p. 1199.

15. Bob Woodward, *The Commanders*, (New York: Simon & Schuster, 1991), p. 225.

16. Ibid., p. 230.

17. Ibid., pp. 260–61.

18. Fred Barnes, "The Unwimp," *The New Republic* (March 18, 1991), pp. 17–18.

19. Ibid.

20. FM 100-1, *The Army* (Washington, D.C.: Department of the Army, 1986), p. 17.

21. Dave R. Palmer, *Summons of the Trumpet: U.S.-Vietnam in Perspective* (Novato, Calif.: Presidio Press, 1978), p. 69.

22. Ibid., p. 84.

23. Lawrence W. Lichty, "Comments on the Influence of Television on Public Opinion," in *Vietnam as History*, ed. Peter Braestrup (Washington, D.C.: University Press of America, 1984), p. 158.

24. *Vietnam: 10 Years Later* (Fort Benjamin Harrison, Ind.: Defense Information School, 1984), p. 52.

25. William M. Hammond, *Public Affairs: The Military and the Media 1962–1968* (Washington, D.C.: U.S. Government Printing Office, 1988), p. 387.

26. "The Report of the Sidle Panel," Appendix to *Battle Lines: Report of the Twentieth-Century Fund Task Force on the Military and the Media*, ed. by Peter Braestrup, (New York: Priority Press Publications, 1985), pp. 169–75. *Battle Lines* provides an excellent overview of military-media relations from World War II through Grenada. See also Harry G. Summers, Jr., "Western Media and Recent Wars," *Military Review* (May 1986).

27. *Operation Desert Shield Ground Rules/Guidelines for News Media*, U.S. Central Command (January 14, 1991).

28. See, for example, Malcolm W. Browne, "The Military vs. The Press," *New York Times Magazine* (March 3, 1991). p. 26. See also 101st Cong., 2nd sess., Senate Hear-

ings Before the Committee on Governmental Affairs, *Pentagon Rules Governing Media Access to the Persian Gulf War* (Washington, D.C.: U.S. Government Printing Office, 1991). For the Pentagon viewpoint, see Pete Williams, "The Press and the Persian Gulf War," *Parameters: U.S. Army War College Quarterly*, vol. xxi, no. 3, Autumn 1991, pp. 2–9.

29. Riley D. Mixon, "Where We Must Do Better," *U.S. Naval Institute Proceedings* (August 1991), pp. 38–39.

30. Brent Baker, "Last One in the Pool . . . ," *U.S. Naval Institute Proceedings* (August 1991), p. 71.

31. FM 100-1, *The Army* (Washington, D.C.: Department of the Army, 1981), p. 16.

32. Clausewitz, *On War*, p. 199.

14

Unity of Command and Coalition Warfare

The courage and the success of the RAF pilots, of the Kuwaiti, Saudi, French, the Canadians, Italians, the pilots of Qatar and Bahrain, all are proof that for the first time since World War II, the international community is united. The leadership of the United Nations, once only a hoped-for ideal, is now confirming its founders' vision. . . .

President George Bush
State of the Union address (January 29, 1991)[1]

Coalition Warfare and the Soviet Union

"The first time since World War II." That phrase was the leitmotiv of the Persian Gulf war. The reason, as President Bush said, was that for the first time since World War II the international community was united. More specifically, for the first time since that war the United States and the USSR were united in a common cause. And that made all the difference in the world.

In a real sense the war was decided on the very day it began. On August 2, 1990, the Soviet Union voted with the United States in the U.N. Security Council to condemn Iraqi aggression and to demand their immediate withdrawal from Kuwait. That vote set the stage for all that followed.

"You have launched what history will judge as one of the most important deployments of allied power since 1945," said President Bush to the 1st Marine Division in Saudi Arabia in November 1990. "To force Iraq to comply, we and our allies have forged a strong diplomatic, economic and military strategy."[2]

That strategy could have been killed aborning by a Soviet veto in the U.N. Security Council. Such a veto would have been a certainty during the Cold War, especially since Iraq had long been an ally of the Soviet Union. But times had changed. Thanks to the efforts of Secretary of State James Baker and Thomas Pickering, the U.S. ambassador to the United Nations, Saddam Hussein was deprived of his Soviet protector.

Baker and Pickering were thus the architects of victory as much as Cheney and Schwarzkopf, for they, too, had struck at a center of gravity. As the Vietnam war had proved, it was one even more critical than defeat of the Iraqi military in battle. "In small countries that rely on large ones," said Clausewitz in his definition of centers of gravity—*the hub of all power and movement, on which everything depends*—"it is the army of their protector. Among alliances it is the community of interest."[3]

Convinced that in the post-Cold War world their long-term interests were with the United States, not with Iraq, the Soviets cast their lot—and their votes in the U.N. Security Council—with the United States. As the Soviet-Iraqi community of interest evaporated, Saddam Hussein found himself no longer under the protective shield of Soviet nuclear power; cut off from the primary source of new arms and equipment to replace battlefield losses; and, more critically, cut off from supply of spare parts for the arms and equipment already on hand. As long as the U.S.–Soviet alliance held, the end for Iraq was inevitable.

But, once forged, the U.S. unwritten alliance with the Soviet Union itself became a center of gravity. "Political unity is a matter of degree," said Clausewitz. "The question is then whether each state is pursuing an independent interest and has its own independent means of doing so, or whether the interests and forces of most of the allies are subordinate to those of the leader."[4] Subordinating themselves to the United States was uncomfortable for the Soviet Union, and they soon became restive.

On February 9, 1990, after the air war began, Soviet president Mikhail Gorbachev announced that those attacks threatened to exceed the mandate of the United Nations and that he was sending his personal envoy, Yevgeny M. Primakov, to Baghdad. A Soviet peace proposal ensued, and on February 21, 1990, Iraqi foreign minister Tariq Aziz arrived in Moscow with Saddam Hussein's acceptance of that proposal.

Some called it a "nightmare scenario." Iraq had been presented with a strategic vulnerability they were quick to exploit. Not only was the U.S. alliance with the Soviet Union in jeopardy, so was the war itself. "The Soviet-brokered plan announced last night for Iraqi withdrawal from Kuwait has put the United States and its coalition partners in a difficult bind and finally realized the fears of many policy-makers about a proposed 'partial solution' that could stall the military campaign short of allied objectives," noted *The Washington Post*.

"Military planners believe that it will be difficult for coalition forces to remain in their current state of high readiness for a ground assault for very long. At the same time, if the momentum of the military campaign is broken now, the alliance will find it hard to resume hostilities later should Iraq stall or make new demands or go back on its word."[5]

Caught on the horns of a dilemma—alienating the Soviet Union on one hand and jeopardizing his war aims on the other—President Bush disengaged himself from the first horn with a thirty-three-minute telephone call with President Gorbachev. The Soviets were mollified and the alliance endured. Soviet-American interests had again proved paramount.

And instead of a battlefield cease-fire, as the Iraqis had hoped, that very day Bush demolished the other horn with a twenty-four-hour ultimatum for immediate and unconditional Iraqi withdrawal from Kuwait. When that ultimatum was rejected, he ordered the ground war to begin. Once more the initiative was with the United States, and one hundred hours later it was all over. As Clausewitz had said, no matter what the enemy's center of gravity might be, "the defeat and destruction of his fighting forces remain the best way to begin."[6]

The Arab Coalition

As improbable as an alliance between the United States and the Soviet Union might have seemed to Saddam Hussein, even more unlikely was the emergence of an Arab coalition arrayed against him. Saddam Hussein knew, and the United States knew as well, that without such a coalition—without the authority to base troops and aircraft on the Arabian Peninsula—it would be almost impossible for the United States to mount an effective military operation to counter the Iraqi invasion of Kuwait.

As Bob Woodward relates, one of President Bush's first acts before he decided to intervene was to talk with Saudi Arabia's King Fahd ibn Abdul Aziz, and then with King Hussein of Jordan and President Hosni

Mubarak of Egypt, who were then meeting together in Alexandria. On August 3, 1990, Bush met with Saudi Arabia's ambassador to the United States, Prince Bandar bin Sultan.

America's reputation had preceded it: "To be an enemy of the United States can be uncomfortable," Senator Daniel Patrick Moynahan had reputedly said after the fall of Saigon, "but to be a friend of the United States can be fatal." Prince Bandar's major concern was, "Do you guys have the guts or don't you? 'We don't want you to put out a hand and then pull it back, and leave us with this guy on our border twice as mad as he is now.' "

For his part, Bush was "upset that Kuwait had not asked for help from the U.S. until apparently a half hour or a few minutes before Iraq invaded" and feared the Saudis would do the same.

" 'I give my word of honor,' Bush finally told Bandar. 'I will see this through with you.' Bandar felt his hair stand up. The President of the United States had just put his personal honor on the line."[7] On August 6, 1990, Secretary of Defense Dick Cheney and CENTCOM commander General H. Norman Schwarzkopf arrived in Saudi Arabia at the president's behest to meet with King Fahd and gain his approval for U.S. forward deployments.

"Following these meetings," said President Bush in an address to the nation on August 8, 1991, "the Saudi government requested our help, and I responded to that request by ordering U.S. air and ground forces to deploy to the kingdom of Saudi Arabia. . . . U.S. forces will work together with those of Saudi Arabia and other nations to preserve the integrity of Saudi Arabia and to deter further Iraqi aggression. . . ."

And while military defensive forces moved into position, the U.S. diplomatic offensive went into high gear. "Secretary of Defense Cheney has just returned from valuable consultations with President [Hosni] Mubarek of Egypt and King Hassan of Morocco,'' the president said. ''Secretary of State Baker has consulted with his counterparts in many nations, including the Soviet Union. And today he heads for Europe to consult with President [Turgut] Ozal of Turkey, a staunch friend of the United States. And he'll then consult with the NATO foreign ministers.''[8]

The diplomatic offensive was a resounding success, isolating Saddam Hussein almost entirely from the world community. Not only did the majority of the Arab world condemn his aggression, they also backed up their words with military forces. In addition to the considerable combat aircraft from Saudi Arabia and the Gulf states, Saudi lieutenant general Prince Khalid bin Sultan's Joint Arab Islamic Command included the eight-plus armored and mechanized brigades of the Saudi Army and the two mechanized brigades of the Saudi National Guard; several surviving brigades of the Kuwaiti Army; and the Peninsula Shield Force with combat units from Bahrain, Oman, Qatar, and the United Arab Republic.

From North Africa came the 6th Moroccan Mechanized Battalion; and, second in size only to the U.S. and Saudi Arabian forces, the Egyptian II Corps, with its 3rd Mechanized Division and 4th Armored Division. One of the big surprises was the inclusion of Syria, a close ally of the Soviet Union, in the Arab coalition. Damascus and Riyadh had been at opposite poles in the Arab world for decades, and Syria had been on America's list of nations that supported international terrorism. But the strategic environment had changed, and the Syrian 9th Armored Division and 45th Commando Brigade were arrayed against Iraq.

Other non-Arab Islamic nations also provided combat forces, including Afghani Mujaheddins, the 1st East Bengal Infantry Battalion from Bangladesh, the

Pakistani 7th Armored Brigade, and an infantry battalion from Niger and Senegal.[9]

Coalition Cohesion

"I can't prove it," Fred Barnes wrote in *The New Republic,* "but my assumption is that Saddam thought breaking the coalition would be easy. Attack Israel, prompt a retaliation, and Bush wouldn't be able to hold Arab countries in the alliance." But when Saddam Hussein launched Scud missiles at Israel, "Bush changed his war plans to keep Israel from retaliating. . . . American warplanes, diverted from other missions to knock out Scud launchers, notched some successes. Bush wooed Israeli Prime Minister Yitzhak Shamir in three phone calls. And Israel didn't retaliate."[10]

Barnes, like Saddam Hussein, gives too much credit to Israel. It was not Israeli forbearance, admirable as it was, that held the coalition together. Even if Israel had retaliated, the alliance would have endured. Egypt and Syria intimated as much at the time when they acknowledged the right of a state to protect itself.

The reason it endured was rooted in the reason it came together in the first place. "War is not a matter of senseless passion," said Clausewitz, "but is controlled by its political object."[11] Countering Saddam Hussein's aggression brought the coalition together; countering Saddam Hussein's aggression was the adhesive that held it together. Just as in World War II the menace of Adolf Hitler held the United States and the Soviet Union together in an unholy alliance, so the menace of Saddam Hussein held the Arab coalition together in the Persian Gulf war.

Other Coalition Forces

The Soviet alliance and the Arab coalition were essential political foundations for the conduct of the war. If either had collapsed, the United States would have been undone. But they were not the only coalition partners.

As usual, Australia and New Zealand sent ships and planes to help its American ally, and for the first time since the Korean war, West European allies provided bases and military forces to assist the United States on the battlefield.

Turkey provided vital airfields, and British, French, Canadian, and Italian aircraft took part in the initial air assault. The United Kingdom, Canada, France, Belgium, the Netherlands, Denmark, Norway, Italy, Spain, and Greece provided warships to patrol the Gulf and enforce the U.N. sanctions. On the ground France dispatched its Daguet Division, essentially the 6th Light Armored Division reinforced, and the United Kingdom its 1st Armored Division.[12]

All in all some forty nations joined together in opposing Saddam Hussein, including former Warsaw Pact adversaries such as Czechoslovakia, Hungary, and Rumania, who provided chemical warfare experts. It was the largest allied coalition since World War II. The over 200,000 friendly forces in the Gulf (including Arab coalition forces) far exceeded the 39,000-man U.N. forces in Korea and the 68,889 Free World Military Force sent to help in Vietnam.

Combined Command Unity

"Who will command it?" That is the question posed by the final principle of war, *unity of command*. Given the numbers of nations involved and their delicate political sensitivities, it was obvious that the textbook answer—"For every objective, ensure unity of effort under one responsible commander"—could not apply to the entire Gulf command. Recognizing that fact, FM 100-1 states that while "vesting a single commander with the requisite authority over all forces" is the best way to do it, "coordination may be achieved by cooperation."[13]

In fact, that method has been the norm in operations involving combined (i.e., multinational) forces. In World War I, General John J. Pershing, the commander of the American Expeditionary Force, was adamant that U.S. forces, with minor exceptions, operate independently and serve only under U.S. commanders. And in World War II, just after Pearl Harbor, Great Britain and the United States established a combined military command, the Combined Chiefs of Staff, to shape their coalition strategy and conduct their coalition war effort.[14]

The Korean war was an exception, for there the United Nations created a "United Nations Command (UNC)"—in fact, General Douglas MacArthur's Far East Command under another name—for the conduct of the war, and all allied forces (including, at their request, the South Korean forces) were subordinated to that command.[15]

In the Vietnam war there was no such unified command. The COMUSMACV (commander, U.S. Military Assistance Command Vietnam), the senior U.S. military commander in Vietnam, commanded only U.S. military forces in-country and exercised no command over the armed forces of the Republic of Vietnam (ARVNAF), the two South Korean divisions and its Marine Brigade, the 1st Australian Task Force, or any other allied force. As General Maxwell D. Taylor, who had served as U.S. Eighth Army commander in the closing days of the Korean war, explained:

Many leading American officials, including some senior military officers, had thought from the beginning of the US troop build-up that General Westmoreland [the CO-MUSMACV from 1964 to 1968] should receive operational control over the South Vietnamese forces as the American Eighth Army commander had controlled the Korean forces from 1950 to 1953. However, in Korea the American commander was a representative of the United Nations, and he exercised operational control of all UN forces in that capacity.

In South Vietnam, no such UN authority existed and a demand for operational control by the Americans would be likely to raise serious resistance among the Vietnamese whose nationalist pride was as intense as their repugnance to the charge of being American puppets.

Westmoreland was firmly against such an action and strongly recommended that command relationships be regulated by the principle of cooperation and mutual support, a view which eventually prevailed.[16]

Although, like Korea, the allied deployment to the Persian Gulf had been under U.N. Security Council auspices, no U.N. command had been created, and Arab national pride was, if anything, even more intense than that of the South Vietnamese.

In an agreement reached by Secretary of State James Baker and King Fahd of Saudi Arabia on November 5, 1991, a system similar to the Combined Chiefs of Staff in World War II was created, this time at the operational rather than the strategic level of command. General H. Norman Schwarzkopf, the commander of all U.S. forces in the Gulf, would work in tandem with Saudi Lieutenant General Khalid bin Sultan, who commanded all Saudi and Arab forces there. All allied forces in the Gulf would be under one of these two headquarters. While Schwarzkopf and

Khalid were given authority over operational matters, the decision to go to war remained "at the highest political levels."[17]

Any doubts whether such a system would work were removed on the first day of the air war, when the strikes on Baghdad and across Iraq and Kuwait by combat aircraft of seven different national air forces were coordinated without a hitch. And thirty-nine days later the feat was duplicated when the allied armies jumped off on their attack. While there was no one single commander, there was no doubt there was unity of effort. That's what the principle of unity of command is all about.

Joint Command Unity

But while unity of effort was achieved at the combined coalition level through cooperation, at the joint or multiservice level at U.S. Central Command it was achieved the old-fashioned way: through assignment of "one responsible commander."

This was made possible by the restructuring of the U.S. military's command and control system in the mid-1980s by the Congress of the United States in legislation proposed by then senator Barry Goldwater and Representative Bill Nichols.

It was a restructuring long overdue, for the system had begun to come apart during the Korean war. Testifying before the Senate during the 1951 "Great Debate" on that war, Secretary of Defense George C. Marshall said that "it became apparent that General MacArthur had grown so far out of sympathy with the established policies of the United States that there was *grave doubt as to whether he could any longer be permitted to exercise the authority in making decisions that normal command functions would assign to a theater commander.*"[18]

Over thirty years later, in a conversation with MacArthur's successor, General Matthew B. Ridgway, those very words were recalled. "And from that time on," General Ridgway said, "no theater commander has ever again been able to exercise that authority in making decisions."[19]

That was certainly true in Vietnam, where there was a gross mismatch between the U.S. and enemy commanders. General Westmoreland was seen by many as the counterpart of North Vietnamese general Vo Nguyen Giap. But in fact it took at least five people in the U.S. chain of command to duplicate Giap, and Westmoreland was not even among them.

Giap was a deputy premier in the North Vietnamese government, a member of the Politburo, the minister of defense, and the commander in chief of the People's Army of Vietnam—the counterpart of the American vice president, national security adviser, secretary of defense, and chairman of the Joint Chiefs of Staff in Washington, and the commander in chief, Pacific Command (CINCPAC), in Honolulu, who was the U.S. theater commander. None was any closer than five thousand miles to the war.

Westmoreland was only the field commander in Vietnam. He had no control over air strikes against the Ho Chi Minh Trail, the enemy's main line of supply and communication, or over air attacks on North Vietnam. And he had no control over naval operations outside the territorial waters of South Vietnam. As he noted in his autobiography:

MACV functioned not directly under the Joint Chiefs of Staff in Washington but through CINCPAC [commander in chief, Pacific Command]. . . . What many failed to realize was that not I but [Admiral U. S. Grant Sharp in Honolulu] was the theater commander in the sense that General Eisenhower, for example, was the theater commander in World War II. My responsibilities and prerogatives were basically confined within the borders of South Vietnam.[20]

It was an inane way to run a war, and it reflected the near bankruptcy of the joint system created by the Defense Reorganization Act of 1947, as amended. The World War II Army-Navy-Air Force-Marine Corps unity of effort that legislation had sought to perpetuate at the national level had deteriorated.

Under Article I, Section 8 of the Constitution, the Congress has the power to "make rules for the government and regulation of the land and naval forces." And that's just what it did. The Goldwater-Nichols Department of Defense Reorganization Act of 1986 made several important changes in the military's national and theater-level organization for combat and chain of command.

It strengthened the role of the chairman of the Joint Chiefs of Staff (CJCS), making him the principal military adviser to the president, the National Security Council, and the secretary of defense. While continuing the de jure restriction that the CJCS cannot exercise military command over the armed forces, it substantially increased his clout by de facto putting him in the military chain of command by permitting the president to direct that communications from the combatant commands be transmitted through the CJCS and by allowing the secretary of defense to assign the CJCS responsibility for overseeing the activities of the combatant commands.

The reorganization act also strengthened the authority of the combatant command CINCs (commanders in chief) and greatly strengthened the joint system by making joint service (i.e., service on interservice staffs and in interservice assignments) a prerequisite for promotions and high-level assignments. After its enactment, Congressman Ike Skelton (D., Mo.), who was instrumental in its passage, held a series of hearings to ensure that the curriculum of the military's war and staff colleges reflected this joint orientation.[21]

The result was that when the Persian Gulf crisis erupted three years later, there was a pool of trained joint service staff officers on hand, and the military's chain of command had been purged of its arteriosclerosis. Authority flowed from President Bush to Secretary of Defense Cheney through General Powell, the CJCS, to General Schwarzkopf, the CINC of the U.S. Central Command in the Gulf. Unlike Westmoreland, this time the commander in the field truly had unity of command.

Schwarzkopf's ground component commander was the commanding general, Third Army. His air component commander was the commanding general, Ninth Air Force. His naval commander was the commander, Seventh Fleet, and his marine commander was the commanding general, I Marine Expeditionary Force. Like General Eisenhower in World War II, General Schwarzkopf was "permitted to exercise the authority in making decisions that normal command functions would assign to a theater commander."

But there were more than structural changes involved. By chance and by circumstance the right people were in the right place at the right time. President Bush, to everyone's amazement, turned out to be the best wartime commander in chief since Franklin D. Roosevelt in World War II. As Secretary of Defense Cheney had said, he was of the "Don't screw around school of military strategy" who believed in sending enough troops to do the job and not tieing the hands of the commander.

For the first time in years the phrase "national command authority" was not heard in Washington. A euphemism for whoever it was who was making the key decisions, the phrase was created to evade responsibility. But Bush seized responsibility. There was no doubt in anyone's mind who would make the decision to intervene, who would make the decision to begin the air war, who would make the decision to begin the ground war, and who would decide when to call it off. It was the president of the United States, George Herbert Walker Bush.

And Secretary of Defense Cheney proved to be a godsend, among the best secretaries of defense to occupy that position since its creation in 1947. By force of personality he was able to maintain firm control of the military while at the same time garnering maximum cooperation. He and General Powell, the chairman of the Joint Chiefs of Staff, worked together hand-in-glove like an Old Army company commander and first sergeant to guide, support, and control the leaders in the field.

For his part, General Powell reprised the role of General George Marshall and Admiral Ernest King in World War II, working closely with his civilian superiors and providing strategic direction to the field commander without attempting to micromanage the war. As a result of this unity of command General Schwarzkopf was able to play General Eisenhower. "Operation Desert Shield/Desert Storm was certainly the classic example of a multi-service operation," he later observed, "a truly joint operation."[22]

NOTES

1. George Bush, "Text of the State of the Union Address," *The Washington Post* (January 30, 1991), p. A14.

2. George Bush, "President Bush: An Unforgettable Visit," (remarks to the 1st Marine Division near Dhahran, Saudi Arabia, November 22, 1990) *Defense Issues,* vol. 5, no. 45 (1990), p. 2.

3. Carl von Clausewitz, *On War,* trans. and ed. Michael Howard and Peter Paret (Princeton, N.J.: Princeton University Press, 1976), pp. 595–96.

4. Ibid.

5. David Hoffman and Ann Devroy, "Soviet Plan Puts Allies in a Bind: Military Campaign Could Be Stalled," *The Washington Post* (February 22, 1991), p. 1.

6. Clausewitz, *On War,* p. 596.

7. Bob Woodward, *The Commanders* (New York: Simon & Schuster, 1991), pp. 232, 240–41.

8. George Bush, "America Will Stand By Her Friends" (address to the nation on August 8, 1990), *Defense Issues,* vol. 5, no. 32 (1990), p. 2.

9. "The Joint Arab Command" in Frank Chadwick and Matt Caffrey, *Gulf War Fact Book* (Bloomington, Ill.: GDW, Inc., 1991), pp. 62–63.

10. Fred Barnes, "The Unwimp," *The New Republic* (March 18, 1991), p. 18.

11. Clausewitz, *On War,* p. 92.

12. Joseph P. Englehardt, *Desert Shield and Desert Storm: A Chronology and Troop List for the 1990–1991 Persian Gulf Crisis* (Carlisle Barracks, Pa.: Strategic Studies Institute, U.S. Army War College, 1991), pp. 8–10.

13. FM 100-1, *The Army* (Washington, D.C.: Department of the Army, 1986), p. 16.

14. Russell F. Weigley, *The American Way of War: A History of U.S. Military Strategy and Policy* (New York: Macmillan Publishing Company, 1973), p. 318.

15. Harry G. Summers, Jr., "United Nations Command (UNC)," *Korean War Almanac* (New York: Facts on File, 1990), pp. 288–89.

16. Maxwell D. Taylor, *Swords and Plowshares* (New York: W. W. Norton & Company, 1972), p. 350.

17. David Hoffman, "Baker, Fahd Set Command Plan," *The Washington Post* (November 6, 1990), p. 1.

18. 82nd Cong., 1st sess., Senate Joint Committee on Armed Services and Foreign Relations, *Military Situation in the Far East,* Part 1 (Washington, D.C.: U.S. Government Printing Office, 1951), p. 325. Emphasis added.

19. Author's notes.

20. William C. Westmoreland, *A Soldier Reports* (Garden City, N.Y.: Doubleday & Company, 1976), pp. 75–76.

21. 99th Cong., 2nd sess., conference report, *Goldwater-Nichols Department of Defense Reorganization Act of 1986* (Washington, D.C.: U.S. Government Printing Office, 1986).

22. H. Norman Schwarzkopf, ''A Tribute to the Navy-Marine Corps Team,'' *U.S. Naval Institute Proceedings* (August 1991), p. 44.

Epilogue

The New World Order

> And when we [succeed in the Gulf] the world can . . . seize this opportunity to fulfill the long-held promise of a new world order where brutality will go unrewarded and aggression will meet collective resistance.
>
> Yes, the United States bears a major share of leadership in this effort. Among the nations of the world, only the United States of America has both the moral standing and the means to back it up. We are the only nation on this Earth that could assemble the forces of peace.
>
> President George Bush
> State of the Union address (January 29, 1991)[1]

The New World Order

President Bush called it a "new world order," but what makes that future a certainty is not so much the U.S. and allied success in the Persian Gulf in February 1991, but the West's far more significant success in the Cold War with the USSR.

Whether it will indeed be a world "where brutality will go unrewarded and aggression will meet collective resistance," however, is by no means a foregone conclusion. President Woodrow Wilson held out that same hope in the aftermath of the First World War, when he also proclaimed a new world order and championed the formation of the League of Nations to help bring it about. But, in part because of American unwillingness to participate in shaping such a new world, collective security never materialized, and the resulting "new world order" turned sinister indeed.

Instead of the benevolent world Wilson envisioned, it became a malevolent world shaped and defined by the rise of totalitarian Communist and fascist dictatorships. Most virulent and long-lasting of those dictatorships was Marxism-Leninism—i.e., "communism"—which gained total power in Russia in 1921.

Not counting the estimated fifteen million people who died in the 1917–1921 turmoil and civil war that preceded that takeover, accounts by Soviet researchers reveal that from 1921 to the death of Josef Stalin in 1953 more than twenty million citizens were murdered to perpetuate that evil empire in power.[2] And as official KGB and Kremlin files are opened in the wake of communism's demise, those terrible figures will undoubtedly increase.

Already they dwarf the wider-known death toll of Adolf Hitler's National Socialist (Nazi) Holocaust, which from 1933 to 1945 massacred more than ten million people, including over six million European Jews. And these Soviet figures do not include those considerable numbers massacred elsewhere in the Communist world—Angola, Cambodia, Cuba, Eastern Europe, Ethiopia, Laos, Mongolia, North Korea, and Vietnam—in the name of party purity.

Exceeding the grisly Soviet death lists, some believe, are the millions of Chinese who were slaughtered by Mao Tse-tung and his successors after the Communist takeover there in 1949. As recently as June 1989, these atrocities continued, with the massacre in Beijing's Tiananmen Square, where some five thousand prodemocracy protesters were killed and another ten thousand injured.

But Asian despotism is now an anomaly. Elsewhere the seventy-year post-World War I totalitarian era is at an end. Marxism-Leninism is dead. No matter by what name we choose to call it, a new world order is at hand. But whether it will be a benevolent or a malevolent world remains to be seen. Even more than in Woodrow Wilson's time, America has it within its power to shape that future.

The Solitary Superpower

Ironically, Saddam Hussein played a major role in making that fact apparent. "The end of the cold war changed the structure of the world," noted *The New Republic*'s Charles Krauthammer. "The Gulf war merely revealed it."[3] And it was revealed just in time, for on the eve of the Persian Gulf war it appeared that the United States was slipping back into the antimilitarism, euphoria, and isolationism of the 1920s and 1930s that betrayed the earlier "new world order."

Unilateral disarmament seemed to be a real possibility. In fact, on August 2, 1990, the very day the Iraqi invasion of Kuwait began, the Pentagon and the Congress agreed to massive cuts in the defense budget and a one-quarter reduction in the size of the armed forces. By 1995, defense spending was slated to shrink to 3.6 percent of the gross national product, the lowest level since the 1930s.

While not reversing these cuts, the Gulf war did, for the time being at least, halt further erosion of American military strength. Euphoria was replaced by a widespread recognition that even with the end of the Cold War and the death of communism, the world was still a dangerous place. The military still had a vital role to play in providing for U.S. national security and, it would seem, for the peace and security of the rest of the world as well. For with the collapse of the

Soviet Union, the United States finds itself in a new and unprecedented position as the world's solitary superpower.

Seventeenth in rank among the world's armed forces in 1939, when World War II began in Europe, America emerged from its traditional isolationism during that war and became a world power. Soon after its end the United States became locked in a quarter-century bipolar confrontation with the Soviet Union.

By the early 1970s, as the world post-World War II recovery became complete, the power of both the United States and the Soviet Union appeared to be in relative decline as other power centers began to emerge. The U.S.-Soviet bipolar world seemingly gave way to a multipolar world, where China, Japan, and Western Europe began to exert influence. With the United States allied with two of these emerging power centers—Japan and Western Europe—and with its Soviet and Chinese adversaries also adversaries with each other, the main thrust of American military strategy, it was argued, was to maintain the United States in that position of relative advantage.[4]

But while these emerging powers continued their economic development, the Gulf war revealed that they were severely limited in their means—and, in some cases, their will—to exercise power in the international arena. Most of the NATO nations did make a military contribution to the Persian Gulf war, with the United Kingdom and France sending substantial land, sea, and air combat forces to the area to reinforce the American commitment.

But Germany and Japan, which on the eve of the war had been seen as emerging world superpowers, opted out of the conflict, even though both were heavily dependent on the Middle East oil. Their subsequent monetary contributions could not disguise the fact that they lacked the will even to defend their own vital

interests. Economic powers they might be, but it was
obvious that neither were superpowers. With the
breakup of the Soviet Union, that status was reserved
for the United States alone.

That fact was to some degree clouded by the Gulf
war. One of the myths of that conflict, Krauthammer
argues, is the myth of multilateralism. "That victory
is said to be an example of a new era of collective
security," he said, "of the indispensability of coalition
politics, of the resurgence of the U.N. This is pious
nonsense. The Gulf war was an example of pseudo-
multilateralism."

But, he admits, "Americans insist on the multilat-
eral pretense. A large segment of American opinion
doubts the legitimacy of unilateral American action,
but accepts action taken under the rubric of the 'world
community.' "

There is more to it than pretense. As was discussed
in the previous chapter, without the cooperation of the
Soviet Union and the assistance of the Arab coalition
the Gulf war could not have been fought in the first
place. But Krauthammer's attack on the multilateralism "myth" carries a critical strategic message.

"Multilateralism is fine," he goes on to say. "It
provides cover for what are essentially unilateral
American actions." The danger is "that we will mistake the illusions—world opinion, U.S. resolutions,
professions of solidarity—for the real thing, which is
American power. . . . The ultimate problem with
multilateralism is that if you take it seriously you
gratuitously forfeit American freedom of action."[5]

The Strategic Offensive

That would be disastrous, for American freedom of
action is the very foundation of post-Cold War American military strategy. "Every age," said Clausewitz,

has "its own kind of war, its own limiting conditions, and its own peculiar preconceptions."[6] The Cold War was fought on the strategic defensive, its inherent offensive nature limited by the bipolar U.S.-Soviet nuclear standoff. For the United States the conflict was defined by the U.S. national policy of containment and its supporting military strategy of deterrence (i.e., the strategic defensive). But with the collapse of the Soviet Union and the end of the Cold War, that age is at an end.

The Gulf war marked the beginning of a new age, a unipolar world where the United States defends its vital interests not with deterrence and the strategic defensive but with assurance and the strategic offensive. As the principles of war dictate, the objective of the strategic offensive is to seize, retain, and exploit the initiative. Thus freedom of action is key.

The myth of multilateralism is not the only threat to that freedom of action. So is the myth that America is in decline and cannot afford to take such a leadership role. But, as Krauthammer noted, the war in the Gulf showed the fatuity of that excuse for inaction:

Before the Gulf crisis American declinists were lamenting America's fall from its perch atop the world in—their favorite benchmark year—1950. Well, in 1950 the United States engaged in a war with North Korea. It lasted three years, cost 54,000 American lives, and ended in a draw. Forty-one years later the United States engaged in a war with Iraq, a country of comparable size. It lasted six weeks, cost 143 American lives, and ended in a rout. If the Roman empire had declined at such a rate, you would be reading this in Latin.

But, say the declinists, you cannot compare the two wars. In Korea, did not the United States have to contend with China as well as North Korea? That is precisely the point. In the 1950s our adversaries had strategic depth. They had the whole Communist world behind them. That is why we were not able to prevail in Vietnam and Korea. In 1991, with the cold war won, our greatest adversaries are in retreat. The enemies we do encounter today, like Saddam, have to face us on their own. Because of that, they don't stand a chance. The difference between Korea and Iraq lies in the fact that in the interim the cold war was won and the world became unipolar.[7]

From Deterrence to Assurance

That unipolar world dictates a major shift in how the United States acts to protect its worldwide interests, chief among which, as a status quo nation, is continued maintenance of worldwide peace and security. For over forty years that task was accomplished through *deterrence*, in military terms, as discussed earlier, a euphemism for the strategic defensive.

Its essence, as Admiral of the Fleet Sir Peter Hill-Norton put it, was ''to raise the fearful doubt in the mind of any potential aggressor that any possible gain was not worth the inevitable risk.'' While it worked where it counted most—the deterrence of direct Soviet attack—it was a negative defensive strategy, which, especially in Third World conflicts with Soviet surrogates, surrendered the initiative to the aggressor.

But hidden within that negative defensive strategy was a positive offensive element, the *assurance* of allies (and, to some degree, of adversaries as well) that the United States would use its power, if need be, to support certain fundamental values. Among these values were the NATO commitment to the defense of Western Europe, and the security guarantees to Japan and South Korea.

And by assuring West Germany and Japan that

America was committed to their defense, the United States obviated the need for those nations to rearm massively, thereby assuring the Soviet Union and China against their legitimate fears of German and Japanese revanchism.

Now, with the end of the Cold War, that positive *assurance* dimension has become dominant, with *deterrence* relegated primarily to maintaining the strategic nuclear standoff. The Gulf war marked the onset of that change. For the first time since World War II, the United States went on the strategic military offensive, not only to protect its own interests but also to assure the world of its commitment to world peace and stability. That assurance was backed up by the deployment of over half a million American servicemen and -women to the Arabian Peninsula, more than 70 percent of the total allied forces deployed.

As President Bush said, if "the long-held promise of a new world order where brutality will go unrewarded and aggression will meet collective resistance" is to be fulfilled, the United States must play the leading role. If it does not, the job will go undone, for without the United States, there will be no "collective resistance." And as after the First World War, the whole world, including the United States, will be the worse for it.

Whether we like it or not—and most Americans do not like it in the least—we live in a unipolar world where the United States reigns supreme. For better or for worse, the "new world order" will be a world of America's making. As President Bush said, "among the nations of the world, only the United States of America has both the moral standing and the means to back it up. We are the only nation on this Earth that could assemble the forces of peace."

The Forces of Peace

What are the factors that determine the size and composition of these forces of peace? "To deal with this new and uncertain future," said General Colin L. Powell, the chairman of the Joint Chiefs of Staff, "one must understand certain fundamental realities of the post-Cold War and post-Desert Storm world, a world of *emerging realities* and also a world of *enduring realities*.

"The most important *emerging reality*," said General Powell, "is the end of the Cold War and the resulting redefined relationship with the Soviet Union. The reality of the future is that the old security context we knew and understood is *gone,* and is not coming back."

First among the *enduring* realities, he said, "is the reality of *Soviet military power*. While the Soviet military threat is finally being reduced, it will hardly disappear. The Soviet Union will remain the one country in the world with the means to destroy the United States in 30 minutes in a single devastating attack. . . ."

Putting substance to President Bush's earlier remarks, Powell emphasized that "Our national strategy is founded on the promise that America will continue to provide the leadership needed to preserve global peace and security. Consequently, our military strategy continues to rely on the basic elements that made possible the historic success of containment and assured the favorable outcome of dozens of lesser military conflicts and missions over the past 45 years." Among those basic elements were deterrence, power projection, and maritime, aerospace, and technological superiority.[8]

Deterrence Forces

Deterrence was once the centerpiece of U.S. military defensive strategy, but the changing world strategic environment has reduced deterrence—more specifically, nuclear deterrence—to a smaller but still vital role within that now primarily offensive strategy of assurance.

Although their battlefield utility has been almost completely dismissed, as witnessed by the 1987 Treaty on Intermediate Nuclear Forces (INF) and the 1991 unilateral U.S. elimination of short-range nuclear weapons, nuclear weapons cannot be disinvented. As General Powell noted, Soviet strategic nuclear weapons—ICBMs (intercontinental ballistic missiles) and SLBMs (sea-launched ballistic missiles)—are the primary threats to the American homeland.

The 1991 START (Strategic Arms Limitations Talks) agreement has, for the first time, begun the reduction in U.S. and Soviet nuclear warheads. But while arms control can significantly reduce the number of warheads required for deterrence, it cannot completely eliminate the nuclear threat. Not only are Soviet stockpiles not likely to be reduced to zero, but also nuclear proliferation continues. In 1991, North Korea and Pakistan were suspected of being on the verge of joining the United States, the USSR, China, Great Britain, France, India, Israel, and South Africa as nuclear powers.

What this means is that for the immediate future the Cold War nuclear strategy of MAD (mutually assured destruction) must remain as an essential part of U.S. military strategy. America must retain sufficient nuclear weapons to ride out an enemy first strike and still be able to destroy the enemy homeland in retaliation.

Post-Cold War defense planning thus envisions re-

tention of land and sea nuclear forces, with Trident II
ballistic missile submarines armed with C-4 and D-5
missiles and land-based ICBMs. Also included are
funds for development of the Strategic Defense Initiative (SDI) to provide a defensive screen against incom-
ing enemy missiles.[9]

But these forces should be only a stopgap measure.
As START reductions continue and as the Soviet
nuclear threat attenuates, deterrent forces should
evolve as rapidly as possible toward a more stable
long-term posture. This would include a reduced-force
level ICBM-SLBM dyad proportionate to the remaining Soviet threat and a deployed antiballistic missile
(ABM) system.

One way to hasten that development would be the
renunciation—unilaterally, if need be—of the 1972
U.S.-Soviet ABM Treaty. The illogic that promoted
deployment of offensive weapons of mass destruction—ICBMs, SLBMs, and manned penetration
bombers—to hold the Soviet civilian population hos-
tage as a defense against nuclear attack (and that
required the U.S. civilian population to be held hos-
tage as well) far exceeds even Douhet's wildest night-
mares. The time is fast approaching when that reign of
terror can be ended.

MAD should give way as soon as is practical to the
SDI defensive systems now under research and development. The political effect of the Iraqi use of Scud
missiles, and the success of the Patriot weapons system against those missiles, was one of the more dra-
matic aspects of the Gulf war. The ABM is now a
system whose time has come. In today's unipolar
world, the old arguments that such defensive deployments would destabilize the bipolar nuclear balance
and spur a nuclear arms race have been overtaken by
events. To hold on to MAD when nonthreatening
defensive systems are possible would truly be mad.

Power Projection

While nuclear deterrence remains a small part of post-Cold War military strategy, the main thrust of that new strategy should be assurance. Although not called by that name, a start in that direction is contained in current JCS plans for power projection. Such power projection is vital if the United States is truly to take the lead in maintaining world peace and security. Rhetoric alone will not suffice. The United States must be demonstrably capable of getting to the scene of potential conflicts with sufficient force to make a difference.

To assure Europe, the Middle East, the Mediterranean, Africa, and Southwest Asia, current plans call for an Atlantic force that includes, said General Powell, "a forward presence in Europe of a heavy Army corps with at least two divisions; a full-time Navy and Marine presence in the Mediterranean; and Air Force fighter wings possessing the full spectrum of tactical capability." These forward deployed forces would be backed up by "active component reinforcements in COMUS (Continental U.S.)" and the "bulk of the Reserve Components of the Services."

"America's military presence also guarantees a stable security environment in the Pacific," say the JCS planners. "Since World War II, the United States has fought two wars—Korea and Vietnam—in the Far East against regional troublemakers. We cannot ignore the fact that today the seven largest armies in the world operate in this region." Pacific forces include reduced-level forward deployments in Japan and Korea, as well as dedicated active and reserve component forces in Alaska and Hawaii.

"Finally," said General Powell, there is "the enduring reality of the *unknown and the uncertain;* not just across the Atlantic and Pacific, but in *all regions* of the world that continue to harbor danger and turmoil; regions where crises will occur when least expected." To meet this reality, contingency forces "provide global crisis and contingency response capability across the spectrum of conflict from counterinsurgency to major conventional conflict.

"The Army contributes a mix of heavy, light, and supporting forces. The Air Force brings the entire range of tactical forces, plus conventional bombers, command and control aircraft, intelligence platforms, refueling aircraft and so forth. Carrier-based naval air power is an essential ingredient . . . as is the amphibious combat power of the Marine Corps. . . . The Special Operations Forces of all Services are also a major ingredient of the contingency forces.

"The force deployed from the United States during Desert Shield/Storm provide an accurate gauge of current thinking regarding appropriate sizing of contingency forces," General Powell concluded. "Recall, however, that the total force drew upon not just U.S.-based forces, but forces from the Atlantic, Pacific, and Europe as well. Through in-depth reviews of the operation, we will now refine that estimate to configure our future contingency forces."[10]

Assurance Forces

Those reviews should include a realization that such current geographically based power projection plans are tenuous at best. Once the keystone of U.S. conventional force strategy, forward basing of U.S. forces abroad is unlikely to endure in the post-Cold War world. It is only a matter of time before domestic pressures at home and rising nationalism abroad will force the withdrawal of U.S. forces from Europe and Northeast Asia and from bases elsewhere in the world.

Instead of parceling out forces by geographic

regions, the U.S. assurance strategy should be based on an echeloned use of force applied by stages in proportion to the degree of the threat and to the intensity of the vital interests involved.

The first response to a crisis abroad should be the deployment of an intervention force, primarily naval forces, including carrier battle groups and embarked marine expeditionary units (MEU). Initially such forces would "show the flag" and signal U.S. assurances to peace and security in the area.

But that signal must be genuine. The political decision to fight, if need be, to demonstrate those assurances must be made before the task force is deployed. Marine expeditionary units are ideally designed for this initial intervention. From a military standpoint they have naval logistical support, naval gunfire support, and carrier-based naval and marine air support immediately at hand.

And from a political standpoint, they send exactly the right signal. They put all parties on warning that major U.S. vital interests are involved and that the United States is prepared to use force, if need be, to protect those interests. But unlike Army forces, they do not inexorably involve the United States in the crisis.

There is a major political difference between sending in the Marine Corps and sending in the Army. Naval and marine forces are seen as transitory. They can as easily be withdrawn as they were committed. And the same is true to a lesser degree of the Air Force. But when you commit the Army, you commit the nation.

That decision should not be made lightly. Only if the threat is beyond the capability of the naval and marine intervention force to contain, and only if major U.S. vital interests are involved, should the reinforcing force be committed. First would be the deployment of

Air Force tactical fighter wings and conventional bombers, followed closely by heavy Army brigades and divisions as well as active and reserve component combat, combat support, and combat service support units, with the firepower and sustainability to defeat the enemy and break his will to resist.

As it now stands, the current contingency force is designed primarily for low-intensity conflict. But low-intensity conflict was a reciprocal of high-intensity conflict, and as the high-intensity Soviet threat attenuates, so does the threat of low-intensity conflict. Although such conflicts will undoubtedly continue, the absence of Soviet involvement diminishes their threat to American interests.

Instead of the light Army divisions now committed to low-intensity conflict, such threats can better be contained by special operations forces working in conjunction with the armed forces of the nations under attack. The more likely threat to U.S. interests, as I argued at a November 1989 International Security Studies Program conference on the future of the Army at Tuft University's Fletcher School of Law and Diplomacy, is midintensity conflict.[11] Nine months later, that prophesy was realized with Iraq's invasion of Kuwait.

That midintensity threat did not end with the Gulf war. It continues to be the most likely eventuality for future U.S. military involvement. As General Powell said, "the force deployed . . . during Desert Shield/Storm provide an accurate gauge of current thinking regarding appropriate sizing of contingency forces." As did the Soviet threat before it, midintensity conflict should be the "defining threat" that shapes the force structure of America's conventional assurance forces.

Maritime, Aerospace, and Technological Superiority

But midintensity conflict is not the only defining factor. As the Gulf War made clear, so is the geographic reality that the United States is a world island, isolated from most world crises by the Atlantic and Pacific oceans. Before the United States can exert its influence it must first get to the crisis area. And as was true in the Gulf war, that dictates that future operations be joint—that is, involve not just one but all of the services.

"The Army suffers from the disease of jointness," former secretary of the navy John Lehman once told me.[12] But as I reminded him, "jointness" for the Army is not a disease. It is a strategic reality. The Army, and the Marine Corps as well, are joint services whether they like it or not, for both depend on the Navy and the Air Force to get them to the scene of the action, and to protect and support them once they arrive on the field of battle.

That reality places a premium on sea and air control, for without it strategic maneuver would be impossible. Today the U.S. Navy dominates the oceans, and even with the planned cutback from 13 carriers and 15 air wings to 12 carriers and 13 air wings (11 active) by 1995 and the cut from 545 to 451 battle force ships, it will remain unchallenged on the high seas for the foreseeable future.

And when it comes to air control, Low Observable (LO) platforms—Stealth technology—"have *fundamentally* changed the nature of air combat," said Air Force chief of staff General Merrill A. McPeak in an August 1991 briefing. "By itself the F-117 [stealth fighter] has made all other air forces obsolete . . . overnight. The United States is pushing the technology area with B-2 and ATF [the F-22 advanced tactical fighter]. Continued stealth investment will keep us in a *league by ourselves for a long time*."

While of questionable value as a manned penetration nuclear bomber, the role the Air Staff believed was its primary justification, the B-2 bomber has a major role to play in the projection of conventional U.S. power. The B-2 bomber "can hold virtually every target in the world at risk within twenty-four hours." Flying from bases in the United States, Guam, and the British Indian Ocean territory of Diego Garcia, it can cover the global landmass and deliver a forty-thousand-pound payload with but one aerial refueling. "The B-2 combines survivability of the F-117 with the payload and range of the B-52—the best of both worlds."[13]

Nuclear propulsion and aerial refueling have solved the conundrum posed by Alfred Thayer Mahan at the turn of the century. While steam gave the Navy great tactical mobility, since it was no longer dependent on the wind gauge for maneuver, it was at the price of strategic mobility.

While a properly provisioned sailing ship could sail anywhere in the world, a steamship was dependent on foreign coaling stations for strategic maneuver. This was the genesis for the worldwide system of American naval bases, ports of call, and, more recently, air bases for the projection of U.S. power.

But that structure may at long last be coming to an end. Modern technology, especially nuclear propulsion and under-way replenishment, has cut the Navy loose from such bases. While such naval bases as Subic Bay in the Philippines may be desirable, they are no longer critical. And with advances in aerial refueling and increased aircraft range, the Air Force, too, is no longer dependent on foreign air bases and the attendant political restrictions on their operations.

Once solely under the control of the Strategic Air Command, the Air Force plans to transfer some of its tanker fleet to the U.S. Transportation Command, the real future "strategic" command. "Transportation capability comes to the fore in every contingency," noted General Powell, "as it delivers combat power to the region and sustains that power through the contingency and redeployment. No other country possesses such a comprehensive combination of airlift, sealift, and prepositioned resources."[14]

Having said that, sealift and airlift are the U.S. military's major strategic limiting factors. While the C-17 transport is slated to replace the aging C-141 cargo fleet, America's sealift capabilities continue to deteriorate. In 1950, American-flagged vessels carried half of the nation's exports and imports. In 1990 they carried less than 4 percent. While acquisition of more fast Navy cargo ships will help, revitalization of the American merchant marine should be a priority U.S. project.

Providing for the New World Order

Technology and research and development can, in General Powell's words, "put the best available weapons and supporting systems in the hands of American forces." But unless those forces have the will and the training to use those weapons, they are just so much useless junk. "The quintessential 'strategic lesson learned' from the Vietnam war," read the conclusion to the first version of *On Strategy,* "is that we must once again become masters of the profession of arms."[15]

That's what the renaissance in doctrine in training throughout the armed forces over the past twenty years has been all about. Technology provided the means to win the Gulf war, but it was leadership, the painstaking creation of a quality force, and years of hard training that brought that victory about. The lessons of the Vietnam war had been learned and learned well.

But while training will remain important in the post-Cold War world, education must now be given priority in the military's staff colleges and war colleges. One can train for the known, but only education can prepare the military for the unknown and unknowable futures that lie ahead. Flexibility must be the watchword. Arms and equipment must more than ever be designed to operate in a variety of climates across the geographic spectrum.

Even more important than equipment design will be the development of the flexibility of mind among our servicemen and -women necessary to cope with the unexpected. In a computer age where certitude is the norm, that is the one thing the strategic environment will not provide.

Only a quality force can cope with such complexities, but maintaining such a force may prove difficult. There is a danger that as the Soviet Union continues to disintegrate, escalating defense cuts will lead to a hollow military incapable of power projection abroad to assure world peace and security.

In its recovery from Vietnam, the American military proved that it could learn from defeat and pull itself up by its bootstraps. But given its past history, it is not at all certain that the country at large will learn from its victories in the Cold War and the Persian Gulf or whether it will follow the path to precipitous disarmament that has led to renewed aggression so many times in the past. Until that critical issue is resolved, the shape and character of the "new world order" remains to be seen.

NOTES

1. George Bush: "Text of the State of the Union Address," *The Washington Post* (January 30, 1991), p. A14.

2. For example, see Roy Medvedev's *Let History Judge: The Origins and Consequences of Stalinism* (trans. and ed. George Shriver) (New York: Columbia University Press, 1989).

3. Charles Krauthammer, "The Lonely Superpower," *The New Republic* (July 29, 1991), pp. 23–27.

4. See Harry G. Summers, Jr., *The Astarita Report: A Military Strategy for the Multipolar World* (Carlisle Barracks, Pa.: Strategic Studies Institute, U.S. Army War College, 1981).

5. Krauthammer, "The Lonely Superpower," p. 26.

6. Carl von Clausewitz, *On War,* trans. and ed. Michael Howard and Peter Paret (Princeton, N.J.: Princeton University Press, 1976), p. 593.

7. Krauthammer, "The Lonely Superpower," p. 24.

8. Colin L. Powell, *chairman, JCS, Testimony to Defense Base Closure Commission* (Washingon, D.C.: office of the chairman, the Joint Chiefs of Staff, April 26, 1991), pp. 3–6.

9. Ibid., pp. 7–8.

10. Ibid., pp. 5, 9–14.

11. Harry G. Summers, Jr., "Mid-Intensity Conflict: The Korean War Paradigm," in *The United States Army: Challenges and Missions for the 1990s,* ed. Robert L. Pfaltzgraff, Jr., and Richard H. Schultz, Jr. (Lexington, Mass.: Lexington Books, 1991), pp. 43–53.

12. Author's notes.

13. Author's notes. Briefing by General Merrill A. McPeak, chief of staff, U.S. Air Force, "B-2 Stealth Bomber: Global Reach—Global Power for the 21st Century" (August 12, 1991).

14. Powell testimony, p. 14.

15. Harry G. Summers, Jr., *On Strategy: A Critical Analysis of the Vietnam War* (New York: Dell Publishing, 1984), p. 258.

APPENDIX

Schwarzkopf: The Strategy Behind Desert Storm

February 27, 1991

Good evening, ladies and gentlemen. Thank you for being here. I promised some of you all a few days ago that as soon as the opportunity presented itself I would give you a complete rundown on what we were doing, and more importantly, why we were doing it; the strategy behind what we were doing. I've been asked by Secretary Chaney to do that this evening, and so if you will bear with me, we're going to go through a briefing. I apologize to the folks over here who won't be able to see the charts, but we're going to go through a complete briefing of the operation.

This goes back from seven August to seventeen January. We started our deployment on the seventh of August. Basically, what we started out against was a couple hundred thousand Iraqis that were in the Kuwait theater of operation. I don't have to remind you all that we brought over, initially, defense forces in the form of the 101st, the 82nd, the 24th Mechanized Infantry Division, the 3rd Armored Cavalry, and in essence we had them arrayed to the south, behind the Saudi task force. Also, there were Arab forces over here in this area, arrayed in defensive positions. And that, in essence, is the way we started.

In the middle of November the decision was made to increase the force, because by that time huge numbers of Iraqi forces had flowed into the area and therefore we increased the forces and built up more forces.

We made a very deliberate decision to align all of those forces within the boundary, looking north towards Kuwait; this being King Kahlid Military City over here. So, we aligned those forces so it very much looked like they were all aligned directly on the Iraqi positions. We also, at that time, had a very active Naval presence out in the Gulf. And, we made sure that everybody understood about that Naval presence. One of the reasons why we did that is because it became very apparent to us early on that the Iraqis were quite concerned about an amphibious operation across the shores to liberate Kuwait; this being Kuwait City. They put a very very heavy barrier of infantry along here and they proceeded to build an extensive barrier that went all the way across the border, down and around, and up the side of Kuwait.

Basically, the problem we were faced with was this: When you looked at the troop numbers, they really outnumbered us about three to two. And, when you consider the number of combat service support people we had, that's logisticians and that sort of thing, in our armed forces, as far as fighting troops we were really outnumbered two to one. In addition to that, they had about 4,700 tanks versus our 3,500 when the buildup was complete. And, they had a great deal more artillery than we do.

I think any student of military strategy would tell you

that in order to attack a position you should have a ratio of approximately three to one in favor of the attacker. And, in order to attack a position that is heavily dug in and barricaded, such as the one we had here, you should have a ratio of five to one in the way of troops, in favor of the attacker. So, you can see basically what our problem was at that time. We were outnumbered, at a minimum, three to two as far as troops were concerned. We were outnumbered as far as tanks were concerned. And, we had to come up with some way to make up the difference.

Next chart, please. I apologize for the busy nature of this chart, but I think it's very important for you to understand exactly what our strategy was. What you see here is a color coding where green is a go sign or a good sign as far as our forces are concerned. Yellow would be a caution sign. And red would be a stop sign. Green represents units that have been attrited below fifty percent strength. The yellow are units that are between fifty and seventy-five percent strength. And, of course, the red are units that are over seventy-five percent strength.

What we did, of course, was start an extensive air campaign. One of the purposes of that extensive air campaign was to isolate the Kuwaiti theater of operation by taking out all of the bridges and supply lines that ran between the north and the southern part of Iraq. That was to prevent reinforcement and supply coming into the southern part of Iraq and the Kuwaiti theater of operation. We also conducted a very heavy bombing campaign. And many people questioned why the extensive bombing campaign. This is the reason why. It was necessary to reduce these forces down to a strength that made them weaker, particularly along the front-line barrier that we had to go through.

We continued our heavy operations out in the sea because we wanted the Iraqis to continue to believe that we were going to conduct a massive amphibious operation in this area. And I think many of you recall the number of amphibious rehearsals we had, to include Imminent Thunder, that was written about quite extensively for many reasons. But we continued to have those operations because we wanted him to concentrate his forces, which he did.

I think this is probably one of the most important parts of the entire briefing I could talk about. As you know, very early on we took out the Iraqi Air Force. We knew that he had very very limited reconnaissance means, and therefore when we took out his Air Force, for all intents and purposes we took out his ability to see what we were doing down here in Saudi Arabia. Once we had taken out his eyes, we did what could best be described as the "Hail Mary" play in football. When the quarterback is desperate for a touchdown at the very end, what he does is he steps up behind the center and all of a sudden every single one of his receivers goes way out to one flank, and they all run down the field as fast as they possibly can, and into the end zone, and he lobs the ball. In essence, that's what we did. When we knew that he couldn't see us anymore, we did a massive movement of troops all the way out to the west—to the extreme west—because at that time we knew that he was still fixed in this area with a vast majority of his forces. And once the air campaign started, he would be incapable of moving out to counter this move, even if he knew we made it out.

There were some additional troops out in this area, but they did not have the capability or the time to put in the barrier that had been described by Saddam Hussein as "an absolutely impenetrable tank barrier that no one would ever get through." I believe those were his words. So, this was absolutely an extraordinary move. I must tell you, I can't recall any time in the annals of military history when this number of forces have moved over this distance to put themselves in a position to be able to attack. But what's more important, and I think it's very very important that I make this point, and that's these logistics bases. Not only did we move the troops out there, but we literally moved thousands and thousands of tons of fuel, of ammunition, of spare parts, of water and of food out here into this area because we wanted to have enough supplies on hand so that if we launched this and we got into a slug-fest battle, which we very easily could have gotten into, we would have enough supplies to last for sixty days. It was an absolutely gigantic accomplishment and I can't give credit enough to the logisticians and the transporters who were able to pull this off; to the superb support we had from the Saudi government; the literally thousands and thousands of drivers, really of every national origin, who helped us in this move out here. And, of course, great credit goes to the commanders of these units who were also able to maneuver their forces out here and put them in this position.

But, as a result, by the twenty-third of February what you found is this situation. The front lines had been attrited down to a point where all of these units were at fifty percent or below. The second level, basically, that we had to face, and these were the real tough fighters that we were worried about, right here, were attrited to someplace between fifty and seventy-five percent, although we still had the Republican Guard located here and here, and part of the Republican Guard in this area that were very strong; and the Republican Guard up in this area, strong. And we continued to hit the bridges all across this area to make absolutely sure that no more reinforcements came into the battle. This was the situation on the twenty-third of February.

Next, please. Oh, wait, I shouldn't forget these fellows. That SF stands for Special Forces. We put Special Forces deep into the enemy territory. They went out on strategic reconnaissance for us, and they let us know what was going on out there. And they were the eyes that were out there, and it's very important that I not forget those folks.

Next, please. This, then, was the morning of the twenty-fourth. Our plan, initially, had been to start over here in this area and do exactly what the Iraqis thought we were going to do, and that's take them on, head on, into their most heavily defended area. Also, at the same time we launched amphibious feigns and naval gunfire in this area so that they continued to think that we were going to be attacking along this coast, and therefore fix their forces in this position. Our hope was that by fixing the forces in this position, and with this attack through here in this position, we would basically keep the forces here and they wouldn't know what was going on out in this area. And I believe we succeeded in that very well.

At four o'clock in the morning, the marines—the 1st Marine Division and the 2nd Marine Division—launched attacks through the barrier system. They were accompanied by the Tiger Brigade—the U.S. Army Tiger Brigade—of the 2nd Armored Division.

At the same time over here, two Saudi task forces also launched a penetration through this barrier. But, while they were doing that, at four o'clock in the morning over here, the 6th French Armored Division, accompanied by a brigade of the 82nd Airborne, also launched an overland attack to their objective up in this area, Alcimon Airfield. And we were held up a little bit by the weather, but by eight o'clock in the morning the 101st Airborne Air Assault launched an air assault deep in the enemy's territory to establish a forward operating base in this location right here.

Let me talk about each one of those moves. First of all, the Saudis over here on the east coast did a terrific job. They went up against a very very tough barrier system. They breached the barrier very very effectively. They moved out aggressively and continued their attack up the coast.

I can't say enough about the two marine divisions. If I use words like "brilliant," it would really be an under-description of the absolutely superb job that they did in breaching the so-called "impenetrable barrier." It was a classic—absolutely classic—military breaching of a very very tough minefield, barbed wire, fire trenches–type barrier. They went through the first barrier like it was water. They went across into the second barrier line even though they were under artillery fire at the time. They continued to open up that breach. And then they brought both divisions streaming through that breach. Absolutely superb operation; a textbook. And I think it'll be studied for many many years to come as the way to do it.

I would also like to say that the French did an absolutely superb job of moving out rapidly to take their objective out here, and they were very very successful, as was the 101st. And, again, we still had the Special Forces located in this area.

What we found is as soon as we breached these obstacles here, and started bringing pressure, we started getting a large number of surrenders. And I think I talked to some of you all about that this evening when I briefed you on the evening of the twenty-fourth. We found we got a large number of surrenders. We also found that these forces right here were getting a large number of surrenders and were meeting with a great deal of success.

We were worried about the weather. The weather, it turned out, was going to get pretty bad the next day, and we were worried about launching this air assault. And we also started to have a huge number of atrocities, of really the most unspeakable type, committed in downtown Kuwait City, to include reports that the desalinization plant had been destroyed. And when we heard that, we were quite concerned about what might be going on. Based upon that, and the situation as it was developing, we made a decision that rather than wait for the following morning to launch the remainder of these forces, we'd go ahead and launch those forces that afternoon.

Next. So, this was the situation you saw the afternoon of the twenty-fourth. The marines continued to make great progress going through the breach in this area, and were moving rapidly north. The Saudi task force on the east coast was also moving rapidly to the north and making very very good progress. We launched another Egyptian/Arab force in this location and another Saudi force in this location, again, to penetrate the barrier, but once again to make the enemy continue to think that we were doing exactly what he wanted us to do, and that's make a headlong assault into a very very tough barrier system—a very very tough mission for these folks here.

But, at the same time, what we did is continue to attack with the French. We launched an attack on the part of the entire 7th Corps, where the 1st Infantry Division went through, breached an obstacle and mine-field barrier here, and established quite a large breach, through which we passed the 1st British Armored Division. At the same time we launched the 1st Armored Division and the 3rd Armored Division. And because of our deception plan and the way it worked, we didn't even have to worry about a barrier. We just went right around the enemy and were behind him in no time at all. And the 2nd Armored Cavalry Division and the 24th Mech Division also launched out here in the far west. And I ought to talk about the 101st because this is an important point. Once the 101st had their forward operating base established here, they then went ahead and launched into the Tigris and Euphrates valley.

There's a lot of people who are still saying that the object of the United States of America was to capture Iraq and cause a downfall of the entire country of Iraq. Ladies and gentlemen, when we were here, we were 150 miles from Baghdad and there was nobody between us and Baghdad. If it had been our intention to take Iraq, if it had been our intention to destroy the country, if it had been our intention to overrun the country, we could have done it unopposed, for all intents and purposes, from this position at that time. But that was not our intention. We had never said it was our intention. Our intention was purely to eject the Iraqis out of Kuwait and to destroy the military power that had come in here. So, this was the situation at the end of February the twenty-fourth, in the afternoon.

Next, please. The next two days went exactly like we thought they would go. The Saudis continued to make great progress up on the eastern flank, keeping the pressure off the marines on the flank here. The Special Forces went out and started operating small boat operations out in this area to help clear mines, but also to threaten the flanks here and to continue to make them think that we were, in fact, going to conduct amphibious operations.

The Saudi forces and Arab forces that came in and took these two initial objectives turned to come in on the flank, heading toward Kuwait City, located right in this area here.

The British UK passed through and continued to attack up this flank. And, of course, the 7th Corps came in and attacked in this direction, as shown here. The 24th Infantry Division made an unbelievable move all the way across into the Tigris and Euphrates valley and proceeded in blocking this avenue of egress, which was the only avenue of egress left because we continued to make sure that the bridges stayed down. So there was no way out once 24th was in this area, and the 101st continued to operate in here. The French, having succeeded in achieving all of their objectives, then set up a flanking position— a flank guard position here—to make sure that no forces could come in and get us from the flank.

By this time we had destroyed or rendered completely ineffective over twenty-one Iraqi divisions.

Next, please. And, of course, that then brings us to

today. Where we are today is we now have a solid wall across the north, of the 18th Airborne Corps, consisting of the units shown right here, attacking straight to the east. We have a solid wall here, again, of the 7th Corps, also attacking straight to the east. The forces that they are fighting right now are the forces of the Republican Guard. Again, today we had a very significant day when the Arab forces, coming from both the west and the east, closed in and moved into Kuwait City, where they are now in the process of clearing Kuwait City entirely and assuring that it's absolutely secure. The 1st Marine Division continues to hold Kuwaiti International Airport. The 2nd Marine Division continues to be in a position where it blocks any egress out of the city of Kuwait so no one can leave.

To date, we have destroyed over twenty-nine—destroyed or rendered inoperable . . . I don't like to say destroyed because that gives you the visions of absolutely killing everyone, and that's not what we're doing. But we have rendered completely ineffective over twenty-nine Iraqi divisions and the gates are closed. There is no way out of here. There is no way out of here. And the enemy is fighting us in this location right here. We continue, of course, to have overwhelming air power. The air has done a terrific job from start to finish in supporting the ground forces, and we also have had great support from the Navy, both in the form of naval gunfire and in the support of carrier air. That's the situation at the present time.

Next, please. Peace is not without a cost. These have been the U.S. casualties to date. As you can see, these were the casualties that we had in the air war. Then, of course, we had the terrible misfortune of the Scud attack the other night, which again, because the weapon malfunctioned, caused death, unfortunately, rather than in a proper function. And then of course these are the casualties in the ground war to date; the total being as shown here.

Next. Hold it. Hold it. Hold on for one second. One second is up. Next, please. We'll put all of these charts up and have them available for you afterwards.

Now I would just like to comment briefly about that casualty chart. The loss of one human life is intolerable to any of us who are in the military. But I would tell you that casualties of that order of magnitude, considering the job that's been done and the number of forces that are involved, is almost miraculous as far as the light number of casualties. It'll never be miraculous to the families of those people, but it is miraculous.

Anyhow, this is what's happened to date with the Iraqis. They started out with over four thousand tanks. As of today, we have over three thousand confirmed destroyed. And I do mean destroyed or captured. And, as a matter of fact, that number is low because you can add seven hundred to that as a result of the battle that's going on right now with the Republican Guard. So that number is very very high and we've almost completely destroyed the offensive capability of the Iraqi forces within the Kuwaiti theater of operation.

The armored-vehicle count is also very very high. And, of course, you can see we're doing great damage to the artillery. The battle is still going on, and I suspect that these numbers will mount rather considerably.

Next. I wish I could give you a better number on this. To be very honest with you, this is just a wild guess. It's an estimate that was sent to us by the field today at noontime, but the prisoners out there are so heavy and so extensive, and obviously we're not in the business of going around and counting noses at this time to determine precisely what the exact number is. But we're very very confident that we have well over fifty thousand prisoners of war at this time, and that number is mounting on a continuing basis.

I would remind you that the war is continuing to go on. Even as we speak right now there is fighting going on out there. Even as we speak right now there are incredible acts of bravery going on. This afternoon we had an F-16 pilot shot down. We had contact with him. He had a broken leg on the ground. Two helicopters from the 101st, and they didn't have to do it, but they went in to try and pull that pilot out. One of them was shot down and we're still in the process of working through that. But that's the kind of thing that's going on out on that battlefield right now. It is not a Nintendo game. It is a tough battlefield where people are risking their lives at all times, and they're great heroes out there and we ought to all be very very proud of them.

That's the campaign to date. That's the strategy to date. And I'd now be very happy to take any questions anyone might have.

Press Conference Questions and Answers

Q. I want to go back to the air war. The chart you showed there with the attrition rates of the various forces was almost the exact reverse of what most of us thought was happening. It showed the front-line troops attrited to seventy-five percent or more, and the Republican Guards, which a lot of public focus was on when we were covering the air war, attrited at less than seventy-five. Why is that? I mean, how did it come to pass?

A. Let me tell you how we did this. We started off, of course, against the strategic targets, and I briefed you on that before. At the same time, we were hitting the Republican Guard. But the Republican Guard, you must remember, is a mechanized armored force for the most part, that is very very well dug in and very very well spread out. So in the initial stages of the game we were hitting the Republican Guard heavily, but we were hitting them with strategic-type bombers rather than pinpoint precision bombers.

For lack of a better word, what happened is the air campaign shifted from the strategic phase into the theater, and we knew all along that this was the important area. The nightmare scenario—the nightmare scenario for all of us—would have been to go through, get hung up in this breach right here, and then have the enemy artillery rain chemical weapons down on troops that were in a gaggle in the breach right there. That was the nightmare scenario. So, one of the things that we felt we must have established is an absolute—as much destruction as we could possibly get of the artillery—the direct support artillery—that would be firing on that wire. That's why we shifted, and in the very latter days we punished this area very heavily, because that was the first challenge. Once we got through this and were moving, then it's a different war. Then we're fighting our kind of war. Before we get through that, we're fighting their kind of war, and that's what we didn't want to have to do. At the same time, we continued to attrite the Republican Guard. And that's why I would tell you that, again, the figures that we're giving you are conservative. They always have been conservative. But we promised you at the outset we weren't going to give you anything inflated; we were going to give you the best we had.

Yes, sir, right here.

Q. Sir, you seem to have about—he seems to have about five or six hundred tanks left out of more than four thousand, as just an example. I wonder, if in an overview, despite these enormously illustrative pictures, you could say what's left of the Iraqi Army in terms of how long could it be before he could ever be a regional threat or a threat to the region again?

A. Well, there's not enough left at all for him to be a regional threat to the region—an offensive regional threat. As you know, he's got a very large army, but most of the army that is left north of the Tigris-Euphrates valley is an infantry army. It's not an armored army. It's not an armor-heavy army, which means it really isn't an offensive army. So it doesn't have enough left, unless someone chooses to rearm them in the future.

Q. General, you said you've got all these divisions along the border which were seriously attrited. It figures to be about two hundred thousand troops maybe that were there. You've got fifty thousand prisoners. Where's the rest of them?

A. There were a very very large number of dead in these units; a very very large number of dead. We even found them when we went into the units ourselves and found them in the trench lines. There were very heavy desertions. At one point we had reports of desertion rates of more than thirty percent of the units that were along the front here. As you know, we had quite a large number of POWs that came across. And so I think it's a combination of desertions; there's a combination of people that were killed; there's a combination of the people that we've captured; and there's a combination of some other people who are just flat still running.

Yes, back here.

Q. General, that move on the extreme left, which got within 150 miles of Baghdad, was it also part of the plan that the Iraqis might have thought that it was going to Baghdad, and would that have contributed to the deception?

A. I wouldn't have minded at all if they'd gotten a little bit nervous about it.

(Laughter)

And I mean that very sincerely. I would have been delighted if they'd gotten very very nervous about it.

Frankly, I don't think they ever knew it was there. I think they never knew it was there until the door had already been closed on them.

Back in the back, please.

Q. Yes. Sir, you talked about heavy press coverage of Imminent Thunder early on and how it helped fool the Iraqis into thinking that it was a serious operation. I wondered if you could talk about other ways in which the press contributed to the campaign?

(Laughter)

A. First of all, I don't want to characterize Imminent Thunder as being only a deception, because it wasn't. We had every intention of conducting amphibious operations if they were necessary. And that was a very very real rehearsal, as were the other rehearsals. I guess the one thing I would say to the press that I was delighted with is in the very very early stages of this operation, when we were over here building up, and we didn't have very much on the ground, you all were giving us the credit for a whole lot more over here. And, as a result, that gave me quite a feeling of confidence that we might not be attacked quite as quickly as I thought we were going to be attacked. Other than that, I would not like to get into the remainder of that question.

Over here, yes, sir.

Q. General, what kind of fight is going on with the Republican Guard and is there any more fighting going on in Kuwait or is Kuwait essentially out of the action?

A. No. Every fight that's going on with the Republican Guard right now is just a classic tank battle. You've got fire and maneuver. They are continuing to fight and shoot at us as our forces move forward, and our forces are in the business of outflanking them and taking them from the rear; using our attack helicopters; using our advanced technology. I would tell you that one of the things that has prevailed, particularly in this battle out here, is our technology. We had great weather for the air war. But right now, and for the last three days, it's been raining out there. It's been dusty out there. There's black smoke and haze in the air. It's an infantryman's weather. God loves the infantryman, and that's just the kind of weather the infantryman likes to fight in. But I would also tell you that our sights have worked fantastically well in their ability to acquire, through that kind of dust and haze, the enemy targets. And the enemy sights have not worked that well. As a matter of fact, we've had several anecdotal reports today of enemy who were saying to us that they couldn't see anything through their sights, and all of a sudden their tank exploded when their tank was hit by our sights. So, that's one of the indications of what's going on.

Q. So if there's no air support, are you saying—

A. Very very tough air embarkment, obviously, as this box gets smaller and smaller, okay, and in the bad weather it gets tougher and tougher to use the air. And, therefore, the air is acting more in an interdiction role than any other.

Back in the back. Yes, sir.

Q. Yes, sir, General. Could you tell us why the French, who went very fast in the desert the first day, stopped in Cimon and were invited to stop fighting after thirty-six hours?

A. Well, that's not exactly a correct statement. The French mission, okay, on the first day was to protect our left flank. What we were interested in is making sure we confined this battlefield, both on the right and the left, and we didn't want anyone coming in and attacking these forces, which was the main attack, coming in from their left flank. So the French mission was to go out and not only seize Al Cimon, but to set up a screen across our left flank, which was absolutely vital to ensure that we weren't surprised. So they definitely did not stop fighting. They continued to perform their mission and they performed it extraordinarily well.

Yes, sir.

Q. When Iraq's Air Force disappeared very early in the air war, there was speculation they might return to provide cover during the ground war. Were you expecting that? Are you surprised they never showed themselves again?

A. I was not expecting it. We were not expecting it. But I would tell you that we never discounted it and we were totally prepared in the event it happened.

Q. *(Inaudible)*

A. Huh?

Q. Have they been completely destroyed? Where are they?

A. There's not an airplane that's flown. I'll tell you where they are. A lot of them are disbursed throughout civilian communities in Iraq. I have proof of that, as a matter of fact.

Yeah, right here.

Q. How many divisions of the Republican Guard now are you fighting and any idea how long that will take?

A. We're probably fighting on the order of—we fought—there were a total of five of them up here. Okay, one of them we had probably destroyed yesterday. We've probably destroyed two more today, and I would say that that leaves us a couple that we're in the process of fighting right now.

Yeah.

Q. Could I ask you two questions? First, did you think that this would turn out—I realize a great deal of strategy and planning went into it—but when it took place, did you think this would turn out to be such an easy cakewalk as it seems? And, secondly, what are your impressions of Saddam Hussein as a military strategist?

A. *(Laughing)* First of all, if we'd thought it would have been such an easy fight, we definitely would not have stocked sixty days' worth of supplies in these log bases. So as I've told you all for a very very long time, it is very very important for a military commander never to assume away the capabilities of his enemy. And when you're facing an enemy that is over five hundred thousand strong, has a reputation that they've had of fighting for eight years, being combat-hardened veterans, had the number of tanks and the type of equipment they had, you don't assume away anything. So we certainly did not expect it to go this way.

As far as Saddam Hussein being a great military strategist, he is neither a strategist nor is he schooled in the operational art, nor is he a tactician, nor is he a general, nor is he a soldier. Other than that, he's a great military man. I want you to know that.

(Laughter)

Q. You went over very quickly the special operations folks. Could you tell us what their role was?

A. We don't like to talk a lot about what the special operations do, as you're well aware. But in this case, let me just cover some of the things I did. First of all, with every single Arab unit that went into battle, we had Special Forces troops with them. The job of those Special Forces was to travel and live right down at the battalion level with all those people, to make sure that they could act as the communicators with friendly, English-speaking units that were on their flanks. And they could also call in air strikes as necessary. They could coordinate helicopter strikes and that sort of thing. That's one of the principal roles that they played, and it was a very very important role. Secondly, they did a great job in strategic reconnaissance for us. Thirdly, the special forces were one hundred percent in charge of the combat search and rescue. And that's a tough mission. When a pilot gets shot down out there in the middle of nowhere, surrounded by the enemy, and you're the folks that are required to go in and go after them, that is a very tough mission, and that was one of their missions. And, finally, they also did some direct action missions, period.

Q. Many of the reports in the pools we've got from your field commanders and the soldiers were indicating that these fortifications were not as intense or as sophisticated as they were led to believe. Was this a result of the pounding that they took, that you described earlier, or is it that they were perhaps overrated in the first place?

A. Have you ever been in a minefield?

Q. No.

A. Okay, all there's got to be is one mine, and that's intense. Okay, there were plenty of mines out there. There was plenty of barbed wire. There were fire trenches, most of which we set off ahead of time, but there were still some that were out there. The Egyptian forces had to go through fire trenches. There were a lot of booby traps, a lot of barbed wire, and not a fun place to me. I've got to tell you that probably one of the toughest things that anyone ever has to do is to go up there and walk into something like that and go through it, and consider that while you're going through it, and clearing it at the same time, you're probably under fire by the enemy artillery.

Q. Is the Republican Guard your only remaining military objective in Iraq? And I gather there have been some heavy engagements. How would you rate this army you faced, from the Republican Guard on down?

A. Rating an army is a tough thing to do. A great deal of the capability of an army is its dedication to its cause and its will to fight. You can have the best equipment in the world, you can have the largest numbers in the world, but if you're not dedicated to your cause, if you don't have a will to fight, then you're not going to have a very good army. One of the things that we learned right prior to the initiation of the campaign that, of course, contributed, as a matter of fact, to the timing of the ground campaign, is that so many people were deserting, and I think you've heard this, that the Iraqis brought down execution squads, whose job was to shoot people, okay, in the front lines. Now, I've got to tell you that a soldier doesn't fight very hard for a leader who is going to shoot him, okay, on his own whim. That's not what military leadership is all about. And so I attribute a great deal of the failure of the Iraqi Army to fight to their own leadership. They committed them to a cause that they did not believe in. They all are saying that they didn't want to be there; they didn't want to fight their fellow Arab; they were lied to; they were deceived, and when they went into Kuwait they didn't believe in the cause. And then, after they got there, they had a leadership that was so uncaring for them, okay, that they didn't properly feed them, they didn't properly give them water, and in the end, they kept them there only at the point of a gun. Now, the Republican Guard is entirely different. The Republican Guard are the ones that went into Kuwait in the first place. They get paid more. They get treated better. And, oh, by the way, they also were well to the rear here, okay, so they could be the first ones to bug out when the battlefield started folding, while these poor fellows up here, who didn't want to be here in the first place, bore the brunt of the attack. Well, it didn't happen.

Q. General?

A. Yes, sir.

Q. Could you tell us something about the British involvement and perhaps comment on today's report of ten dead through friendly fire?

A. Yeah. The British, I've got to tell you, have been absolutely superb; the members of this coalition from the outset. I have a great deal of admiration and respect for all the British that are out there, and particularly General Sir Peter Delebya, who is not only a great general but he's also become a very close personal friend of mine. They played a very very key role in the movement of the main attack. I would tell you that what they had to do was go through this breach in one of the tougher areas, because I told you they had reinforced here, and there were a lot of forces here. And what the Brits had to do was go through the breach and then set up the block, so that the main attack could continue on without forces over here—the mechanized forces over here—attacking that main attack in the flank. And that was the principal role of the British. They did it absolutely magnificently, and then they immediately followed up in the main attack, and they're still up there fighting right now. So, they just did a great job.

Yeah, right here.

Q. General, these forty thousand Kuwaiti hostages, taken by the Iraqis, where are they right now? That's quite a few people. Are they in the line of fire? Do we know where they are?

A. No, no, no. We were told, and again a lot of this is anecdotal, okay—we were told that they were taken back to Basra. We were also told that some of them were taken all the way back to Baghdad. We were told a hundred different reasons why they were taken; number one, to be a bargaining chip if the time when bargaining chips were needed. Another one was for retribution because of course at that time Iraq was saying that these people were not Kuwaitis; they were citizens of Iraq, and therefore they could do anything they wanted to with them. So, I just pray that they'll all be returned safely before long.

Right here, yeah.

Q. Is there a military or political explanation as to why the Iraqis did not use chemical weapons?

A. We got a lot of questions about why the Iraqis didn't use chemical weapons, and I don't know the answer. But I just thank God that they didn't.

Q. Is it possible that they didn't use them because they didn't have time to react?

A. Okay, you want me to speculate. I'll be delighted to speculate. Nobody can ever pin you down when you speculate. Number one, we destroyed their artillery. We went after their artillery big-time. They had major desertions in their artillery, and that's how they would have delivered their chemical weapons, either that or by air. And we all know what happened to the air. So we went after the artillery big-time, and I think we were probably highly highly effective in going after their artillery. There's other people who are speculating that the reason why they didn't use chemical weapons is because they were afraid that if they used chemical weapons, there would be nuclear retaliation. There's other people that speculate that they didn't use their chemical weapons because their chemical weapons degraded, and because of the damage that we did to their chemical production facilities, they were unable to upgrade the chemicals within their weapons as a result of their degradation. That was one of the reasons, among others, why we went after their chemical production facilities early on in the strategic campaign. I'll never know the answer to that question, but as I say, thank God that they didn't.

All the way back in the back.

Q. General, are you still bombing in northern Iraq, and if you are, what's the purpose of it now?

A. Yes.

Q. For what purpose?

A. I'm sorry?

Q. What's being achieved now?

A. Military purposes that we—it is exactly the same things we were trying to achieve before. Okay, the war is not over, and you've got to remember people are still dying out there, okay, and those people that are dying are my troops. And I'm going to continue to protect those troops in every way I possibly can until the war is over.

Yes, sir, right here.

Q. How soon, after you've finally beaten those Republican Guards, the yellow forces who threaten you, will you move your troops out of Iraq, either into Kuwait or back into Saudi?

A. That's not my decision to make.

Q. General, what are you doing to try and bring to justice the people responsible for the atrocities in Kuwait City, and also could you comment on the friendly-fire incident in which nine Britains were killed?

A. Yeah, I'm sorry. That was asked earlier and I failed to do that. First of all, on the first question, we have as much information as possible on those people that were committing the atrocities, and of course we're going through a screening process, and whenever we find those people that did in fact commit those atrocities, we try and separate them out. We treat them no differently than any other prisoner of war, but the ultimate disposition of those people, of course, might be quite different from the way we would treat any other prisoner of war.

With regard to the unfortunate incident yesterday, the only report we have is that two A-10 aircraft came in and they attacked two scout cars—British armored cars—and that's what caused the casualties. There were nine KIA. We deeply regret that. There's no excuse for it. I'm not going to apologize for it. I am going to say that our experience has been that based upon the extremely complicated number of different maneuvers that were being accomplished out here, according to the extreme diversity of the number of forces that were out here, according to the extreme differences in languages of the forces that are out here, and the weather conditions, and everything else, I feel that we were quite lucky that we did not have more of this type of incident. I would also tell you that because we had a few earlier that you know about, we went to the extraordinary lengths to try and prevent that type of thing from happening. It's a terrible tragedy and I'm sorry that it happened.

Q. Was it at night?

A. I don't know. I'm sorry. I . . . I don't believe so because I believe the information I had that a forward air controller was involved in directing that would indicate that it was probably during the afternoon. But it was when there was very very close combat going on out there in that area.

Yeah.

Q. General, the United Nations General Assembly is talking about peace, and as a military man, you look at your challenge and you're going to get some satisfaction out of having achieved it. Is there some fear on your part that there will be a cease-fire that will keep you from fulfilling the assignment that you have? Is your assign-

ment as a military man separate from the political goals
of the—

A. Do I fear a cease-fire?

Q. Well, do you fear that you will not be able to
accomplish your ends? That there will be some political
pressure brought on the campaign?

A. I think I've made it very clear to everybody that
I'd just as soon the war had never started and I'd just as
soon never have lost a single life out there. That was not
our choice. We've accomplished our mission and when
the decision makers come to the decision that there
should be a cease-fire, nobody will be happier than me.

All the way back, in the back. I'll take a couple of
more questions, then I have to go.

Q. General, we were told today that an A-10, returning from a mission, discovered and destroyed sixteen
Scuds. Is that a fact and where were they located?

A. Most of those Scuds were located in western Iraq.
I would tell you that we went into this with some intelligence estimates that I think I have since come to believe
were either grossly inaccurate or our pilots are lying
through their teeth. And I choose to think the former
rather than the latter, particularly since many of the pilots
have backed up what they've been saying by film and
that sort of thing. But we went in with a very very low
number of these mobile erector launchers that we thought
the enemy had. However, at one point we had a report
that they may have had ten times as many. I would tell
you, though, that yesterday the pilots had a very very
successful afternoon and night as far as the mobile erector launchers; most of them in western Iraq, which would
have been used against Israel.

One question here.

Q. General, you've said many times in the past that you do not like body counts. You've also told us tonight that the enemy casualties were very very large. I'm wondering, with the coalition forces already burying the dead on the battlefield, will there ever be any sort of accounting or head counts made or anything like that?

A. I don't think there's ever, in the history of warfare, been a successful count of dead. And that's because it's necessary to lay those people to rest for a lot of reasons, and that happens. So I would say that no, there will never be an exact count. But probably in the days to come you're going to hear many many stories, either overinflated or underinflated, depending upon who you hear them from. The people who will know best, unfortunately, are the families that won't see their loved ones come home.

One more question. Right here, yes, sir.

Q. If the gate is indeed closed, as you've said several times, and the theories about where these Kuwaiti hostages are, perhaps Basra, perhaps Baghdad, where could they be? And a quick second question. Was the timing for the start of the ground campaign a purely military choice or was it a military choice with political influence on the—

A. That's two questions.

Q. That's right.

A. When I say the gate is closed, I don't want to give you the impression that absolutely nothing is escaping. Quite the contrary. What isn't escaping is heavy tanks. What isn't escaping is artillery pieces. What isn't escaping is that sort of thing. That doesn't mean that civilian vehicles aren't escaping. That doesn't mean that innocent civilians aren't escaping. That doesn't mean that unarmed Iraqis aren't escaping. And that's not the gate I'm talking about. I'm talking about the gate that is closed on the war machine that is out there.

Now, your other question was?

Q. The time for the beginning of the ground campaign.

A. Oh, yeah. Okay. The timing for the beginning of the ground campaign. We made a military analysis of when that ground campaign should be conducted. I gave my recommendation to the Secretary of Defense and General Colin Powell. They passed that recommendation on to the President and the President acted upon that recommendation. Why? Do you think we did it at the wrong time?

(Laughter)

Q. I'm wondering if your recommendation and analysis was accepted without change?

A. I'm very thankful for the fact that the President of the United States has allowed the United States military and the coalition military to fight this war exactly as it should have been fought. And the President, in every case, has taken our guidance and our recommendations to heart and has acted superbly as the Commander and Chief of the United States. Thank you very much.

Transcribed by Billy G. Krueger, 56 TTW/JA,
MacDill Air Force Base, Florida.

INDEX